LAND USE LAW AND DISABILITY

Planning and Zoning for Accessible Communities

In *Land Use Law and Disability*, Robin Paul Malloy argues that our communities need better planning to be safely and easily navigated by people with mobility impairment and to facilitate intergenerational aging in place. To achieve this, communities will need to think of mobility impairment and inclusive design as land use and planning issues, in addition to understanding them as matters of civil and constitutional rights.

Although much has been written about the rights of people with disabilities, little has been said about the interplay between disability and land use regulation. This book undertakes to explain mobility impairment, as one type of disability, in terms of planning and zoning. The goal is to advance our understanding of disability in terms of planning and zoning to facilitate cooperative engagement between disability rights advocates and land use professionals. This in turn should lead to improved community planning for accessibility and aging in place.

Robin Paul Malloy is the E. I. White Chair and Distinguished Professor of Law, and Kauffman Professor of Entrepreneurship and Innovation at Syracuse University. He is a recognized expert on property development law, land use law, and real estate transactions. He has authored eight books, including two earlier books with Cambridge University Press and a leading casebook on real estate transactions; edited eight additional books; and authored numerous articles and book chapters. He is an editor of three different book series, including the Cambridge Disability Law and Policy series (with Peter Blanck).

CAMBRIDGE DISABILITY LAW AND POLICY SERIES

Edited by Peter Blanck and Robin Paul Malloy

The Cambridge Disability Law and Policy series examines these topics in inter-disciplinary and comparative terms. The books in the series reflect the diversity of definitions, causes, and consequences of discrimination against persons with disabilities while illuminating fundamental themes that unite countries in their pursuit of human rights laws and policies to improve the social and economic status of persons with disabilities. The series contains historical, contemporary, and comparative scholarship crucial to identifying individual, organizational, cultural, attitudinal, and legal themes necessary for the advancement of disability law and policy.

The book topics covered in the series also are reflective of the new moral and political commitment by countries throughout the world toward equal opportunity for persons with disabilities in such areas as employment, housing, transportation, rehabilitation, and individual human rights. The series will thus play a significant role in informing policy makers, researchers, and citizens of issues central to disability rights and disability antidiscrimination policies. The series grounds the future of disability law and policy as a vehicle for ensuring that those living with disabilities participate as equal citizens of the world.

Books in the Series

Land Use Law and Disability

PLANNING AND ZONING FOR ACCESSIBLE COMMUNITIES

ROBIN PAUL MALLOY

Syracuse University

CAMBRIDGE
UNIVERSITY PRESS

CAMBRIDGE
UNIVERSITY PRESS

32 Avenue of the Americas, New York NY 10013-2473, USA

Cambridge University Press is part of the University of Cambridge.

It furthers the University's mission by disseminating knowledge in the pursuit of education, learning and research at the highest international levels of excellence.

www.cambridge.org
Information on this title: www.cambridge.org/9781316614143

© Robin Paul Malloy 2015

First published 2015
First paperback edition 2016

A catalogue record for this publication is available from the British Library

Library of Congress Cataloguing in Publication data
Malloy, Robin Paul, 1956– author.
Land use law and disability : planning and zoning for accessible communities / Robin Paul Malloy, Syracuse University, College of Law.
    pages cm. – (Cambridge disability law and policy series)
Includes bibliographical references and index.
ISBN 978-0-521-19393-1 (hardback)
1. Barrier-free design – Law and legislation – United States.   2. City planning and redevelopment law – United States.   3. Zoning – United States.   I. Title.
KF5709.3.H35M35   2014
346.7304'5 – dc23   2014035905

ISBN 978-0-521-19393-1 Hardback
ISBN 978-1-316-61414-3 Paperback

For

Margaret, Gina, and Giovanni

Contents

Preface

Over the past couple of years, I witnessed family and friends age and gradually become less mobile. Slowly they drifted into isolation as it became increasingly difficult to participate in the events of everyday life. These observations inspired me to think about property development and the regulation of land use from the perspective of people with mobility impairment. At first, I focused on exploring inclusive design requirements confronting property owners and developers from the perspective of compliance with inclusive design building codes, but I soon concluded that the less explored and richer area of concern for land use lawyers and planning professionals was simply one of understanding mobility impairment as a land use and planning issue.

In this book, I suggest that our communities need better planning to be safely and easily navigated by people with mobility impairment and to facilitate intergenerational aging in place. This requires us to think of mobility impairment and inclusive design as land use and planning issues in addition to understanding them as matters of civil and constitutional rights. Although much has been written about the rights of people with disabilities, little has been said about the interplay between disability and land use regulation. This book undertakes to explain mobility impairment, as one type of disability, in terms of planning and zoning. It is written with the hope that a better understanding of disability in terms of planning and zoning will facilitate more cooperative engagement between disability rights advocates and land use professionals and that this in turn will lead to improved community planning for accessibility and aging in place.

In this regard, the book offers a new perspective because there has been very little challenge to the exclusivity of the civil rights paradigm in thinking about disability. Land use law emanates from the police power of government, and the central issue in the book involves finding an appropriate balance between the police power and civil rights when coordinating and regulating land use and property development. Some guidebooks are on the market that deal with compliance issues concerning accessible and universal design, but these books do not really involve land use law. The books are more akin to manuals prepared for assisting in compliance with a building code. This book is different because it focuses on land use law.

I have written the book for the general reader but hope that it will be of particular interest to planning and zoning professionals as well as to students of planning, property development, and land use. I also intend the book to reach an audience of people interested in disability studies and hope that the book is understood as a useful contributor to our mutual goal of making communities more accessible. At the same time, I do understand that people in disability studies will not be familiar with thinking of disability from a land use perspective. This may cause them to have some initial concerns because analysis under the police power is different than analysis under civil rights; nonetheless, it seems important to move beyond a civil rights paradigm so that we can address the planning and zoning issues we confront in making our communities more accessible.

Having presented issues from this book at various conferences, I understand that some property rights advocates may think that my views do too little to protect property rights from regulation. For example, some property rights people express a view that the government should not have the authority to require a homeowner to alter any aspect of a residential home for purposes of making the home more accessible under federal and state disability law. They express a belief that a homeowner has a right to build a home in any way that she wishes, and they assert this even though they seemingly understand that building codes already restrict this right. At the same time, I understand that some disability rights advocates think that my views do not go far enough to advance all of their goals because they feel that government should ensure universal and absolutely equal access to 100 percent of the built environment, without regard to cost. Some of these people also express the view that local government should have no role in regulating the separation and location of particular uses when a disability right is asserted. I am of a different view. Land use law has traditionally dealt with tensions between land use regulation and other important fundamental rights, such as those represented by the freedom of religion, the right to free speech, the definition of family, freedom of association, the right to travel, the right to a healthy environment, and the protection of property under the Fifth Amendment. Thus, although some advocates of property rights and disability rights may find points of contention with positions taken in this book, I am satisfied that the book develops a view grounded in the traditional jurisprudence of land use law and that it initiates a respectful dialogue concerning the need to mediate competing and deeply held values in our system of governance and in the way that land use regulation interacts with disability.

In addition to being of interest to the general reader and the land use professional, this book may also be used as the basis for a seminar on land use law and disability or as a supplement to a college course in planning and in a class on land use and zoning law. It might also serve as the core of a "short course" or "mini-course" on the subject (such courses are becoming increasingly popular as summer offerings and as bridge courses between academic terms at many colleges and law schools). I have used the materials as a way to introduce my regular land use and zoning law students to key issues regarding disability and aging in place. Typically, this means setting aside two to three weeks of classes during my 13-week course for discussion of the interplay between land use law and disability. In addition, I have used these materials in working with planners and zoning officials seeking guidance on dealing with issues surrounding disability and aging in place. I have found that the book facilitates discussion and gets people thinking about these issues in a new way. Initially, most land use professionals and property developers believe that disability and mobility issues are strictly civil rights matters and that the only questions to address are technical compliance issues with respect to Americans with Disability Act (ADA) design guidelines. Using these materials, we are able to discuss the importance of planning and to sort out the distinctions between ADA design guidelines and the law related to land use regulation.

In the book, I include edited versions of a few of the key cases that seem most pertinent to the issues being discussed. These cases have been edited so as to flow with the text, and they are used to advance the discussion in each chapter. The cases extend and expand on the text and are not used simply to offer an example, although they do illustrate application at the same time as they explain the subject. The cases provide the reader with a good basis for understanding the way that courts approach these issues in practice. Although I have file cabinets (both real and virtual) full of documents and resources, I have intentionally attempted to avoid the tendency in legal journal writing to use an excessive number of long footnotes. My hope is that this will permit the discussion to flow more naturally. At the same time, footnote references should be more than adequate for tracking down additional resources for those readers who are so inclined. I hope that I have been successful in striking a reasonable balance. Footnotes are prepared in Bluebook style for U.S. legal citation.

I provide a table of cases for the book. It is to be noted that the table of cases identifies only those primary cases included and discussed in the text of the book. Cases that simply appear in the footnotes, and cases that are merely cited by a court within an edited case opinion, are not included in this table. Thus, the table of cases includes the case opinions that have been included in edited form and cases specifically identified and discussed in the text, excluding the text of edited case opinions. I consider these to be the primary cases.

In developing my ideas for this book and preparing the manuscript, I benefited from the support of many people. I wish to acknowledge and thank these people. First and foremost, I thank my wife, Margaret, for 36 years of marriage and her continued encouragement and for her willingness to listen to and discuss an endless array of ideas. Second, I wish to thank Dean Hannah Arterian and the Syracuse University College of Law for actively supporting my research and writing on this project over the past two and a half years. In addition, a number of individuals were willing to listen to my ideas and read some draft materials. They have provided valuable feedback and include Keith Bybee; Jennifer Champa Bybee; Jeremy Blumenthal; Christian C. Day, Nestor M. Davidson, Michael Diamond, David Driesen, Deborah Kenn, and Shelley Saxer; and James C. Smith. I thank my friend Jerry Evensky for a willingness to engage in numerous lunchtime conversations concerning aspects of this book project. I also wish to recognize, more generally all the participants in the Syracuse University College of Law faculty workshop series coordinated by Rakesh Anand; the participants in the third annual meeting of the Association for Law, Property, and Society (ALPS); Suzanne Lennard and the participants in the 2012 Livable Cities Conference held in Portland, Oregon; Molly Stuart and the participants in the Bettman Symposium of the 2013 annual meeting of the American Planning Association held in Chicago, Illinois; Peter Blanck, who initially encouraged me to look more deeply into the connections between property development and disability; and Sheila Welch, for her invaluable administrative assistance.

I also want to thank the following for collectively and intermittently providing research assistance for this project, two earlier projects identified later, and other related papers leading up to this book: members of the professional library staff at the Syracuse University College of Law (in particular, Mark Burns and T. J. Holynski) and student research assistants Laura Gagnon, Lesley Germanow, Jason Hirata, Amber Mufale, Matthew Oja, Anthony Osbourne, Anthony Rapa, Melissa Schreiber-Stahl, and Kelly R. Tichacek.

Finally, I want to thank the town of DeWitt for providing me with the privilege of serving on the Zoning Board of Appeal (ZBA), where I have been able to observe and participate in the process of dealing with land use and disability law issues firsthand. Thanks go to Edward Michalenko, town supervisor, for appointing me to the ZBA and to the people with whom I have enjoyed the pleasure of working as a member and as deputy chair, including

Kenneth Alweis, Dylan Bruns, Thomas Carello, Dino Centra, Robert Jokl, Effe O'Hara, Julian Modesti, Robert Sweeney, Matthew Wells, and ZBA attorney Don Doerr. I also extend thanks to our professional staff members, Angela Epolito, Richard Robb, and Andrew Worden.

Some of the ideas discussed in this book were previously explored in Robin Paul Malloy, *Inclusion by Design: Accessible Housing and Mobility Impairment*, 60 HASTINGS L. J. 699–748 (2009), and Robin Paul Malloy, *Accessible Housing and Affordability*, in AFFORDABLE HOUSING AND PUBLIC-PRIVATE PARTNERSHIPS 207–217 (Nestor M. Davidson and Robin Paul Malloy, eds., Ashgate, 2009); Robin Paul Malloy, *Opening Neighborhoods to People with Mobility Impairment: Property, Disability and Inclusive Design Housing*, in THE PUBLIC NATURE OF PRIVATE PROPERTY 133–152 (Robin Paul Malloy and Michael R. Diamond eds., Ashgate 2011).

It goes without saying that I am indebted to the continued support of my editor at Cambridge University Press, John Berger.

Robin Paul Malloy, JD, LLM
E. I. White Chair and Distinguished Professor of Law
Kauffman Professor of Entrepreneurship and Innovation
College of Law, Syracuse University

1

Inclusion by design

Thinking beyond a civil rights paradigm

1.1 PAULI: AGE 28

Pauli was a passenger in an automobile being driven by his mother when they were hit by a drunk driver.[1] The accident left Pauli unable to walk, paralyzed from the waist down. That was 11 years ago. Today, at age 28, Pauli has just been promoted to junior partner of a local management consulting firm.

While he finishes his work for the day, Pauli looks forward to attending a celebratory party for all the newly promoted people in the firm. The party is being held later this night at the home of the firm's senior partner. Pauli organizes his desk, makes a call to request a wheelchair-accessible bus, freshens up in the men's room, and then rolls himself down the hallway to the elevator. He makes his way out the front door of his building and rolls his wheelchair down the sidewalk to the curb cut, where he crosses the street to wait for the wheelchair-accessible bus that will take him to his home. Two regular city buses that cover his route come and go while Pauli waits the 40 minutes that will be required on this day for the accessible bus to arrive with one other passenger already on it. As Pauli waits for his bus, he thinks about the way his life has changed since that accident 11 years ago. In his wheelchair, life is so much different from the time when he played football, ran track, and danced with his high school sweetheart at the junior prom. Although those memories are cherished, he has since adjusted to a new life and reflects positively on the many changes that have recently improved his quality of life, such as curb cuts, accessible buses, roll-in entrances to buildings, bathrooms with lower sinks and light switches, and new building designs with doorways and facilities that provide adequate space for moving and manipulating his wheelchair.

---

[1] Robin Paul Malloy, *Inclusion by Design: Accessible Housing and Mobility Impairment*, 60 HASTINGS L. J. 699 (2009).

He knows that such changes have come slowly and that there is a need for additional design changes, but he also appreciates the increasing community awareness of the need for greater accessibility. While acknowledging that much work needs to be done, Pauli feels lucky because his office is in a new building with many inclusive design features, which was not the case in his prior job location, nor is it the case in many of the office buildings downtown, some of which were built 40 or more years ago and have done a poor job of updating. Pauli also feels fortunate because the city, after threats of litigation, recently purchased two new wheelchair-accessible buses, and he now enjoys being able to take advantage of one of the few bus routes served by such a bus, even if service is often slower than that provided by the regular city bus service. The city still has not looked at demographic trends and the need for future bus routes, but at least Pauli can see improvements in transportation and building designs that are beneficial to many people with low functional mobility, not just people in wheelchairs. Within a few minutes, the bus arrives, and Pauli, aware of all the hard work that has gone into becoming a junior partner, rolls onto the bus and is headed home.

After arriving at home, Pauli changes for the party and, together with his wife, drives to the home of the senior partner. The senior partner lives in a newly developed suburban neighborhood to which Pauli has never been before. By the time they locate the partner's home, there are already a number of cars parked along the street. From their car, they can hear the music of laughter and joyful conversation spilling out into the neighborhood. They park the car and head toward the front of the house. There are no sidewalks in the neighborhood, and Pauli's wheelchair does not work well in the soft grass, so they make their way down the center of the street and past the wall of parked cars. Pauli's sense of excitement dissipates, and his gut wrenches as he looks out at a tiered three-level stone sidewalk terracing up the front lawn to a porch with a two-step entry to a relatively narrow front door. Disheartened, but with a well-practiced smile on her face, Pauli's wife goes to the front door to inquire about another, more suitable entrance to the house.

As she waits at the door, she cannot help but notice the way in which the warm glow of the party inside contrasts with the sullen lines of distress on Pauli's face. The senior partner comes to the door and offers her regrets for not thinking about the issue of Pauli's access to her home. She pauses and thinks for a minute about the entrance from the garage, but that too has steps – three steps up from the garage to the main living room – and the doorway is too narrow. Finally, she suggests that Pauli roll around the side of the house, past the line of garbage cans, and come in through the rear mud room. "This," she says, "is the door we use to let the dogs in and out. I am sure that they won't mind." She goes on to explain that there is only one step at this entrance and that she will send several guests back to help lift Pauli through the doorway – the only doorway in her home wide enough to accommodate a wheelchair. Pauli makes his way past the trash cans thinking of all the family gatherings and all the college and Super Bowl parties hosted at homes in which the same old issue arises. He wonders to himself if people anguish as much over "having" to invite him to their homes as he does over being invited.

1.2 ANN: AGE 15

Sally and Jim have a 15-year-old daughter, Ann, born with a mobility-impairing condition necessitating the use of a wheelchair or scooter.[2] Ann attends the public school, which provides an inclusive and open environment. Ann is a good student, and with the aid of her motorized scooter, she is able to get around the school and participate in some school activities, such as helping to manage the school track team and playing an instrument in the band. Ann has many friends and is well liked by her classmates. All of this is good, but there is a problem: Ann never gets invited to anyone's home for a play date or a sleepover, or for general socializing, not because of personal discrimination but because of exclusion by design in the homes of her classmates and friends. Although her home is a model of accessibility, there are no sidewalks in her neighborhood, and her school friends and extended family members do not have homes able to easily and safely accommodate her use of a wheelchair. Thus, Ann lives in a partitioned world of public inclusion at school and social exclusion after school. Ann lives in a space of truncated social relationships, and indirectly, her parents' relationships are also hindered, as they find it increasingly difficult to visit others who occupy exclusionary housing units. The implications of these truncated relationship networks are isolating and stigmatizing for everyone but perhaps more so for young school-age children and teenagers, because reciprocal social networking is so important to a healthy self-image and to their proper social development.

1.3 CELIA: AGE 74

Celia, a 74-year-old woman, until recently has been living independently in her own home.[3] Celia had lived in the same home for 50 years, ever since she was married to her now deceased husband. She had six children while living in that house and has many cherished memories of the people and events that

---

[2] *Id.* at 701.   [3] *Id.*

filled the home with love and laughter over the years. Now, at age 74, Celia has difficulty living in her home. Celia suffers from arthritis in her joints and occasionally loses feeling in her right foot, causing minor interference with keeping her balance. With her arthritis and her foot problem, she is no longer able to navigate the five concrete steps that lead into and out of her home. Inside of her home, she struggles with the layout of the house, which has all three bedrooms and the only bathroom on the second floor. There is a 12-step stairway between the main floor of the house and the second floor. On flat surfaces she is fine and does not need, or use, either a walker or a wheelchair. Doctors estimate that Celia has many years ahead of her and that she would be able to live independently in her home for several more years if it were not for the presence of so many stairs. Celia prefers to age in place, but she recently had to sell her home and move 10 miles away to a senior living facility in a nearby town because her town has none. This facility is easier to navigate, but it removes her from a neighborhood populated with families and people of all ages and places her in an environment where everyone is her age and older. As was the case with her private residence, the neighborhood by the nursing home has no sidewalks and no form of public transportation.

She misses looking out her window and watching the neighborhood children play and seeing the new moms and dads proudly pushing carriages with newborn babies along the sidewalk. She misses the joy of participating in front yard neighborhood chatter and of the children coming around on Halloween and singing carols at Christmas. The hardest thing to deal with is the realization that in addition to having to leave her own home after so many years, she is no longer able to visit the homes of her children, grandchildren, nephew, sister, and friends, who all reside nearby but occupy houses that are not readily accessible because of entry steps and internal stairways. Despite her lack of need for a wheelchair or even a walker, Celia finds that almost every home that she used to visit now represents a barrier to the normalcy of her prior pattern of social interaction. Celia misses the opportunity to visit the homes of the people she cares so much about and finds herself prematurely disconnected from many of the important social networks that she had enjoyed over the years.

1.4 TIFFANY: AGE 65

Tiffany is 65 years old and lives in a small city, on the third floor of a walk-up apartment building. She no longer drives, and she uses a cane when she walks because of an injury to her right leg. In recent years, going up and down the stairway to her third-floor apartment has become increasingly difficult. As life in the city has changed over time, Tiffany has witnessed the increase in broken sidewalks and the closing up of the downtown drug store, grocery store, and two restaurants, which, in her younger days, were all located within a three-block radius of her home. Tiffany finds it to be increasingly difficult to live independently because of where she is located.

The nearest grocery store, drug store, and restaurant are located several miles away in a suburban shopping center. The shopping center features a new store that is fully accessible. Housing costs in the suburb are too high for Tiffany to afford. The public transit system provides service between the neighborhood of her home in the city and the suburban shopping center, but the four-mile trip takes two hours and requires two transfers. Once in the suburb, there are no sidewalks in the town because property owners do not want to pay for them, and they worry about having to keep them free of snow during the four months when snow is typically on the ground. Across a six-lane highway from the shopping center is a hair salon and a movie theater, but Tiffany has never had the courage to cross the busy road that slices through the town on the way into the city. The grocery store, although fully accessible and having won awards for its inclusive design, is still very difficult for Tiffany to access and enjoy because it is poorly integrated into the surroundings that she must navigate to get there in the first place. Similar difficulties arise when Tiffany attempts to visit the city-based senior citizen's center and when she wishes to visit her local church; sidewalks are in disrepair, and crossing streets is difficult because of traffic and because few intersections have safe crosswalks. Even getting in and out of her home is difficult, because it is an apartment in an older building that still has a difficult stairway to climb. The problem is magnified during winter months, when very few of the sidewalks are properly cleared of snow. Tiffany has found that neither city nor suburban living is necessarily ideal for a person with low functional mobility and living without an automobile.

Unfortunately, the experiences of Pauli, Ann, Celia, and Tiffany are not unique. Their experiences are shared each day by millions of people representing almost 20 percent of American families, and their particular situations simply illustrate the broader set of problems arising from the fact that functional mobility levels vary among people.[4] They also illustrate the fact that many communities are doing a less than ideal job of planning for inclusive design. As indicated in these narratives, we see examples of communities

---

4 *Id.*; Qi Wang, U.S. Dep't of Com., Report No. CENSR-23, Disability and American Families: 2000, at 4 (2005), *available at* http://www.census.gov/prod/2005pubs/censr-23.pdf. *See also* Linda L. Nussbaumer, Inclusive Design: A Universal Need 4–6 (2012).

way affect the right of homeowners to include or exclude people from their homes based on race or any other associational preferences. Consequently, it is important to distinguish the individual rights that we are seeking to protect from the ownership and use of structures, which impact the navigability of the built environment. A more modern and inclusive approach to planning and zoning should allow us to focus on health and safety issues without having to deal with detailed regulatory distinctions for classifying structures as public places, as places of public accommodation, or as private residences. The real focus should be on making the complete and integrated community safe and easy to navigate without regard to the public or private nature of property ownership.

The responsibility of planning for accessible communities ought to rest, to a large extent, with local and regional government rather than with the federal government. Coordinating land uses and promoting the public health, safety, welfare, and morals have long been the province of local government acting pursuant to the police powers. To date, however, many local zoning and planning professionals have failed to fully appreciate the extent to which accessibility relates to their authority to regulate land *uses*. Similarly, many disability rights advocates have failed to understand the positive contribution that property development and land use professionals can offer to the process of making our communities more accessible. Too frequently, issues of inclusion and accessibility are presented to local governments as matters to be addressed by building design guidelines developed pursuant to federal disability law rather than as matters for local government planning. The truth is that effective planning for accessibility and aging in place requires appropriate input from a variety of professionals, including those responsible for local government regulation of property development and land use.

The traditional emphasis on local land use planning and regulation, however, has given way in recent years to a growing trend in favor of regional and national planning.[21] Examples of this trend include federal regulations pursuant to the Clean Water Act, Clean Air Act, and Migratory Bird Act

---

[21] *See* BRIAN W. BLAESSER & ALAN C. WEINSTEIN, FEDERAL LAND USE LAW & LITIGA-TION § 1:1, at 6 (2007); WILLIAM H. HUDNUT, III, CHANGING METROPOLITAN AMERICA: PLANNING FOR A SUSTAINABLE FUTURE (2008) (but the fact that purely local approaches are no longer practicable does not mean that everything should be regulated by the federal government). *See also* John R. Nolan, *Champions of Change: Reinventing Democracy through Land Law Reform*, 30 HARV. ENVTL. L. REV. 1, 45 (2006); Ashira Pelman Ostrow, *Land Law Federalism*, 61 EMORY L. J. 1397 (2012); Ashira Pelman Ostrow, *Process Preemption in Federal Sitting Regimes*, 48 HARV. J. LEGIS. 289 (2011).

and regulations related to wetlands protection and the management of coastal lands.[22] This trend recognizes that many localized land uses have implications that extend beyond the property line and the jurisdictional boundary of the location of the use. For instance, certain uses can impact traffic, air quality, water quality, and noise levels well beyond the jurisdiction of one local government. In many cases, the justification for a national approach is that the cumulative effects of disaggregated local decision making can lead to extensive spillover effects and to numerous negative externalities across jurisdictional boundaries.[23] Another justification, offered in Chapter 4, is less focused on the spillover effects and more concerned with advancing a positive economic environment for communities to grow as dynamic "network enterprises," competing for residents and for businesses on the basis of providing a particular "quality of life."[24] When understood as a "network enterprise," national inclusive design standards for accessibility make sense, just as national standards for cell phone protocols do. At the same time, local and state coordination of land use may continue to best reflect important differences among communities in a diverse and democratic system of governance.

The coordination of land uses among communities might occur in several ways and typically focuses on establishing compatibility measures and performance standards that facilitate desirable outcomes across jurisdictional lines. One way of doing this is by requiring *consistency* in planning among different levels of local government.[25] This might include having local planning and zoning legislation reviewed by regional and state authorities for consistency with state objectives and for evaluation of spillover effects that might be detrimental to surrounding properties located within the legal boundaries of other local governments. Another way of achieving compatibility and standardization is by having planning take place at the national level rather than at the local or state level. To a large extent, the Americans with Disability Act (ADA) has worked to establish uniform national standards with respect to the protection of people with disabilities, and pursuant thereto, detailed national

---

[22] Migratory Bird Treaty Act, 16 U.S.C. § 703–712 (2006); Clean Water Act, Pub. L. No. 95-217, 91 Stat. 1566 (1977) (codified as amended at 33 U.S.C. § 1251 et seq. (2006)); Clean Air Act, 42 U.S.C. § 7401 et seq. (2006); 33 C.F.R. § 323.1 et seq. (2013); 40 C.F.R. § 25.1 (2013); 40 C.F.R. § 124.1 et seq. (2005).

[23] *See* COOTER & ULEN, *supra* note 15, at 40–42; MALLOY, LAW AND MARKET ECONOMY, *supra* note 13, at 97; MALLOY, LAW IN A MARKET CONTEXT, *supra* note 13, at 117; POSNER, *supra* note 15, at 158–160; SHY, *supra* note 15, at 3.

[24] *See* SHY, *supra* note 15. *See also infra* Chapter 4.

[25] U.S. Dep't of Commerce, Standard City Planning Enabling Act § 3 (1928). *See also* Bd. of Cnty. Comm'rs of Brevard Cnty. v. Snyder, 627 So. 2d 469 (Fla. 1993).

ト

guidelines on accessible design and construction have been promulgated.[26] Following the lead of the national government, many states have adopted similar approaches to disability legislation.[27]

Developing these national standards provides people with an expectation that they will receive similar treatment in every state, and it can facilitate interstate activity based on providing a set of predictable, compatible, and standardized guidelines for building design. This eliminates competition on the cost of accessible construction because all developers face the same guidelines, and it enhances mobility because people can more freely relocate to new communities knowing that accessibility design standards are the same in all states.

Even with national standards for prevention of discrimination and for regulating details of building design, it is still important for local government to *coordinate* property development and land *uses* pursuant to the police power because local governments are closest to the land and the community in question. Local governments understand the local geography and circumstances, and they are more likely to be aware of the concerns of local residents. Local land use regulation can also generate local stakeholder support for the values and goals underlying particular efforts at coordinating land use, such as efforts directed at advancing inclusive and accessible design to address the needs of people aging in place as well as the needs of people with mobility impairment. At the same time, the federal government has no inherent expertise and enjoys no significant economies of scale in planning for the best locations for particular land uses within a local community, even if it has such advantages in establishing civil rights guidelines and in setting uniform national design standards for such construction features as doorways and bathrooms.

Modern communities have many planning needs, and it is important to think in terms of planning for mobility in the broader context of addressing

[26] Americans with Disabilities Act of 1990, Pub. L. No. 101–336, 104 Stat. 327 (codified as amended at 42 U.S.C. § 12131 et seq. (2006)); 28 C.F.R. pt. 35.151 (2011); 28 C.F.R. pts. 36.401–36.406 (2011)); 36 C.F.R. Architectural Barriers Act § 1191, *amended by* Accessibility Guidelines; Outdoor Developed Areas, 78 Fed. Reg. 59,476 (Sept. 26, 2013) (to be codified at 36 C.F.R. § 1191). *See also* U.S. Dep't of Housing & Urban Dev. & U.S. Dep't of Justice, Accessibility (Design and Construction) Requirements for Covered Multifamily Dwellings under the Fair Housing Act (2013); U.S. Dep't of Justice, 2010 ADA Standards for Accessible Design (2010), *available at* www.ada.gov/2010ADAstandards_index.htm; Marcela Abadi Rhoads, The ADA Companion Guide: Understanding the Americans with Disabilities Act Accessibility Guidelines (ADAAG and the Architectural Barriers Act (ABA)) (2010).

[27] *See, e.g.,* Ariz. Rev. Stat. Ann. § 41–1401 et seq. (2010); Cal. Code. Regs. tit. 24 § 5–101 et seq. (2011); Md. Code Ann., State Gov't § 20–601 et seq. (West 2013); Md. Code Ann., Health-Gen § 7–101 et seq. (2009); N.Y. Exec. Law § 290 et seq. (McKinney 2013).

a wide range of other needs, such as those related to housing affordability, poverty, sustainability, education, transportation, health care, and financial stability. In this context, there must be an understanding of local and regional input into the planning and zoning process under state law as well as an appreciation of a federal role in advancing the rights of people with disabilities.

Modern property development and land use regulations should be comprehensive in nature and informed by investigation, fact finding, and a combination of expert and community-based input. This means that planning must be done for "complete communities" and that a silo mentality of building inclusive design structures without regard to the connectivity of these structures to the broader community is insufficient. Making an individual house safe and easy to navigate for a person of low functional mobility, for example, does little to improve her quality of life in the community when barriers to safe and easy navigation exist everywhere outside of her home and if she lacks easy access to health care or other goods and services. Understanding this fact and planning for the proper integration of land uses and services across the built environment are traditional functions of local land use and zoning professionals, even if construction design guidelines are standardized at a national level. Moreover, setting detailed guidelines for building construction is not the same thing as planning for the needs of a community and coordinating its land uses to achieve desired outcomes.

A first step in developing better planning for accessibility and aging in place involves thinking of mobility impairment and inclusive design as land use issues. Thinking of ADA accessibility requirements in terms of local zoning and land use regulation should not be difficult. The ADA and related legislation already divide property into different categories of "use," and these categories in turn trigger different requirements and standards for accessibility. For example, under these federal regulations, there are properties identified as public places, places of public accommodation, multifamily residential, and single-family residential.[28] Each of these categories is defined not only in terms of the purpose of a structure that might be located on a property but also in terms of how the place and space are used. It is the "use" of the property as a public place, or as a place of public accommodation, that is important in determining the construction design guidelines for accessibility. This focus on use is central to land use planning and zoning, and the coordination of uses within a community is traditionally a function of local government.

---

[28] Properties identified as public places, places of public accommodation, multifamily residential, and single-family residential. "Places of Public Accommodation," Americans with Disabilities Act of 1990, 42 U.S.C. § 12181(7) (2006).

Local governments have long regulated property development based on different types of use categories, such as residential, retail, light industrial, industrial, and recreational.[29] Consequently, local governments are fully equipped to effectively understand the use categories of federal disabilities law. Furthermore, inasmuch as accessibility and aging in place are facilitated by good coordination of land uses, it is important to develop an understanding of the role of local government in advancing inclusive design as part of protecting the public health, safety, welfare, and morals. The current literature on disability law and policy, however, provides very little focus on issues of zoning and land use regulation. Instead, the literature is dominated by civil rights and constitutional law concerns. Although this literature and focus are important, they do not fully address the issues that must be confronted by property developers and land use regulators concerned with inclusion and accessibility. In part, the lack of a land use focus in the disability law literature might be attributed to the fact that contemporary approaches to disability law and policy are strategically framed with reference to race discrimination. This framing avoids a direct consideration of the land use issues involved in developing inclusive design communities. In fact, the current approach to disability law obscures the inherent link between accessibility, zoning, and land use planning. Perhaps this has been an oversight in the literature, or perhaps it reflects a desire to require mandated design requirements outside of a consideration of the police powers of local governments and to avoid potential challenges from property rights advocates opposing overly aggressive and potentially expensive regulation.

As to property rights advocates, they have been fairly aggressive about trying to limit the extent to which government can regulate land use, and they may interpret the extensive regulatory requirements for accessibility as overreaching, and in some cases as unnecessarily costly to property owners.[30]

---

[29] Standard State Zoning Enabling Act (SZEA) U.S. Dep't of Commerce (1926); *Euclid*, 272 U.S. 365; JULIAN C. JUERGENSMEYER & THOMAS E. ROBERTS, LAND USE PLANNING AND DEVELOPMENT REGULATION LAW §§ 4:1–4:2 (3d ed. 2013). *See generally* J. BERRY CULLINGWORTH, THE POLITICAL CULTURE OF PLANNING: AMERICAN LAND USE PLANNING IN COMPARATIVE PERSPECTIVE, Chapter 2 (1993); ZONING AND THE AMERICAN DREAM: PROMISES STILL TO KEEP (Charles M. Haar & Jarold S. Kayden eds., 1989). Mandelker, *Land Use Law*, §§ 5.01–5.86.

[30] *See* Koontz v. St. John's River Water Mgmt. Dist., 570 U.S. __, 133 S. Ct. 2586 (2013); MALLOY, LAW IN A MARKET CONTEXT, *supra* note 13, at 17; POSNER, *supra* note 15, at 31–88; Echeverria and Hansen-Young, *The Track Record on Takings Legislation: Lessons from Democracy's Laboratories*, 28 STAN. ENVTL. L. J. 439, 444–445 (2009); Mark C. Weber, *Unreasonable Accommodation and Due Hardship*, 62 FLA. L. REV. 1119 (2010). *See also* Juergensmeyer & Roberts, *Land Use*, at 426.

For example, when the law requires buildings to have a zero-step entryway, wheelchair-accessible bathrooms, wider hallways, and elevators to accommodate a person with low functional mobility, it imposes costs on property owners and limits their development and design choices.[31] Property rights advocates may assert that government lacks, or ought to lack, the authority to regulate land use in such a way or to such an extent. Such assertions, as is explained later in this book, are unlikely to be deemed meritorious by anyone who has an informed understanding of the law relevant to land use regulation. Just the same, the strength of the claims to accessibility and inclusion are made stronger by addressing underlying land use questions rather than avoiding them – and the opportunity for good zoning and planning is enhanced when local governments are involved in the process. This is because local land use regulation offers a process for considering a variety of present and future community needs in the context of comprehensive planning, and comprehensive planning can account for the integrated nature of communities while addressing the strategic deployment of scarce resources.

As this introduction indicates, mobility impairment and aging in place are complex issues confronting many communities. They are issues that raise concerns at the interface of disability law and land use regulation. They are shaped by physical, medical, and cultural factors, and they put competing values in tension. Developing successful responses to the challenges raised by mobility impairment and aging in place will require local zoning and land use professionals to be active participants in shaping policy and in developing appropriate regulations. These challenges, although great, are not beyond the ability and expertise of local zoning and planning professionals; local zoning and land use professionals have been addressing similar challenges for years. They have confronted similar challenges in dealing with the tension between a number of deeply held and competing values. For example, the First Amendment protects such things as the right to operate adult entertainment venues, but planners can regulate the location as well as the intensity and density of such operations.[32] Similarly, the First Amendment protects the freedom of religion, but local land use regulators can set site development guidelines and control certain types of auxiliary activities connected with the primary religious use.[33] Local planning and zoning regulations frequently deal

---

[31] *See* 42 U.S.C. § 12131; 28 C.F.R. § 35.151 (2005) amended (2011).

[32] City of Renton v. Playtime Theatres Inc., 475 U.S. 41 (1986); Young v. Am. Mini Theatres, Inc., 427 U.S. 50 (1976); Northend Cinema, Inc. v. City of Seattle, 585 P.2d 1153 (Wash. 1978).

[33] St. John's United Church of Christ v. City of Chicago, 502 F.3d 616 (7th Cir. 2007); Glenside Ctr., Inc. v. Abington Twp. Zoning Hearing Bd., 973 A.D.2d 10 (Pa. Commw. Ct. 2009); Greater Bible Way Temple of Jackson v. City of Jackson, 733 N.W.2d 734 (Mich. 2007).

with freedom of expression by controlling signs and aesthetics,[34] and the rights of association frequently create tension with efforts to zone certain properties for single-family use.[35] The fact that we have a number of deeply held values that frequently come into tension, and that the world is dynamic and ever changing, is exactly why we need planning. We need to plan for change – for demographic, social, political, economic, and cultural change – so that our communities remain vibrant and sustainable over time. Defining, clarifying, and articulating rights is one thing; planning and zoning to effectuate those rights in the design of the built environment is another. Thinking about planning, zoning, and the way in which we effectuate inclusion by design is what this book is all about.

This book does not present a detailed guide to compliance with the Americans with Disability Act or to the requirements for developing building codes for compliance with universal design standards. This book challenges us to rethink the legal frame used to address the issue of inclusion in the way that we develop property and regulate land use. Building better and more inclusive communities is going to require cooperation among local land use regulators and advocates for disability rights, and effective cooperation is more likely when efforts are made to address and reconcile the concerns of inclusive design with the underlying law of zoning and land use regulation.

At this point, it is probably useful to clarify some simple vocabulary that will be used in addressing the overall focus of the book. The definitions offered are meant to be simple and guided by common sense rather than being grounded in any sort of technical, medical, or scientific literature. These definitions are also offered in full recognition of the fact that the discourse of disability is itself somewhat unsettled as to the best or most appropriate term to describe certain conditions or relationships. It is also understood that there are many types of disability, even though this book really only addresses mobility impairment. Likewise, mobility impairment is itself complicated, as it may be related to low functionality in a limb or to visual or hearing impairments that make navigating the built environment more difficult. Setting aside these complications, this

---

[34] Schad v. Borough of Mount Ephraim, 452 U.S. 61 (1981); Metromedia, Inc. v. City of San Diego, 453 U.S. 490 (1981); Central Hudson Gas & Elec. Corp. v. Pub. Serv. Comm'n of N.Y., 447 U.S. 557 (1980); Juergensmeyer & Roberts, *Land Use*, at 445–50.

[35] Hollenbaugh v. Carnegie Free Library, 439 U.S. 1052 (1978); Moore v. City of East Cleveland, 431 U.S. 494 (1977), *overruled by* Samson v. City of Bainbridge Island, 683 F.Supp.2d 1164 (D.Wash. 2010); Village of Belle Terre v. Boraas, 416 U.S. 1 (1974); Doe v. City of Butler, Pa., 892 F.2d 315 (3d Cir. 1989); Borough of Glassboro v. Vallorosi, 568 A.2d 888 (N.J. 1990); City of Santa Barbara v. Adamson, 610 P.2d 436 (Cal. 1980).

book focuses on particular aspects of mobility impairment that seem the most illustrative of issues confronting local community planners.

To begin with, references to various levels of functional mobility are made throughout the book. At one end of the spectrum are people with marginal functional mobility, and by this is meant people who are restricted to bed or who are unable to move with the aid of normal assistive devices without the added intervention of human assistance and supervision. Moving up the functional mobility scale, low functional mobility, also referred to as mobility impairment, means that a person has a "condition that substantially limits one or more basic physical activities such as walking, climbing stairs, reaching, lifting, or carrying."[36] This can include people using such assistive devices as wheelchairs, walkers, canes, and crutches, and it may result from a variety of causes, such as old age, illness, arthritis, injury, cerebral palsy, muscular dystrophy, amputation, and other surgeries as hip or knee replacement. Average functional mobility is just what the term indicates: a range of mobility that is average across a given multigenerational population. High-level functional mobility refers to those people who have better than average mobility – we can think of runners, skiers, athletes, rock climbers, and other such people as representative of this level of functionality.

From a zoning and planning perspective, we need to have places that are safe and healthy for all of the people living in our community, even as we acknowledge that functional mobility varies across a given population. This requires that our communities be safe and easy to navigate as people age in place, and this means that our communities must be designed to meet multiple intergenerational mobility needs to make them sustainable in terms of supporting a lifelong and meaningful opportunity for participation in community life by all residents. Residents should not need to prematurely or involuntarily

---

[36] Qi Wang, U.S. Dep't of Com., Report No. CENSR-23, Disability and American Families: 2000 (2005), *available at* www.census.gov/prod/2005pubs/censr-23.pdf. This definition referred to "substantial" limitations and did not include lesser physical limitations, so the number could be higher. As to the definition of disability more generally, the following sources address the somewhat unsettled terminology. *Community and Culture: Frequently Asked Questions,* NAT'L ASS'N OF THE DEAF, www.nad.org/issues/american-sign-language/community-and-culture-faq (last visited Sept. 17, 2013); John Folkins, *The Language Used to Describe Individuals with Disabilities,* AM. SPEECH-LANGUAGE-HEARING ASS'N (Dec. 1992), www.asha.org/publications/journals/submissions/person_first.htm; Scott Rains, *What Is Universal or Inclusive Design,* ASHOKA CHANGEMAKERS (June 4, 2009), www.changemakers.com/groups/design-disabilities-group/discussion-7; Katie Snow, *People First Language,* www.disabilityisnatural.com/ images/PDF/pfl09.pdf (last visited Sept. 17, 2013); C. Edwin Vaughan, *People-First Language: An Unholy Crusade,* BRAILLE MONITOR (March 2009), *available at* http://nfb.org/Images/nfb/Publications/bm/bm09/bm0903/bm090309.htm.

relocate to another community simply as a result of the normal aging process or as a consequence of declining mobility. Our communities should be planned to provide meaningful pathways and networks to navigability for as many people as possible.

In examining the planning implications of mobility impairment, and its relationship to the aging process, it must be understood that low functional mobility is a physical condition, the meaning and consequences of which are shaped and influenced by the natural and built environments. As to the natural environment, it is easy to appreciate the differences in functional mobility among people. Some people can easily cross rocky paths, climb mountains, wade across river rapids, and traverse rough and varied terrain; others cannot. The built environment, unlike the natural environment, expresses the power of humans to shape their surroundings. This power is not unlimited, however, as buildings, highways, and other human interventions all must correspond in one way or another to the natural geography, typography, and weather conditions of the area. For example, homes built in the city of New Orleans must be elevated from the ground because much of the city is below sea level. Local conditions drive building requirements, and the building requirements make it more difficult to design appropriately ramped entranceways to some structures.[37] Thinking about the influence of local conditions on the

---

[37] On a trip that I made to New Orleans from June 7 to 9, 2006, with Professor James Charles Smith, we interviewed people concerning housing issues and people with disabilities. We discussed emergency relief efforts with several leaders of nonprofit organizations dealing with recovery from Hurricanes Katrina and Rita in New Orleans. The groups we talked with during this period included the Advocacy Center of New Orleans, Catholic Charities, the Greater New Orleans Fair Housing Action Center, the New Orleans Housing Resource Center, the New Orleans Neighborhood Development Collaborative, and the Housing Authority of New Orleans (contact information on file with author). The people with whom we spoke identified a key problem area as one of dealing with people with disabilities. The city was unprepared for the disaster, and all the more so in terms of the needs of people with disabilities. In addition, accessible buildings and housing with inclusive design features were difficult or impossible to find. Working to address the needs of persons with mobility impairment took added time, relative to that spent on people without disabilities, and caused greater delay and frustration for all involved. This view on lack of accessibility and the problems confronted by people with disabilities is also echoed in some of the responses to surveys done of 24 organizations operating in Louisiana and Mississippi. The author was given access to a portion of the survey data used as part of a study by the Burton Blatt Institute of Syracuse University done in conjunction with a report for the Department of Labor titled *Contributions of Disability Program Navigators to Emergency Response and Economic Recovery of People with Disabilities, Post–Hurricane Katrina: Findings and Recommendations* (the author contributed housing-related questions to the broad-based survey) (information on file with author). Approximately 25 percent of Katrina evacuees were people with disabilities, but only between 1 and 2 percent from Louisiana and Mississippi were provided with accessible Federal Emergency Management Agency (FEMA) trailers for housing, and this led to a lawsuit and a settlement agreement where FEMA

accessibility of the built environment takes planning, and planning involves something more than identifying a civil right to access. Similarly, constraints imposed by technology and other scarce resources limit our ability to fully free ourselves from some of the mobility-based advantages and disadvantages that nature imposes. Nonetheless, good zoning and planning can facilitate design and construction that enhance the safety and ease of navigation for many people in a given community.

As we think about the need to ensure a safe and inclusive environment for people to live, work, and play, it is also important to recognize that functional mobility can vary over a lifetime and that diminishing levels of mobility impact people of all ages, races, religions, and ethnicities.[38] Fortunately, many issues of functional mobility can be addressed through technology and design; functional mobility is not an immutable characteristic, and the goal of good zoning and planning ought to be to advance the public health, safety, welfare, and morals. This includes working for inclusive design standards in property development.

To put the problem of mobility into perspective, consider that the traditional view on mobility impairment is that it affects about 1 percent of the population

undertook to make its trailers accessible to the people assigned to them. *See* Susan Finch, *U.S. Judge OKs Accord on Trailers for Disabled: Toll-Free Lines to Help FEMA Reach Out*, NEW ORLEANS TIMES PICAYUNE, Sept. 27, 2006, at METRO; Court Settlement: FEMA Provides Accessible Trailers for Katrina and Rita Victims (Sept. 26, 2006), http://sci.rutgers.edu/forum/showthread.php?t=70349. *See generally* Debra Lyn Bassett, *Place, Disasters, and Disability*, *in* LAW AND RECOVERY FROM DISASTER: HURRICANE KATRINA 51 (Robin Paul Malloy ed. 2009) [hereinafter LAW AND RECOVERY FROM DISASTER]; Janet E. Lord et al., *Natural Disasters and Persons with Disabilities*, *in* LAW AND RECOVERY FROM DISASTER, at 71. One person with whom we spoke in New Orleans, "Charlie," explained his own personal experience of evacuating to housing that was inaccessible, where kitchen appliances could not be reached and the bathrooms could not be used because he could not access them in his wheelchair. Interview with "Charlie," in New Orleans, La. (June 8, 2006). One year later, he was still waiting for accessible and affordable housing back in New Orleans. *Id.* In enhancing our ability to be better prepared for emergencies and to build more inclusive housing, we must work to assist all segments of the community and to make housing both physically and financially accessible. *See generally* Jonathan P. Hooks & Trisha B. Miller, *The Continuing Storm: How Disaster Recovery Excludes Those Most in Need*, 43 CAL. W. L. REV. 21 (2006).

[38] *See* Andrew J. Houtenville, 2004 *Disability Status Reports: United States*, EMP'T AND DISABILITY INST. COLLECTION, Oct. 2005, *available at* www.digitalcommons.ilr.cornell.edu/edicollect/180; H. STEPHEN KAYE ET AL., U.S. DEP'T OF EDUC., DISABILITY STATISTICS CTR., REPORT NO. 14, MOBILITY DEVICE USE IN THE UNITED STATES 7 (2000), *available at* http://dsc.ucsf.edu/pub_listing.php; H. STEPHEN KAYE ET AL., U.S. DEP'T OF EDUC., DISABILITY STATISTICS CTR., ABSTRACT NO. 23, WHEELCHAIR USE IN THE UNITED STATES 1 (2002), *available at* http://dsc.ucsf.edu/publication.php. Sometimes mobility impairment is temporary as when someone breaks a leg, has hip replacement surgery, or suffers a back injury.

of the United States.[39] This 1 percent figure relates to the percentage of people using wheelchairs and to the fact that the wheelchair is the universal symbol for signifying accessibility to people with low functional mobility. The symbolic translation for many people is that they do not see many people in wheelchairs, so low functional mobility must be a rather minor issue. Contrary to the perception, however, the reality is that almost 17 percent of American families have a family member with some form of mobility impairment and that the rate of low functional mobility in the population increases dramatically as a population ages.[40] As of 2006, 23 percent of the population of the United States was aged 55 years and older,[41] and it is anticipated that within the next 10 to 15 years, 25 percent of the population in the United States will be age 65 years or older (this is up from 12.4 percent in the year 2000).[42] People in these age groups have much higher rates of low functional mobility than the general population, with as many as 40 to 50 percent of people over age 65 years having some type of limited mobility.[43] This means that as the general population ages over the next few years (absorbing the baby boomers into the ranks of those 55 years of age and older), we could likely have more than 20 percent of American families dealing with issues of mobility impairment. These changing demographics raise an important set of issues for community developers and planners.

An aging population is not the only factor to consider when planning for needs related to low functioning mobility. There are, of course, always going to be people who experience short-term or long-term declines in mobility without regard to age. People will be born with conditions that cause lowered functional mobility, or they may experience declining mobility as a result of illness, injury, accident, or some other cause. In addition to concerns generated by an aging population, declining functional mobility is likely to increase as a result of other factors. For example, rising rates of obesity and the increasing number of people losing limbs to diabetes and other causes also add to the number of people with low-level mobility.[44] Likewise, as we deal with modern forms of warfare and the ability to save life on the battlefield, we are confronted

---

[39] *Id.*; Qi Wang, *supra* note 4.   [40] Qi Wang, *supra* note 4.

[41] CHERYL RUSSELL, DEMOGRAPHICS OF THE U.S.: TRENDS AND PROJECTIONS 361 (3d ed. 2007).

[42] *Id.* at 362.

[43] NAT'L INST. ON AGING, *The Health and Retirement Study: Growing Older in America* 36–37 (Mar. 2007), *available at* www.nia.nih.gov/health/publication/growing-older-america-health-and-retirement-study (last updated Oct. 17, 2013).

[44] *See* Ctr. for Disease Control, *Long-Term Trends in Diagnosed Diabetes*, U.S. DEP'T OF HEALTH AND HUMAN SERVS. (2011), www.cdc.gov/diabetes/statistics/slides/long_term_trends. pdf; Ctr. for Disease Control, *National Diabetes Fact Sheet*, U.S. DEP'T OF HEALTH AND

with many thousands of surviving combat troops who have returned home from active duty with a need to adjust to decreased levels of mobility resulting from serious injury to or loss of a limb.[45] As a consequence, it is becoming increasingly important for us to rethink the design and navigability of the built environment. We need to expand on the use of inclusive design and develop what I refer to as inclusive design communities (IDCs): communities that take an integrated approach to property development and planning and that enable people to remain active and lifelong participants in community life. Inclusive design communities bring the two worlds of land use regulation and disability rights together to inspire planning and zoning that are inclusive and open to all residents over their entire lifetimes.

For purposes of clarity, I should say that developing IDCs is not the same as promoting inclusionary zoning, although they need not be inconsistent. Inclusive design communities are about making communities safe and easy to navigate for people with low functional mobility, whereas inclusionary zoning is generally focused on provision of low-income and "affordable" housing. Inclusive design communities can be neighborhoods, subdivisions, or even gated communities. They should be developed in a regional context of providing reasonable housing and employment opportunities for people of varying backgrounds and incomes. At the same time, local variations in economic access to property are inherent in a market society that provides choice on the basis of equal opportunity without necessarily assuring equality of outcome. Thus, while inclusionary zoning may be compatible with IDCs, I consider inclusionary zoning, for the purposes of this book, to be a separate political issue. Consequently, the use of the words *inclusion* and *access* relates to mobility and disability rather than to income.

In thinking about planning for IDCs, I believe that there are four key qualities that an IDC should strive to promote. These qualities include being intergenerational, intermodal, interoperable, and interjurisdictional. Inclusive design communities should be intergenerational to meet the needs of multiple generations of individuals and to provide safe and easy navigation for people in all ages of development, from children to senior citizens. Inclusive design communities should be intermodal to enhance interconnectivity across the built

HUMAN SERVS. (2011), www.cdc.gov/diabetes/pubs/pdf/ndfs_2011.pdf; Ctr. for Disease Control, *Crude and Age-Adjusted Percentage of Adults with Diagnosed Diabetes Reporting Any Mobility Limitation, United States, 1997–2011*, U.S. DEP'T OF HEALTH AND HUMAN SERVS., www.cdc.gov/diabetes/statistics/mobility/health_status/fig2.htm (last visited Oct. 1, 2013).

[45] David Wood, *U.S. Wounded in Iraq, Afghanistan Includes More Than 1,500 Amputees*, THE HUFFINGTON POST (Nov. 7, 2012, 5:38 PM EST), www.huffingtonpost.com/2012/11/07/iraq-afghanistan-am_n_2089911.html.

environment, taking into account multiple systems of private and public transport, including such alternatives as automobiles, buses, trains, bicycles, and walking. They should be interoperable, meaning that they should be planned and developed to enable multiple methods for providing accessible designs and uses. They should facilitate development by multiple providers and still have everything able to function interchangeably with maximum connectivity across the built environment. Finally, IDCs should be interjurisdictional in the way that they facilitate development of infrastructure networks across the built environment, making certain that roads, power lines, sidewalks, and other infrastructure function in a reasonably seamless manner to serve the entire community, even if multiple jurisdictions are involved.

In discussing IDCs, it is important to clarify that the term *inclusive design* does not necessarily mean the same thing as *universal design*.[46] Universal design is a term often invoked by people working in the field of disability rights and policy. It can have multiple meanings in terms of the actual construction requirements to be met when thinking about the complexity of our built environment. From a land use planning and regulation perspective, therefore, universal design is not a very helpful term because the law requires different factors to be accounted for in making different buildings and properties accessible, and different standards of accessibility are referenced in the literature. In constructing residential housing, for instance, we can find accessibility standards addressing different levels of what is referred to as *visitability*[47] as well as standards designated as meeting universal design, and individual components of a house, such as doors or light switches, may be built to universal design standards while the totality of the house is not. Similarly, construction requirements can vary with considerations of what is reasonable, as in making a *reasonable accommodation* in the design of a work environment for a person with mobility impairment,[48] and in relationship to financial constraints.[49] There are, in fact, many ways of dealing with accessibility, and inclusive design considers the relative value of construction choices by accounting for

---

[46] Design Research Ctr., *What Is Inclusive Design*, OCAD Univ., http://idrc.ocad.ca/index.php/about-the-idrc/49-resources/online-resources/articles-and-papers/443-whatisinclusivedesign (last visited Oct. 1, 2013).

[47] U.S. Dep't of Hous. and Urban Dev., Accessibility: Who Is Protected & the Importance of "Visitability," http://portal.hud.gov/hudportal/HUD?src=/program_offices/comm_planning/affordablehousing/training/web/crosscutting/equalaccess/accessprotected (last visited Jan. 31, 2014); Jordana L. Maisel et al., AARP Public Policy Inst., Increasing Home Access: Designing for Visitability (2008), *available at* www.nwccog.org/docs/rrr/seniors2009/seniors_housing/aarp_2008_Increasing_home_access.pdf. *See also* Malloy, *Inclusion by Design, supra* note 1.

[48] 42 U.S.C. § 12111(9) (2009).   [49] 42 U.S.C. § 12111(10)(B)(ii) (2009).

available technology, costs, and the balancing of a variety of other factors relevant to protecting the public health, safety, welfare, and morals. Consequently, inclusive design is a term meant to express the goal of advancing safe and easy navigation for people with low functional mobility while recognizing the inherent limitations that may prevent a community from universally achieving a singular level of access across the entire built environment.

In achieving the goal of safe and easy navigation, IDCs acknowledge that good zoning and planning involve not only the design of individual buildings and spaces but also the integration of places and spaces such that individuals can interact and exchange with each other in multiple settings and on a variety terms – so that they can enjoy meaningful access to the various venues in which life is experienced and played out. Making certain that a community is inclusive and accessible is a natural part of using the governmental police power to protect and advance the public interest, and this is the function of zoning and planning.

In developing IDCs, therefore, land use regulators must work strategically to coordinate a community's property resources, both public and private, in a way that advances the public health, safety, welfare, and morals. At the same time, land use regulation is an administrative process, and zoning and planning officials are subject to acting within legal guidelines that ensure due process and equal protection.[50] Regulation of property is also limited by the Fifth Amendment prohibition against *takings*.[51] Making property uses more accessible, however, does not mean that a property right has been taken, nor does it mean that the right to exclude is being diminished. Accessibility deals with the regulation of design preferences and not with the right to exclude. Thus, individuals may still exclude people from their private property or chose to live in gated communities that control entry, and local governments may still exclude certain uses from particular areas of a community pursuant to their police powers. The simultaneous need to advance the public health, safety, welfare, and morals while respecting legal constraints on the exercise of the police power requires local governments to act in a rational and balanced manner in developing approaches that are sensitive to competing interests and values in our system of governance. The balancing act that is oftentimes

---

[50] *See e.g.* City of Cleburne v. Cleburne Living Ctr., Inc., 473 U.S. 432 (1985); Euclid, 272 U.S. 365. *See also* Juergensmeyer & Roberts, *Land Use*, at 435–440; DANIEL R. MANDELKER, LAND USE LAW §§ 2.39, 2.41, 2.44 (5th ed. 2003).
[51] Pa. Coal Co. v. Mahon, 261 U.S. 393 (1922). *See also* STEPHEN J. EAGLE, REGULATORY TAKINGS (5th ed. 2012); RICHARD A. EPSTEIN, TAKINGS: PRIVATE PROPERTY AND THE POWER OF EMINENT DOMAIN (1985); Juergensmeyer, *Land Use*, at 390–427; Mandelker, *Land Use Law* §§ 2.01–2.38.

required in exercising the police power in protecting the public health, safety, welfare, and morals can be difficult, but traditional approaches to land use law offer a well-developed set of legal tools for addressing it.[52]

In developing a plan for this book, it has been puzzling to observe the lack of local planning and zoning on the subject of inclusive design. Communities across the country are actively engaged in conversations and actions directed at reducing their carbon footprint,[53] advancing green development,[54] promoting sustainable growth,[55] focusing on "complete streets,"[56] and creating healthy and walkable environments,[57] but little or nothing, in all of these efforts, is focused on the specific need for more inclusive design. There is overlap and synergy among all of these planning efforts, and inclusive design seems relevant to almost every one of the others. After all, what is the point of a sustainable community that has no plan for facilitating the process of intergenerational aging in place? For whom are these communities hoping to make the community sustainable if not for current and future generations of residents? Likewise, the "complete street" movement can improve navigation for people with disabilities at the same time as they do so for bike riders and others, and communities seeking to reduce their carbon footprint can benefit from making paths, sidewalks, and urban design friendlier to people with mobility impairment at the same time as they try to make them more walkable and better suited to mass transit. Good planning benefits everyone, and everyone benefits from inclusive design; thus, accessibility and the needs of people aging in place should be an express part of comprehensive planning in every community.

[52]   FGL & L Prop. Corp., 66 N.Y.2d 111; Euclid, 272 U.S. 365. Juergensmeyer & Roberts, *Land Use* at 1–5; Mandelker, *Land Use Law* § 1.04.

[53]   *See* SMART GROWTH NETWORK, INT'L CITY/CNTY. MGMT. ASS'N, GETTING TO SMART GROWTH: 100 POLICIES FOR IMPLEMENTATION, *available at* www.smartgrowth.org/pdf/gettosg.pdf (last modified Feb. 3, 2014); Sarah B. Schindler, *Following Industry's LEED®: Municipal Adoption of Private Green Building Standards*, 62 FLA. L. REV. 285 (2010).

[54]   *See* Robert H. Freilich & Neil M. Popowitz, *The Umbrella of Sustainability: Smart Growth, New Urbanism, Renewable Energy and Green Development in the 21st Century*, 42 URB. L. 1 (2010); Keith H. Hirokawa, *At Home with Nature: Early Reflections on Green Building Laws and the Transformation of the Built Environment*, 39 LEWIS & CLARK L. REV. 507 (2009); Janice C. Griffith, *Green Infrastructure: The Imperative of Open Space Preservation*, 42/43 URB. L. 259 (2011).

[55]   *See* JOHN M. DEGROVE, PLANNING POLICY AND POLITICS: SMART GROWTH AND THE STATES (2005).

[56]   *See* James A. Kushner, *Car-Free Housing Developments: Towards Sustainable Smart Growth and Urban Regeneration through Car-Free Zoning, Car-Free Redevelopment, Pedestrian Improvement Districts, and New Urbanism*, 23 UCLA J. ENVTL. L. & POL'Y 1 (2005).

[57]   *See id.*

In elaborating on issues raised in this first chapter, the book proceeds in several steps. Chapter 2 explains the traditional basis for local regulation of property development and land use. This involves discussion of the police power and of the various legal constraints on the exercise of the police power. Chapter 3 summarizes the current requirements for accessibility and puts these requirements into the context of an aging population with an increasing need for safe and easy navigation across the built environment. Chapter 4 explores some of the market dynamics that are relevant to understanding inclusive design and the idea of a community as a network enterprise. This chapter extends the discussion developed in Chapters 2 and 3 and offers additional ideas for thinking about the relationship between land use law and disability in the context of market and network considerations. Chapter 5 discusses additional zoning concepts as they relate to inclusive design and regulation of land use, including, for example, such concepts as the area and use variance, the special or conditional use permit, the nonconforming use, and some tools that might assist in encouraging additional production of inclusive design beyond the level of minimal compliance with federal disability law standards. Finally, Chapter 6 offers a few concluding thoughts.

In following the plan for this book, I hope to cover the key issues that arise in the process of planning and zoning for accessible communities. Admittedly, some readers may identify additional issues that they believe I should have covered or additional arguments that I might have made. I welcome these observations and comments, as the purpose of this book is to begin, rather than to conclude, a new conversation about the relationship between disability rights and land use law.

2

Planning and zoning under the police power

Planning and land use regulation in the United States dates back to the colonial period.[1] At that time, regulations addressed basic street layout, spacing of buildings, open space, lot layout, and some building code requirements, such as those to reduce the risk of spreading fire.[2] Some cities, including Philadelphia in 1681 and Washington, D.C., in 1791, developed early "comprehensive plans" to shape their growth patterns, and by the mid 1800s, many cities were realizing that lack of sanitation systems, overcrowding, poor drainage systems, lack of potable water, and conflicting land uses were posing problems for public health and safety.[3] In the mid 1800s, cities were often dirty and smelly places with stagnant waste water and raw sewage on the street. These conditions facilitated a number of diseases, such as yellow fever, cholera, typhoid, scarlet fever, and diphtheria.[4] In response to the danger that such conditions posed to the public health, the *sanitary reform movement* emerged, and regulations started to be adopted to reduce the presence of waste, nuisances, and other conditions associated with threats to the public health and

---

[1] See John F. Hart, *Colonial Land Use Law and Its Significance for Modern Takings Doctrine*, 109 HARV. L. REV. 1252 (1995–1996).

[2] *Id.*; JULIAN CONRAD JUERGENSMEYER & THOMAS E. ROBERTS, LAND USE PLANNING AND DEVELOPMENT REGULATION LAW § 2:2 (3d ed. 2007).

[3] JUERGENSMEYER & ROBERTS, *supra* note 2, § 2:3; William L. Andreen, *The Evolution of Water Pollution Control in the United States – State, Local, and Federal Efforts, 1789–1972: Part 1*, 22 STAN. ENVTL. L. J. 145 (2003); John B. Blake, *The Origins of Public Health in the United States*, 38 AM. J. OF PUB. HEALTH 1539 (1948); Richard A. Epstein, *In Defense of the "Old" Public Health: The Legal Framework for the Regulation of Public Health*, 69 BROOK. L. REV. 1421 (2003–2004).

[4] John Duffy, *Social Impact of Disease in the Late Nineteenth Century*, 47 BULL. N.Y. ACAD. MED. 797 (1971); Rodney M. Wishnow & Jesse L. Steinfeld, *The Conquest of the Major Infectious Diseases in the United States: A Bicentennial Retrospect*, 30 ANN. REV. MICROBIOL. 427 (1976).

safety.[5] By the time of the 1893 Chicago World's Fair, cities were becoming more crowded, and the *City Beautiful Movement* emerged to address issues that went beyond the concerns of the sanitary reform movement.[6] The City Beautiful Movement focused on aesthetics and purely health-related land use goals and regulations.

Out of these early movements, a sense of need for bringing order, beauty, and cleanliness to rapidly growing communities led to more formal planning and zoning in the early 1900s.[7] The First National Conference on City Planning was held in the nation's capital in 1909, and New York City enacted the first comprehensive zoning ordinance in 1916.[8] By 1924, the U.S. Department of Commerce had already passed the Standard State Zoning Enabling Act as a model for state legislatures to adopt in delegating the police power to zone to local municipalities, and 564 cities and towns had adopted zoning ordinances.[9] In 1926, the first legal challenge to the constitutionality of zoning reached the U.S. Supreme Court. The challenge was presented in the landmark case of *Village of Euclid v. Ambler Realty Co.*[10] In the *Euclid* case, the Supreme Court upheld the authority of local governments to regulate land uses through zoning and thereby paved the way for continued expansion of the public regulation of property development. Although the Court in *Euclid* did not specifically address issues related to inclusive design, the opinion did provide the foundation for authorizing local planning and zoning under the police power.

It is important to understand that land use regulation is focused on *use* of property and not on the particular characteristics of a user (such as race, religion, or disability). Likewise, the form of ownership of the property is generally not relevant to the matter of regulating land use; thus, it should not be relevant if the property in question is owned by an individual, a partnership, a corporation, or a not-for-profit organization. Traditional justifications for property regulation include the prevention of nuisances; controlling for spillover effects (externalities); and protecting the public health, safety, welfare, and

---

[5] Jon A. Peterson, *The Impact of Sanitary Reform upon American Urban Planning*, 13 J. Soc. Hist. 83 (1979).

[6] William H. Wilson, The City Beautiful Movement (1994).

[7] Michael M. Bernard, *The Development of a Body of City Planning Law*, 51 A.B.A. J. 632 (1965).

[8] Alfred Bettman, *Constitutionality of Zoning*, 37 Harv. L. Rev. 834 (1924); Charles M. Haar, *In Accordance with a Comprehensive Plan*, 68 Harv. L. Rev. 1154 (1955).

[9] Juergensmeyer & Roberts, *supra* note 2, § 3:6; Daniel R. Mandelker, Land Use Law § 4.15 (5th ed. 2003); Bettman, *supra* note 8.

[10] Vill. of Euclid v. Ambler Realty Co., 272 U.S. 365 (1926).

morals.[11] In Chapter 4, another justification is suggested based on the idea of government using regulation to facilitate positive functionality to produce a desired quality of life for a community understood to be operating as a kind of "network enterprise."[12]

In this chapter, discussion begins with background information concerning nuisance and the idea of regulating externalities. This discussion serves as a prelude to consideration of the *Euclid* case. After *Euclid*, the chapter addresses the distinction between planning and zoning and explains the legal relationship between a community's comprehensive plan and its zoning ordinance. It then discusses the difference between legislative and adjudicative action in the context of a local government developing and implementing a land use plan. Finally, it discusses some of the major legal constraints and limitations imposed on government in regulating land use under the police power. In all of this discussion, the focus will be on explaining the way in which inclusive design fits within the traditional local planning and zoning process and how the local land use planning and zoning process might be used to improve intergenerational accessibility across the built environment.

2.1 PRELUDE TO *EUCLID*

In an idealized world, complex property relationships could be easily coordinated by innumerable individuals negotiating among themselves to achieve reasonably and mutually beneficial outcomes. Such outcomes would be consistent with the image that Adam Smith, the founder of modern-day economics, offered in his conception of the *invisible hand*.[13] For Smith, the idea of an invisible hand was that individuals, pursuing their own self-interest, are

---

[11] JUERGENSMEYER & ROBERTS, *supra* note 2, § 3:13; DANIEL R. MANDELKER, *supra* note 9, at § 4.16. *See generally* FRED BOSSELMAN, DAVID L. CALLIES, & JOHN BANTA, THE TAKINGS ISSUE: AN ANALYSIS OF THE CONSTITUTIONAL LIMITS OF LAND USE CONTROL Chapters 5–6 (1973).

[12] The idea of city as a network enterprise is discussed in Chapter 4. Important books on the idea of networks more generally include MANUEL CASTELLS, THE RISE OF THE NETWORK SOCIETY: THE INFORMATION AGE – ECONOMY, SOCIETY, AND CULTURE Vol. 1 (2010); YOCHAI BENKLER, THE WEALTH OF NETWORKS: HOW SOCIAL PRODUCTION TRANSFORMS MARKETS AND FREEDOM (2006); OZ SHY, THE ECONOMICS OF NETWORK INDUSTRIES (2001); KECHENG LIU, SEMIOTICS IN INFORMATION SYSTEMS ENGINEERING (2000).

[13] ROBIN PAUL MALLOY, LAW AND MARKET ECONOMY: REINTERPRETING THE VALUES OF LAW AND ECONOMICS 90–99 (2000); ROBIN PAUL MALLOY, LAW IN A MARKET CONTEXT: AN INTRODUCTION TO MARKET CONCEPTS IN LEGAL REASONING 27–30 (2004); Robin Paul Malloy, *Adam Smith in the Courts of the United States*, 56 LOY. L. REV. 33 (2010); Robin Paul Malloy, *Mortgage Market Reform and the Fallacy of Self-correcting Markets*, 30 PACE L. REV. 79 (2009).

guided by an invisible hand that leads them to promote the public interest, even though the public interest is no part of their original intention.[14] In other words, people with good information and an ability to negotiate with each other ought to be able to attain desirable outcomes that simultaneously maximize their own individual preferences as well as those of the community more generally. This means that marginal private costs are equal to marginal social costs and that marginal private benefits are equal to marginal public benefits.[15] In such a situation, there is no variance between public and private interests and presumably no need for government to be involved in regulating property development and the coordination of land uses.

In practice, we know that Smith's idealized world does not exist. Coordinating property uses in a highly complex and integrated world is difficult for individuals, and when acting in their own self-interest, they are generally unlikely to achieve perfect unity between private and public interest. There are multiple reasons for this: problems of incomplete information; lack of clearly defined property rights; transactions costs; problems of coordinating collective action with neighbors; difficulty enforcing performance and enforcing remedies when an agreement is achieved; and the problem of wealth effects, which may skew outcomes in favor of higher-income property owners.[16] The point is that in an idealized world, we might not need land use regulation, but in the real world, we need some mechanism for coordinating land uses – and this mechanism must be able to mediate the tensions arising from the push and pull of competing preferences among self-interested individuals. These tensions are not just economic but also political, social, cultural, and emotional. To achieve beneficial and acceptable results in a very diverse community of individuals, the coordinating mechanism must be deemed fair, accessible, predictable, and rational (not arbitrary, capricious, or completely subjective), and because many people feel that the distribution of resources is itself unfair, the mechanism cannot simply be driven by a desire to confirm private market arrangements among people of economic means.

For better or for worse, in the absence of a perfect identity between private and public interest, government has taken on the role of mediating the coordination of land uses. Importantly, it should be understood that this role for government is not altogether inconsistent with Adam Smith's idea of the invisible hand, because Smith also suggested a role for an *impartial spectator*, who would constrain and temper the pursuit of individual

---

[14] *See* sources cited *supra* note 13.   [15] *Id.*
[16] Robert Cooter & Thomas Ulen, Law & Economics (3d ed. 2000); Oz Shy, The Economics of Network Industries (2001); Richard A. Posner, Economic Analysis of Law (7th ed. 2007); Malloy, Law and Market Economy, *supra* note 13; Malloy, Law in a Market Context, *supra* note 13.

self-interest.[17] In some ways, therefore, representative government acting pursuant to the rule of law provides the mediating presence required of Smith's impartial spectator. Moreover, appreciating a role for government in the regulation of property development and land use need not be considered an antimarket view; Adam Smith, after all, was himself a government agent working in a customhouse in Scotland, and the idea of representative government functioning as an impartial spectator in certain situations would probably not have struck him as overly problematic.[18]

Given acceptance of the idea that government regulation of land use is important in situations where individuals cannot themselves easily coordinate such uses, let us consider an example that illustrates some of the background issues that shape an understanding of land use regulation. As a starting point, let us begin with an example based on the facts of the well-known case of *Boomer v. Atlantic Cement Co.*, 257 N.E.2d 870 (N.Y. 1970).[19]

The *Boomer* case involved a private nuisance dispute among adjoining property owners.[20] Atlantic Cement owned property on which it operated a facility that discharged pollutants into the ambient air. These discharges affected the property of surrounding landowners, and in response, they brought a lawsuit seeking to enjoin further operation of the cement facility. In deciding the case, the court considered the potential for development of new technology to mitigate future discharges but noted that the company was using current technology at the time. The court found that enjoining the operation of the facility would cost Atlantic Cement in excess of $45 million, whereas the negative impact of the operation on surrounding property owners was less than $1 million. In this case, the decision was made to permit Atlantic Cement to continue operating. As an alternative to closing down the facility, the surrounding property owners were compensated for the negative impact on the value of their property. One way of looking at this outcome is that awarding $1 million to correct the problem (making surrounding property

---

[17] D. D. RAPHAEL, THE IMPARTIAL SPECTATOR: ADAM SMITH'S MORAL PHILOSOPHY (2007); COOTER & ULEN, *supra* note 16, at 40–42; MALLOY, LAW AND MARKET ECONOMY, *supra* note 13, at 66–69; POSNER, *supra* note 16, at 158–160.

[18] *See generally*, RAPHAEL, IMPARTIAL SPECTATOR, *supra*, note 17; JERRY EVENSKY, ADAM SMITH'S MORAL PHILOSOPHY: A HISTORICAL AND CONTEMPORARY PERSPECTIVE ON MARKETS, LAW, ETHICS, AND CULTURE (2005); CHARLES L. GRISWOLD, JR., ADAM SMITH AND THE VIRTUES OF ENLIGHTENMENT (1999); IAN SIMPSON ROSS, THE LIFE OF ADAM SMITH (1995).

[19] Boomer v. Atl. Cement Co., 257 N.E.2d 870 (N.Y. 1970). *Boomer* was a case involving an action for private nuisance, but the basic fact pattern can be used to illustrate several points, including nuisance, externality, transaction costs, and the difficulty of cooperative action.

[20] *Id.*

owners "whole" by awarding compensation) was much cheaper than enjoining the operation of the facility at a cost to its owner of more than $45 million.[21] In addition, because the company employed a number of people and added value to the local economy, closing the plant would have had negative economic repercussions for the entire community, beyond the $45 million cost to Atlantic Cement.

The action in this case was brought as a private nuisance, meaning that the operation of the facility was a nuisance to a limited number of people and that the operation of such a facility (a cement factory) was not a nuisance to the public in general.[22] Under similar facts, an action might have been brought by a public official to enjoin the activity as a public nuisance if the operation of the facility posed a threat to public health, perhaps because it could be shown that the discharging of dust and dirt into the ambient air is a triggering factor in lung disease – although this was not the situation in *Boomer*.[23] Under traditional land use law, a property owner has no right to operate a nuisance on his property, and the government can enjoin the particular use under its police power to protect the public health, safety, welfare, and morals.[24] Moreover, because a property owner has no right to operate a nuisance, preventing a use that amounts to a nuisance is not a taking under the Fifth Amendment to the U.S. Constitution.[25] As a starting point, therefore, one must appreciate that nuisance law has long been a source of authority for government to limit the use rights of a property owner; it is a traditional background legal principle supporting the exercise of the police power.

Modern land use law now limits many more uses than those that rise to the level of a nuisance. Let us consider the *Boomer* situation in terms of externalities and the problem of transaction costs to suggest a further basis for government regulation of land uses. In the *Boomer* case, Atlantic Cement was making a use of its property that imposed costs and burdens on adjoining

---

[21] COOTER & ULEN, *supra* note 16, at 43–44; MALLOY, LAW AND MARKET ECONOMY, *supra* note 13, at 108, 154–155; MALLOY, LAW IN A MARKET CONTEXT, *supra* note 13, at 189–190; POSNER, *supra* note 16, at 13–26.

[22] Keshbro, Inc. v. City of Miami, 801 So. 2d 864 (Fla. 2001); Wernke v. Halas, 600 N.E.2d 117 (Ind. App. 1992); Lussier v. San Lorenzo Valley Water Dist., 253 Cal. Rptr. 470 (1988); JUERGENSMEYER & ROBERTS, *supra* note 2, § 14:4.

[23] 44 Plaza, Inc. v. Gray-Pac Land Co., 845 S.W.2d 576 (Mo. Ct. App. 1992); Padilla v. Lawrence, 685 P.2d 964 (N.M. Ct. App. 1984).

[24] Udell v. Haas, 235 N.E.2d 897 (N.Y. 1968); *see also*, Bove v. Donner-Hanna Coke Corp., 258 N.Y.S. 229 (N.Y. App. Div 1932).

[25] M & J Coal Co. v. U.S., 47 F.3d 1148 (Fed. Cir. 1995); Osceola Cnty. v. Best Diversified, Inc., 936 So. 2d 55 (Fla. Dist. Ct. App. 2006); Dep't of Health v. The Mill, 887 P.2d 993 (Colo. 1994).

properties. The discharge of pollutants into the ambient air, resulting in dirt and dust on adjoining properties, is a classic spillover effect (also known as an externality),[26] and because the spillover imposes burdens and costs on the adjoining properties, to the detriment of the owners, it is identified as a negative externality.[27] In the language of property, Atlantic Cement is obtaining a free negative servitude over the adjoining properties because it is, in effect, using the adjoining property to deposit dust and dirt that it is unable to contain on its own property but that it must generate as part of its normal operations (dust and dirt are normal by-products of the production process).[28] In other words, if Atlantic Cement wanted to avoid having a spillover effect on adjoining properties, it would need to acquire much more land to encircle its operations and "catch" all of the particles escaping from its facility. In the alternative, it would need to invest in a way to reduce and eliminate the discharge.

Determining if the negative servitude in this example is free might turn on the question of who was there first: Atlantic Cement or the adjoining property owners. If the adjoining property owners were there first, then Atlantic Cement moved in and its operations imposed costs on the adjoining property owners, and diminishing the value of their land. In this case, Atlantic Cement obtains the servitude for free, unless it pays the adjoining owners for the cost of the servitude – and the owners may be unwilling to sell. Conversely, if Atlantic Cement were located on its property prior to the arrival of adjoining property owners (a residential subdivision is built several years later), it could be argued that the adjoining owners moved to the nuisance and were able to acquire the property at a discounted price because of the presence of its operation next door.[29] In the situation of moving to the nuisance, it might be held that the homeowners have already been compensated for the impact of the servitude

---

[26] Brett M. Frischmann, *Law in a Networked World: Speech, Spillovers, and the First Amendment*, 2008 U. Chi. Legal F. 301 (2007); Brett M. Frischmann & Mark A. Lemley, *Spillovers*, 107 Colum. L. Rev. 257 (2007); Daniel B. Kelly, *Strategic Spillovers*, 111 Colum. L. Rev. 1641 (2011); Gideon Parchomovsky & Peter Siefelman, *Cities, Property, and Positive Externalities*, 54 Wm. & Mary L. Rev. 211 (2012).

[27] Cooter & Ulen, *supra* note 16, at 154–155; Malloy, Law and Market Economy, *supra* note 13, at 90–91; Malloy, Law in a Market Context, *supra* note 13, at 192–193; Posner, *supra* note 16, at 72.

[28] Juergensmeyer & Roberts, *supra* note 2, § 16:3(A).

[29] Spur Indus., Inc. v. Del E. Webb Dev. Co., 494 P.2d 700 (1972); Bove v. Donner-Hanna Coke Corp., 236 A.D. 37 (1932). This case discusses the idea of the homeowner getting a discounted price up front on the purchase of the property because her reasonable investment-backed expectations should have included an expectation that further industrial development and pollution would occur in the future. Inasmuch as the up-front purchase price was already discounted, there was no cause for awarding damages for the same reason at a later date.

at the time of purchase, as a result of the discounted purchase price. In other words, the negative effects of the Atlantic Cement operations result in a lower cost of acquiring nearby property, and this lower acquisition price reflects an up-front compensation for the discharge of dust and dirt on surrounding lands.[30] Situations such as this raise conflict among property owners, and the greater the number of property owners involved, the more complex and difficult an amicable resolution becomes.

The situation in *Boomer* is made more difficult for private parties to coordinate as the number of adjoining property owners increases and as the specificity of property rights and the costs and benefits on all sides become less clear. Government can sometimes assess the problem better than the immediately affected individuals and work out a regulatory arrangement that might be more tolerable than that which they might try to accomplish on their own. To get a better sense of the problem, let us continue with this basic fact pattern and assume that the parties would be willing to work together to achieve an efficient market-based outcome, if they were simply permitted to do so on their own.

Let us assume the following additional facts.[31] First, let us assume that there are six households adjoining the property owned by the cement company and that the dirt and dust emitted from the cement company primarily cause a negative effect on adjoining property owners by making the interior of their homes dirty, requiring more frequent cleaning. Second, assume that the damage caused to each household adjoining the cement company is determined to equal $100. Third, the emissions can be controlled in one of two ways. One option is for the cement company to install a filter on its cement production facility that would capture and remove the dust before the air exits to the outside neighborhood. The second option is that households can purchase individual air filters to install in their homes to capture dust and dirt and thus mitigate the impact of the cement company emissions. The factory filter is priced at $300. The individual home filters are priced at $75 each. The overall situation is one that results in $600 of damages to adjoining property owners (six households × $100 damages each) as the spillover and negative externality of the use being made by the cement company. One option for dealing with this externality, if we do not wish to enjoin operation

---

[30] In addition to these complexities, poor people sometimes end up being disproportionally concentrated near industrial activities because the presence of industrial uses with negative spillover effects lowers the cost of neighboring property, which makes the homes in that area more affordable to lower-income individuals.

[31] *See* MALLOY, LAW AND MARKET ECONOMY, *supra* note 13, at 90; MALLOY, LAW IN A MARKET CONTEXT, *supra* note 13, at 177.

of the cement company, is for the company to pay the adjoining property owners for their damages (collectively, $600). Another option is not to require payment by the cement company and to let the households deal with the $100 damages that they each face. Of course, it should occur to someone that the $600 of damages can be prevented either by having the cement factory acquire and install a filter for $300 or by having the households spend $75 each for individual home filter systems at a collective cost of $450. In other words, a $600 problem can be solved for as little as $300, and in general, society would desire that problems such as this be resolved at the least total cost so that scarce resources might be available for doing other things.[32] If this problem can be corrected for $300 rather than $600, the community has $300 that can be used for other goods and services, such as for more health care, improved education, or better roads.

Now, let us imagine that we are positioned on a nearby hilltop observing the cement factory and the six adjoining households with all of this carefully calculated information known to us. Imagine that we are in many respects observing the activity below in much the same way as Adam Smith's impartial spectator might view it. The question we might be interested in is, if the factory and the households have all of the information that we have, and they have a costless way of negotiating to reach the most efficient way of solving this externality problem, what might they do? In other words, let us assume that everyone has perfect information, that there are no transaction costs, and that there are no barriers to free negotiation. Furthermore, let us assume that the current state of the law does not address the problem of externalities such that property owners are free to use their land for any lawful use; thus, the cement company is free to conduct it operations without any legal obligation to account for the cost of the spillover effects. In such a situation, what might we expect economically rational homeowners to do? From an economic perspective, each household would know that it is suffering $100 of damage as a result of the spillover from the cement company operations. Each household would also know that it could avoid this damage by spending $75 each for a home filter system. They would also know that the damage can be avoided by the cement company having a filter installed at a cost of $300 – a cost that amounts to $50 per household if they can reach an agreement to purchase such a filter and gift it to the cement company to use. The economically rational course of action is for the households to work together to purchase a filter for the cement company. This permits them to solve their problem at the least cost

---

[32] COOTER & ULEN, *supra* note 16, at 154–155; MALLOY, LAW IN A MARKET CONTEXT, *supra* note 13, at 151–152.

($50 rather than $75 or $100 each), and it permits the community to resolve this problem for a total cost of $300 rather than at a collective cost of $450 or $600.

As hypothetical impartial spectators, we might ask if it makes a difference if the state of the law does address the problem of externalities. For example, let us consider the rational economic outcome in a situation where the local land use regulation requires property owners to account for and internalize the cost of all spillover effects related to their use of land. This regulation would essentially make the cement company responsible for correcting the spillover effect and hold it liable for damages. In this situation, we should expect that the cement company will consider its options; it can pay $600 in damages ($100 × 6 households), or it can buy each household an individual home filter for a total cost of $450 ($75 × 6 households), or it can purchase a filter for the cement plant at $300.[33] The rational economic outcome is for the cement company to purchase the $300 filter for its facility; this is the same outcome as under the alternative rule. Consequently, under conditions of perfect information, no transaction costs, and no barriers to free negotiation, the economically efficient outcome is achieved without regard to the legal rule. It should be noted, however, that even as the efficient outcome is achieved in each case, the distributive impact is different.[34] In the first case, the homeowners bear the cost, and in the second case, the cement company does. This could be an important factor for political reasons based on the political influence of the competing parties. It also has implications based on the ability of the parties to spread costs – as in the potential for the cement company to spread the cost of correcting for the spillover by adding slightly to the price of its goods and services to consumers. If the cement company can spread the cost over numerous users of its products, the people ultimately paying to correct the externality may be far removed from the actual location of the facility (assuming that many sales are to nonlocals). These consumers will have no voice in local politics (including planning and zoning), whereas the

[33] For example, sometimes airport authorities pay for soundproofing for nearby homes as one way of mitigating an expansion of a runway or the introduction of larger or noisier jets at the airport. *See Sound Insulation*, FED. AVIATION ADMIN., www.faa.gov/airports/airport_development/omp/FAQ/Sound_Insulation (last visited Feb. 27, 2014); C. Kell-Smith & Associates, Inc., *Ted Stevens Anchorage International Airport*, http://kell-smith.com/?page_id=64 (last visited Feb 10, 2013); Tim Waters, *Soundproof Homes Offer Joy of Silence Near LAX*, LOS ANGELES TIMES, May 6, 1988, http://articles.latimes.com/1988-05-06/local/me-2647_1_soundproof-homes (last visited Oct. 28, 2013).

[34] *See* Guido Calabrese & A. Douglas Melamed, *Property Rules, Liability Rules, and Inalienability: One View of the Cathedral*, 85 HARV. L. REV. 1089 (1972); Alice Kaswan, *Distributive Justice and the Environment*, 81 N.C. L. Rev. 1031 (2003).

local residents will have a potentially strong voice.[35] Furthermore, whereas nearby property owners will be highly motivated to organize and lobby for a rule making the company liable, the distant consumers will have little or no incentive to organize on this issue because they will only experience a small incremental price increase, and even this is probably not transparent. The ability of the cement company to pass these costs on to consumers will depend on how competitive the market is for its products.[36] The more competitive the market, the less ability the cement company will have to pass on costs, and this could hurt the company financially.[37] Consequently, even in a world of no or nominal transaction costs, the political dynamics and the economic context are both important to understanding the potential implications of policy choices that have differing distributional consequences.

Now, let us assume a more realistic world that operates in a dynamic of transaction costs and where information is less than perfect. Let us assume that it is costly to work with other people, to negotiate, to gather information, and to arrange for certain multiparty transactions. To keep it simple, let us assume that as impartial spectators on our hilltop, we know that the transaction costs of having to take collective and coordinated action with multiple parties impose $40 on each party. Acting individually is still relatively costless. Now consider the economically rational outcomes under the alternative legal states discussed earlier. When the cement company is not responsible for spillovers, the households have to take care of the problem. In such a situation, they now can either suffer $100 damages each (total cost of $600), pay $75 each for a home filter (total cost of $450), or collectively agree to purchase a filter for the cement company at $90 each ($50 each plus $40 transaction costs each, for a total of $540). The economically rational choice is for each household to purchase an individual home filter system (costing each household $75 rather than $90). This means that $450 will be spent to correct a problem that can be solved for $300. Under the alternative rule, the cement company is responsible for spillover effects. The cement company can make a decision on what course of action to take without having to coordinate with other parties. Thus, the cement company confronts the same choices as it did previously and should elect to spend $300 to acquire the filter for its facility. The economically efficient outcome is achieved by having a land use regulation that requires the cement company to internalize the cost of spillover effects. Even if the cement company and the homeowners are unable to calculate all of this,

---

[35] Maxwell L. Stearns & Todd J. Zywicki, Public Choice Concepts and Applications in Law (2009).

[36] Cooter & Ulen, *supra* note 16, at 25–38; Posner, *supra* note 16, at 419–421.

[37] Sources cited *supra* note 36.

we, as impartial spectators on the hill with experts to assist us, may be able to appreciate the issues associated with the coordination of these competing land uses.

Let us take this example a step further. Assume that the people in the six households adjoining the property of the cement company are low-income residents with very little discretion in their budget. In other words, they are living on the margin and basically just able to cover the cost of living in their homes. They do not have discretionary funds for home improvements and things of that sort. In this situation, we might observe something identifiable as the "wealth effect."[38] The wealth effect might make our outcome even worse if we have a rule that makes the households responsible for addressing the spillover problem rather than the cement company. For instance, in our preceding examples, if our households have no extra "out-of-pocket" funds to purchase an air filter system, they will not be able to pay for any option that requires a financial contribution, and they will each simply suffer $100 in damages. In the short term, at least, dealing with the impact of damages requires no out-of-pocket resources, and it is the one option they each have, even though they will be living in dirty and dusty homes. From a community perspective, this is the worst outcome of the options presented in the sense that a problem capable of being solved for $300 is permitted to impose $600 of costs on the households in this community.

As a final consideration at this point, some thought should be given to the problems of taking coordinated and collective action. As previously indicated, collective action can impose transaction costs beyond those associated with learning about options and calculating trade-offs. An additional set of costs arises when thinking about the potential for people to cheat on their bargains and promises. For example, in the preceding hypotheticals, it was assumed that one option to solve the spillover externality was for the households to get together and collectively purchase a filter to be placed in the cement company facility. This option required each household to contribute $50 to the purchase price. Let us assume that our households (households 1–6) all agree to this arrangement and sign a contract to contribute $50 each. Under the terms of the agreement, household 1 agrees to act as the "point person" and actually order the filter system. Households 2–6 all agree to each contribute $50 against the ordering receipt marked "paid" and issued by the filter system manufacturer. The agreement to pay against the receipt is based on a concern that several of the households expressed with respect to giving household 1 all of the money in advance and perhaps not being able to make sure that it will all be properly

---

[38] *See* MALLOY, LAW AND MARKET ECONOMY, *supra* note 13, at 93; MALLOY, LAW IN A MARKET CONTEXT, *supra* note 13; POSNER, *supra* note 16, at 14–15.

applied to the purchase of the system (they are worried that household 1 might abscond with the funds). Basically, the agreement they enter into means that each household will solve a $100 problem for $50, and everyone desires this outcome. After ordering the filter system and presenting everyone with the purchase receipt, however, household 3 simply refuses to pay. Household 3 seeks to obtain a $100 benefit for no out-of-pocket expenditure (household 3 seeks to be a "free rider" in the sense of getting the benefit without paying) and assumes that none of the other households will be willing or able to sue him for what amounts to an additional $10 a piece that the other five households will have to pay as a result of household 3's failure to perform ($300 ÷ 5 = $60).[39] The way household 3 calculates it, the cost of a lawsuit (assume $40 per household) will be more than the additional $10 a piece that each of the remaining households will have to pay to cover household 3's failure to contribute. Even though this means that the remaining households have to pay $60 each to acquire the company filter rather than $50 each, it is still less costly than the alternatives of buying the individual home air filter systems ($75 each), enduring the $100 in damages, or bringing a $40 lawsuit while also having to pay $50 toward the purchase of the company filter ($90 each). This example illustrates that there may be incentives and disincentives that work against successful collaboration and that costs will be involved in policing and enforcing an agreement. These costs should also be considered in evaluating collective action.

The preceding examples illustrate some of the issues involved in coordinating property development and land use. The examples are very simple; in the real world, there are innumerable competing users and uses and many complex spillover effects. Likewise, determining the available technologies, best options, and actual costs and benefits of all potentially reasonable courses of action is difficult. Furthermore, many people do not consider the choices among competing land uses to be matters that should be resolved by employing only the values represented by the calculus of economic efficiency. Coordinating land uses does involve consideration of costs and benefits, but it frequently also involves a need to mediate deep and intense differences among people based on competing political, social, cultural, and aesthetic values. For all of these reasons, it may be difficult for individuals to achieve good community-wide outcomes when everyone simply seeks to pursue his own self-interest. Unlike the individual decision to purchase a home or to rent

---

[39] COOTER & ULEN, *supra* note 16, at 42, 107; MALLOY, LAW IN A MARKET CONTEXT, *supra* note 13, at 122; Victor P. Goldberg, *The Free-Rider Problem, Imperfect Pricing, and the Economics of Retailing Services*, 79 NW. U. L. REV. 736 (1984).

a particular apartment, the coordination of multiple and complex land uses across an entire community is difficult. Sometimes having access to experts and a little distance from an underlying relationship or conflict, as in being a kind of impartial spectator, is beneficial.

As a further prelude to addressing the *Euclid* case, it should be noted that all of the preceding examples involved the fact that the use of one property for a cement company resulted in discharge of dust and dirt that "spilled over" onto adjoining properties. An "invasion" of dust, dirt, noise, or something else is often an element of a classic spillover externality, but it is not a requirement. For example, an adjoining property owner may construct or modify a building in a way that is aesthetically undesirable, thus causing the value of surrounding property to fall. Similarly, a property owner might wish to place a series of large billboards on a residential lot or shelter numerous animals in a backyard. In a very real sense, these types of uses do not involve a physical "invasion" of adjoining property in the same way as dirt, dust, and noise might, but they do have a negative effect on the use and enjoyment of the surrounding property and likewise affect the public health, safety, welfare, and morals. Consider, too, a popular grocery store or restaurant that locates in a quiet residential neighborhood. Even if the store and restaurant are built with ample parking, and can be more or less self-contained on the property where they are located, it may be that the traffic generated by customers coming and going to these businesses creates a neighborhood impact that is akin to an externality or an associational spillover. Perhaps the roads in the neighborhood need to be widened to safely handle increased traffic loads, or perhaps because of increased automobile traffic, a need for new sidewalks is generated. The presence of these "attractor" uses can also create a type of neighborhood externality for which land use professionals need to account in seeking to effectively coordinate land uses. The point is that externalities in the land use context need not involve any sort of "invasion" or trespass to fall within the regulatory scope of the police power.

2.2 EUCLIDIAN ZONING

In *Village of Euclid v. Ambler Realty Co.*, the U.S. Supreme Court had its first opportunity to evaluate the constitutionality of zoning and land use regulation and to assess the legality of local government restrictions on the use preferences of individual property owners.[40] It held that local governments do have the ability to regulate property development and land uses and that this authority

---

[40] *Euclid*, 272 U.S. 365.

under the police power is not limited to the prevention of nuisances. In the decades since the *Euclid* decision, much effort has gone into defining the scope and limitations of the police power as well as to addressing the process by which it is properly exercised.

As background to the *Euclid* case, it is important to understand the basic foundation of the police powers. The police power of a state is intrinsic to the idea of sovereignty over a given territory.[41] It includes the power to make law, enforce law, and regulate behavior for the protection of the public health, safety, welfare, and morals.[42] In the United States, the federal government has certain police powers granted to it under the Constitution, and likewise, under the 10th Amendment, the states retain police power to the extent not granted to the federal government and not reserved for the people.[43] Local governments and municipalities exercise police power to the extent that there has been a proper delegation of the sovereign's police power to them.[44] Thus, local governments and municipalities exercise police power in accordance with state enabling legislation, and the extent of their authority is as delegated and limited by such legislation.[45] In *Euclid*, the police power of the state of Ohio had been delegated for enumerated purposes to local governments, and the Village of Euclid was one of the recognized units of government to which such authority had been delegated.

Pursuant to its police power, the village of Euclid developed and passed a zoning ordinance to govern the regulation of land within its boundaries. Because the zoning ordinance prevented Ambler Realty Co. from using land it owned in the way it desired, and because the restrictions on use greatly diminished the value of the property, Ambler sued the village to prevent the enforcement of the zoning ordinance. At the time of the *Euclid* case, zoning and land use regulations had not yet been tested for legality under the U.S. Constitution. Many people believed that such regulations would be unconstitutional to the extent that they did not specifically address themselves to the prevention of a nuisance. There had been varied results under state law challenges to zoning, but *Euclid* presented the first opportunity for the U.S. Supreme Court to deliver an opinion as to the constitutionality of local land use regulations – regulations that restricted a private property owner's dominion and control over his own property and that seemed to interfere with

---

[41] U.S. Dep't of Commerce, Standard State Zoning Enabling Act, 1926; Juergensmeyer & Roberts, *supra* note 2, § 3:7.

[42] Sources cited *supra* note 41.   [43] *Id.*

[44] Juergensmeyer & Roberts, *supra* note 2, § 3:7.

[45] *Id. See, e.g.,* Fla. Stat. Ann. § 166.021 (West 2011); 65 Ill. Comp. Stat. Ann. 5/11–13–1 (West 2011); N.Y. Village Law § 7–700 (McKinney 2011).

the natural path of commercial development in a growing industrial region of the country.[46]

Village of Euclid v. Ambler Realty Co.

272 U.S. 365 (1926)

MR. JUSTICE SUTHERLAND delivered the opinion of the Court.

The Village of Euclid is an Ohio municipal corporation. It adjoins and practically is a suburb of the City of Cleveland. Its estimated population is between 5,000 and 10,000, and its area from twelve to fourteen square miles, the greater part of which is farm lands or unimproved acreage. It lies, roughly, in the form of a parallelogram measuring approximately three and one-half miles each way. East and west it is traversed by three principal highways: Euclid Avenue, through the southerly border, St. Clair Avenue, through the central portion, and Lake Shore Boulevard, through the northerly border in close proximity to the shore of Lake Erie. The Nickel Plate railroad lies from 1,500 to 1,800 feet north of Euclid Avenue, and the Lake Shore railroad 1,600 feet farther to the north. The three highways and the two railroads are substantially parallel.

Appellee is the owner of a tract of land containing 68 acres, situated in the westerly end of the village, abutting on Euclid Avenue to the south and the Nickel Plate railroad to the north. Adjoining this tract, both on the east and on the west, there have been laid out restricted residential plats upon which residences have been erected.

On November 13, 1922, an ordinance was adopted by the Village Council, establishing a comprehensive zoning plan for regulating and restricting the location of trades, industries, apartment houses, two-family houses, single family houses, etc., the lot area to be built upon, the size and height of buildings, etc.

The entire area of the village is divided by the ordinance into six classes of use districts, . . . [regulating the type of uses for each district; three height districts, regulating the permissible height of structures; and four area districts, regulating the size of lots and the permissible coverage of lots] . . .

Annexed to the ordinance, and made a part of it, is a zone map, showing the location and limits of the various use, height and area districts . . . The plan is a complicated one and can be better understood by an inspection of the map, though it does not seem necessary to reproduce it for present purposes.

---

[46] Village of Euclid v. Ambler Real Estate Co., 272 U.S. 365 (1926); JUERGENSMEYER & ROBERTS, *supra* note 2, § 3:4(B).

The lands lying between the two railroads for the entire length of the village area and extending some distance on either side to the north and south, having an average width of about 1,600 feet, are left open, with slight exceptions, for industrial and all other uses. This includes the larger part of appellee's tract...

The enforcement of the ordinance is entrusted to the inspector of buildings, under rules and regulations of the board of zoning appeals. Meetings of the board are public, and minutes of its proceedings are kept. It is authorized to adopt rules and regulations to carry into effect provisions of the ordinance. The board is given power in specific cases of practical difficulty or unnecessary hardship to interpret the ordinance in harmony with its general purpose and intent, so that the public health, safety and general welfare may be secure and substantial justice done.

The ordinance is assailed on the grounds that it is in derogation of § 1 of the Fourteenth Amendment to the Federal Constitution in that it deprives appellee of liberty and property without due process of law and denies it the equal protection of the law... The court below held the ordinance to be unconstitutional and void, and enjoined its enforcement.

Before proceeding to a consideration of the case, it is necessary to determine the scope of the inquiry. The bill alleges that the tract of land in question is vacant and has been held for years for the purpose of selling and developing it for industrial uses, for which it is especially adapted, being immediately in the path of progressive industrial development; that for such uses it has a market value of about $10,000 per acre, but if the use be limited to residential purposes the market value is not in excess of $2,500 per acre; that the first 200 feet of the parcel back from Euclid Avenue, if unrestricted in respect of use, has a value of $150 per front foot, but if limited to residential uses, and ordinary mercantile business be excluded therefrom, its value is not in excess of $50 per front foot.

It is specifically averred that the ordinance attempts to restrict and control the lawful uses of appellee's land so as to confiscate and destroy a great part of its value; that it is being enforced in accordance with its terms; that prospective buyers of land for industrial, commercial and residential uses in the metropolitan district of Cleveland are deterred from buying any part of this land because of the existence of the ordinance and the necessity thereby entailed of conducting burdensome and expensive litigation in order to vindicate the right to use the land for lawful and legitimate purposes; that the ordinance constitutes a cloud upon the land, reduces and destroys its value, and has the effect of diverting the normal industrial, commercial and residential development thereof to other and less favorable locations.

The record goes no farther than to show, as the lower court found, that the normal, and reasonably to be expected, use and development of that part of appellee's land adjoining Euclid Avenue is for general trade and commercial purposes, particularly retail stores and like establishments, and that the normal, and reasonably to be expected, use and development of the residue of the land is for industrial and trade purposes. Whatever injury is inflicted by the mere existence and threatened enforcement of the ordinance is due to restrictions in respect of these and similar uses; to which perhaps should be added — if not included in the foregoing — restrictions in respect of apartment houses . . .

The question . . . as stated by appellee: Is the ordinance invalid in that it violates the constitutional protection "to the right of property in the appellee by attempted regulations under the guise of the police power, which are unreasonable and confiscatory?"

Building zone laws are of modern origin. They began in this country about twenty-five years ago. Until recent years, urban life was comparatively simple; but with the great increase and concentration of population, problems have developed, and constantly are developing, which require, and will continue to require, additional restrictions in respect of the use and occupation of private lands in urban communities. Regulations, the wisdom, necessity and validity of which, as applied to existing conditions, are so apparent that they are now uniformly sustained, a century ago, or even half a century ago, probably would have been rejected as arbitrary and oppressive. Such regulations are sustained, under the complex conditions of our day, for reasons analogous to those which justify traffic regulations, which, before the advent of automobiles and rapid transit street railways, would have been condemned as fatally arbitrary and unreasonable. And in this there is no inconsistency, for while the meaning of constitutional guaranties never varies, the scope of their application must expand or contract to meet the new and different conditions which are constantly coming within the field of their operation. In a changing world, it is impossible that it should be otherwise. But although a degree of elasticity is thus imparted, not to the meaning, but to the application of constitutional principles, statutes and ordinances, which, after giving due weight to the new conditions, are found clearly not to conform to the Constitution, of course, must fall.

The ordinance now under review, and all similar laws and regulations, must find their justification in some aspect of the police power, asserted for the public welfare. The line which in this field separates the legitimate from the illegitimate assumption of power is not capable of precise delimitation. It varies with circumstances and conditions. A regulatory zoning ordinance, which would be clearly valid as applied to the great cities, might be clearly invalid as applied to rural communities. In solving doubts, the maxim *sic utere tuo ut alienum non laedas,* which lies at the foundation of so much of the common law of nuisances, ordinarily will furnish a fairly helpful clew. And the law of nuisances, likewise, may be consulted, not for the purpose of controlling, but for the helpful aid of its analogies in the process of ascertaining the scope of, the power. Thus the question whether the power exists to forbid the erection of a building of a particular kind or for a particular use, like the question whether a particular thing is a nuisance, is to be determined, not by an abstract consideration of the building or of the thing considered apart, but by considering it in connection with the circumstances and the locality. A nuisance may be merely a right thing in the wrong place, – like a pig in the parlor instead of the barnyard. If the validity of the legislative classification for zoning purposes be fairly debatable, the legislative judgment must be allowed to control.

There is no serious difference of opinion in respect of the validity of laws and regulations fixing the height of buildings within reasonable limits, the character of materials and methods of construction, and the adjoining area which must be left open, in order to minimize the danger of fire or collapse, the evils of over-crowding, and the like, and excluding from residential sections offensive trades, industries and structures likely to create nuisances.

Here, however, the exclusion is in general terms of all industrial establishments, and it may thereby happen that not only offensive or dangerous industries will be excluded, but those which are neither offensive nor dangerous will share the same fate. But this is no more than happens in respect of many practice-forbidding laws which this Court has upheld although drawn in general terms so as to include individual cases that may turn out to be innocuous in themselves. The inclusion of a reasonable margin to insure effective enforcement, will not put upon a law, otherwise valid, the stamp of invalidity. Such laws may also find their justification in the fact that, in some fields, the bad fades into the good by such insensible degrees that the two are not capable of being readily distinguished and separated in terms of legislation . . .

It is said that the Village of Euclid is a mere suburb of the City of Cleveland; that the industrial development of that city has now reached and in some degree extended into the village and, in the obvious course of things, will soon absorb the entire area for industrial enterprises; that the effect of the ordinance is to divert this natural development elsewhere with the consequent loss of increased values to the owners of the lands within the village borders. But the village, though physically a suburb of Cleveland, is politically a separate municipality, with powers of its own and authority to govern itself as it sees fit within the limits of the organic law of its creation and the State and Federal Constitutions . . .

We find no difficulty in sustaining restrictions of the kind thus far reviewed . . .

The Supreme Court of Illinois, in City of Aurora v. Burns, supra, in sustaining a comprehensive building zone ordinance dividing the city into eight districts, including exclusive residential districts for one and two-family dwellings, churches, educational institutions and schools, said:

> "The constantly increasing density of our urban populations, the multiplying forms of industry and the growing complexity of our civilization make it necessary for the State, either directly or through some public agency by its sanction, to limit individual activities to a greater extent than formerly. With the growth and development of the State the police power necessarily develops, within reasonable bounds, to meet the changing conditions . . ." . . .

. . . [In this case,] before the [Village of Euclid zoning] ordinance can be declared unconstitutional, [it must be shown] that such provisions are clearly arbitrary and unreasonable, having no substantial relation to the public health, safety, morals, or general welfare . . .

The relief sought here is . . . an injunction against the enforcement of any of the restrictions, limitations or conditions of the ordinance. And the gravamen of the complaint is that a portion of the land of the appellee cannot be sold for certain enumerated uses because of the general and broad restraints of the ordinance. What would be the effect of a restraint imposed by one or more of the innumerable provisions of the ordinance, considered apart, upon the value or marketability of the lands is neither disclosed by the bill nor by the evidence, and we are afforded no basis, apart from mere speculation, upon which to rest a conclusion that it or they would have any appreciable effect upon those matters. Under these circumstances, therefore, it is enough for us to determine, as we do, that the ordinance in its general scope and dominant features, so far as its provisions are here involved, is a valid exercise of authority, leaving other provisions to be dealt with as cases arise directly involving them.

And this is in accordance with the traditional policy of this Court . . . It has preferred to follow the method of . . . a systematically guarded application and extension of constitutional principles to particular cases as they arise, rather than [one of] out of hand attempts to establish general rules to which future cases must be fitted. This process applies with peculiar force to the solution of questions arising under the due process clause of the Constitution as applied to the exercise of the flexible powers of police, with which we are here concerned.

Decree reversed.

_____

The *Euclid* case makes a number of important points that are critical to understanding modern planning and zoning law. Although many of these points have been further developed in numerous cases since the 1926 decision in *Euclid*, *Euclid* is still cited as the foundation for the constitutionality of planning and zoning in the United States.

In *Euclid* we learn that the exercise of the police power includes the authority of local government to regulate land use and the way in which improvements are constructed on property. Such regulation is proper when done to promote and protect the public health, safety, welfare, and morals. Significantly, the location of the property and the context of the regulation are important. As to location, the court in *Euclid* informs us that the requirements in a rural community may be different from those governing a large city, and as to context, the court opines that a pig may be appropriate in a barnyard but not in the parlor. Thus, location and context are to be considered in evaluating the exercise of the police power, and there is to be flexibility in evaluating regulation based on the fact that we live in a dynamic rather than a static world. *Euclid* not only validates local planning and zoning but also links the validity of such regulation to changing circumstances arising over time, saying, "for while the meaning of constitutional guaranties never varies, the scope of their application must expand or contract to meet the new and different conditions which are constantly coming within the field of their operation. In a changing world, it is impossible that it should be otherwise."

Today the world is much more crowded and much more complex than it was in 1926. The zoning ordinance in *Euclid* was by modern standards simple and rudimentary. Now we have many more types of land use regulation and multiple approaches to zoning that establish a variety of use and construction standards. Modern zoning is responsive to changes in the way we live and reflects changing understandings of the public health, safety, welfare, and morals. This includes regulatory change in response to the need for inclusive design. As noted earlier in the book, we are in the midst of significant demographic change as our population ages and as the impact of declining functional mobility affects more and more families. At the same time, we have seen a tremendous shift in the way in which we understand and deal with disability. The United States and the world have made significant commitments to accessibility not only because it is a way of promoting equality but also because accessible communities, featuring inclusive design, are important to advancing the public health, safety, welfare, and morals.[47]

Our understanding of the public health, safety, welfare, and morals is different than it was in 1926, and this is easy to illustrate. We now require people to wear seatbelts when driving an automobile, we try to restrict the smoking of cigarettes, and we have regulations regarding secondhand smoke; we also have learned that asbestos is not a desirable component of a healthy building, and we acknowledge the need to regulate land with respect to broader ecosystem implications related to clean water and air and with respect to the needs of agriculture and sustainable habitat for the protection of wildlife. Eliminating barriers to the safe and easy navigation of the built environment is just another example of the ever-changing context in which we must understand the exercise of the police power.

In exercising the police power to develop and enact land use regulations, the standard of review as applied in *Euclid* and applicable today is the rational basis test.[48] This means that there must be a rational basis for believing that the enacted regulations will protect and promote the public health, safety, welfare, and morals. Stated differently, as long as it is at least fairly debatable that the regulation promotes the desired public regarding outcome, a court will not overturn it under a police powers challenge. Importantly, it is the property owner affected by the planning and zoning ordinance that has the burden of establishing that the regulation is not even fairly debatable – not supported by a rational basis.[49] This means that the deference given to local enactment of land use regulations is very high. In defense of this position of deference, courts will often point out that enacting such regulation is a legislative function and

---

[47] *See, e.g.*, Convention on the Rights of Persons with Disabilities, G.A. Res. 61/106, U.N. Doc. A/RES/61/106 (Dec. 13, 2006); *Disability Discrimination Act 1992* (Cth) (Austl.); Canjiren Baozhang Fa [Law on the Protection of Disabled Persons] (promulgated by the Standing Comm. Nat'l People's Cong., Dec. 28, 1990, effective May 15, 1991) 1990–1992 Falü Quanshu 1268 (China), *translated in* 14 P.R.C. Laws and Regs V-03-00-101; Behindertengleichstellungs-gesetz [BGG] [Equal Opportunities for Disabled People Act], May 1, 2002, BGBl. I. at 1467 (Ger.), *available at* www.gesetze-im-internet.de; 7600, Igualdad de Oportunidades para las personas con Discapacidad en Costa Rica [Equal Opportunities for Persons with Disabilities] May 29, 1996, La Gaceta, 2000, sec. 2 (Costa Rica); Canadian Human Rights Act, R.S.C. 1985, c. H-6; Equality Act, 2010, c. 15 (U.K.); Equal Opportunity, Non-Discrimination and Universal Accessibility for People with Disabilities (B.O.E. 2003, 289) (Spain). *See also* DISABILITY RIGHTS IN EUROPE: FROM THEORY TO PRACTICE (Anna Lawson & Caroline Gooding, eds., 2005); Theresia Degener, *International Disability Law – A New Legal Subject on the Rise: The Interregional Experts' Meeting in Hong Kong, December 13–17, 1999*, 18 Berkely J. Int'l. L. 180 (2000).

[48] JUERGENSMEYER & ROBERTS, *supra* note 2, § 5:37; MANDELKER, *supra* note 9, § 1.12.

[49] Sources cited *supra* note 48.

that they should therefore be careful not to violate the separation of powers principle.[50] In addition, courts will often note that local residents have the ability to respond to land use regulations of which they disapprove by voting local officials out of office.

Given this legal framework, *Euclid* remains notable today for several other reasons. First, note that the regulation in question dramatically decreased the market value of Ambler's property. This significant decline in value, resulting from the enactment of the zoning ordinance, was not determinate on the question of a valid exercise of the police power. This was so even though, at the time Ambler acquired the property, it had reasonable expectations that commercial and industrial growth would continue on a path from the city of Cleveland to its property in the village of Euclid. Despite regional development patterns, the village of Euclid had jurisdictional authority under the police power to enact local land use regulations, even though its regulations may have been counter to regional land use expectations and resulted in a significant decline in property value to the owner. A property owner is not entitled to the highest and best use of the land, and land use regulations can properly alter certain investment-based expectations with respect to future and potential uses of the property.[51]

A nuanced wrinkle in the court opinion as it addressed the reasonable expectations for commercial and industrial growth in the village of Euclid is that it indicated a willingness to permit regulation even if it seemed to run counter to natural market forces. This is an important although subtle point given the time period of the case. At the time, there would have been much support for laissez-faire and the ideas of Adam Smith and the invisible hand of progress. Market forces were believed to be powerful and positive in advancing the social order, and government interference with these natural forces was something to be avoided. Recognizing that market forces were expanding commercial and industrial growth into the village, yet accepting the authority of local government officials to stand in the way of such natural forces, reflected a changing attitude about individual self-interest and markets at a level beyond simply dealing with a question of zoning. This set the stage for a number of incremental shifts in attitude that facilitated what is now commonly referred to as the emergence of the administrative state. In the years since 1926, the administrative and regulatory structure of the United States has expanded

---

[50] *Euclid*, 272 U.S. 365; Cooper v. Bd. of Cnty. Comm'rs, 614 P.2d 947 (Idaho 1980); Kyser v. Township, 786 N.W.2d 543 (Mich. 2010); JUERGENSMEYER & ROBERTS, *supra* note 2, § 5:37(A); MANDELKER, *supra* note 9, § 6.26.

[51] Lucas v. S.C. Coastal Council, 505 U.S. 1003 (1992); Penn Cent. Transp. Co. v. City of New York, 438 U.S. 104 (1978); Hadacheck v. Sebastian, 239 U.S. 394 (1915).

dramatically. The incremental design and land use changes required for most efforts at inclusive design would seem to raise few if any problems with respect to the police power authority of local government.

A second noteworthy aspect of *Euclid* involves what the opinion explains about the relationship between zoning and nuisance law. As the opinion points out, valid zoning is not limited to the traditional power of government to prevent a nuisance.[52] In cases up to this point in time, many people accepted that the key land use device available to local governments involved the traditional authority it possessed to prevent a nuisance to protect the public health, safety, welfare, and morals. Regulation of a land use and separation of conflicting land uses were permitted to stop or prevent a nuisance. One way to look at the village of Euclid zoning ordinance is to think of it in terms of trying to anticipate and reduce the potential for a nuisance by creating distinct zones restricting activities in certain areas of the village; industrial uses were separated from single-family residential use, for instance. The opinion, however, made it clear that the constitutionality of zoning ordinances did not turn on the traditional power to regulate and prevent a nuisance. What emerged from the case, and developed more clearly over time, was a sense that planning and zoning were in large part needed to address spillover effects and externalities as well as the difficulties inherent in relying on individual property owners to successfully coordinate a complex set of uses on their own.

Spillover effects involve impacts that affect others off of a property as a result of the use being made on the property. For example, as discussed in the prior section of this chapter, a property owner may lawfully operate a factory on her property and yet smoke and dust may escape into the ambient air and end up having a negative impact on surrounding properties. The impact on others may not be accounted for in the cost of operating the factory, and yet it is a cost of the use being made of the property. At a certain level, the smoke becomes a nuisance, and the use can be prevented under the police power for that reason. At the same time, even without rising to the level of a nuisance, the activity imposes costs on others and raises conflicts with a potential to undermine the enjoyment and value of surrounding properties. If this is determined to pose an adverse impact on the public health, safety, welfare, and morals, appropriate regulation directed at abating the adverse impact may be enacted under the police power, even in the absence of it being held a nuisance.

Some people might suggest that the owner of the factory and the surrounding property owners should simply get together and reach an agreement capable of compensating the surrounding property owners for the adverse impact of

---

[52] *Euclid*, 272 U.S. 365.

operating the factory. This may in fact be one valid approach to addressing the adverse impact. The problem with this suggestion is that we know, as discussed earlier in this chapter, that it is oftentimes difficult for individuals to coordinate and enforce corrective action on their own. We know that there are impediments to individual coordination of complex use arrangements because of market failures and because of coordination problems, information problems, transaction costs, problems associated with poorly defined property rights, wealth effects, and more. Because of these types of problems, government can act under the police power to coordinate and regulate land uses and property development to advance the public health safety, welfare, and morals.

As long as there is a rational basis for land use regulation designed to protect and advance the public health, safety, welfare, and morals, subject to some limitations to be discussed later in this chapter, it is likely to be upheld as a valid exercise of the police power. Thus, local governments have been permitted to regulate land use to address problems related to noise, dust, smoke, vibration, traffic congestion, crowding, and even the casting of shadows caused by the placement of a structure on a given lot.[53] The regulations can address density and intensity of land use; the height, width, and bulk of a structure; the placement and orientation of structures on a lot; ancillary uses; and a variety of other factors.[54] Moreover, the authority to regulate in accordance with the police power includes the ability to regulate for aesthetic purposes; this includes regulating design and the design preferences of property owners.[55] As the U.S. Supreme Court noted in *Berman v. Parker,*

> Public safety, public health, morality, peace and quiet, law and order – these are some of the more conspicuous examples of the traditional application of the police power to municipal affairs. Yet they merely illustrate the scope of the power and do not delimit it... The concept of the public welfare is broad and inclusive. The values it represents are spiritual as well as physical, aesthetic as well as monetary. It is within the power of the legislature to determine that the community should be beautiful as well as healthy, spacious as well as clean, well-balanced as well as carefully patrolled.[56]

---

[53] *See* Fountainbleau Hotel Corp. v. Forty-Five Twenty-Five, Inc., 114 So. 2d 257 (Fla. Dist. Ct. App. 1959); S. Camden Citizens in Action v. N.J. Dep't of Envtl. Prot., 254 F.Supp.2d 486 (D. N.J. 2006); Hyde v. Somerset Air Serv, Inc., 61 A.2d 645 (N.J Ch. 1948); Thomas Farragher, *60 Stories and Countess Tales*, THE BOSTON GLOBE (Sept. 24, 2006), www.boston.com/news/local/massachusetts/articles/2006/09/24/60_stories_and_countless_tales/?page=2.

[54] Westfield Motor Sales Co. v. Town of Westfield, 324 A.2d 113 (N.J. Super. Ct. Law Div. 1974); JUERGENSMEYER & ROBERTS, *supra* note 2, §§ 4:12–4:14

[55] JUERGENSMEYER & ROBERTS, *supra* note 2, § 12:1; MANDELKER, *supra* note 9, § 11.05.

[56] Berman v. Parker, 348 U.S. 26, 33 (1954).

Many cases in the law of land use and zoning validate the authority of government to regulate design and aesthetics. For example, local governments can regulate building designs and facades, establish historic districts, regulate the placement of art, and establish aesthetic criteria for neighborhoods under the police power.[57] These regulations can be based on a variety of rational reasons related to health, safety, welfare, and morals. Consequently, addressing some of the ways in which we achieve accessibility and inclusive design should be well within the police power. This can relate to the design and location of ramps, entranceways, and other architectural elements. It may also include establishing criteria for building materials, colors, and fit with surrounding buildings and landscaping, in addition to regulations as to the placement and orientation of certain construction features on a lot.[58] Admittedly, building exteriors as opposed to interiors are more readily understandable as having a public impact in terms of a rationale for aesthetic design regulation. Ramps, entranceways, driveways, and open spaces all have implications for others beyond the immediate property. Likewise, structures and spaces that are held open for public use or to accommodate the public in a variety of ways may extend or blur the line between public and private aesthetics because such spaces are not fully private, as would be an interior room in a private home. Thus, local planning officials should have some input about inclusive design even if criteria on accessibility are set in accordance with federal disability law. Requiring a ramp for accessibility, for instance, should not mean that a property owner can just build any type of a ramp out of whatever materials he likes. The ramp may be required under federal disability law and certain construction design elements may be established, but local zoning regulations should address the way that such ramps interface with local land uses. Interior spaces are a little different than those spaces that are public or that present a potential externality spillover to public health, safety, welfare, and morals, including aesthetics. Even as to interior spaces, however, health and safety factors have long dictated a number of design and construction requirements consistent with exercise of local police power. Inclusive design requirements

---

[57] Penn Cent. Transp. Co. v. N.Y.C., 438 U.S. 104 (1978); La Salle Nat'l Bank v. City of Evanston, 312 N.E.2d 625 (Ill. 1974); State ex rel. Stoyanoff v. Berkeley, 458 S.W.2d 305 (Mo. 1970); A-S-P Assocs., v. City of Raleigh, 258 S.E.2d 444 (N.C. 1979); City of Santa Fe v. Gamble-Skogmo, Inc., 389 P.2d 13 (N.M. 1964).

[58] Reid v. Architectural Bd. of Review of City of Cleveland Heights, 192 N.E.2d 74 (Ohio Ct. App. 1963); Anderson v. City of Issaquah, 851 P.2d 744 (Wash. Ct. App. 1993); MANDELKER, *supra* note 9, § 11.24; Janet Elizabeth Haws, Comment, *Architecture as Art? Not in My Neocolonial Neighborhood: A Case for Providing First Amendment Protection to Expressive Residential Architecture*, 2005 B.Y.U. L. REV. 1625 (2005).

directed at reducing the number of falls and injuries occurring in buildings, and at enhancing the safe and easy navigation of the built environment for the growing number of people in the population with low and declining mobility, should fall readily within the police power.

A third matter to note about the *Euclid* decision is that even as it discusses the regulation of property and its use, it does not involve an asserted claim of a *taking* in violation of the Fifth Amendment to the U.S. Constitution.[59] A takings claim is something that a modern student of land use and zoning law might well expect to be addressed in this type of lawsuit, but it is not present in the case opinion. This is important because the idea of a regulatory taking is relatively new, and early cases such as *Euclid* struggled to evaluate regulation under the police power in terms of such constitutional constraints as due process and equal protection. A discussion of takings law will be in the last section of this chapter related to limitations on the police power.

At this date in the twenty-first century, we have gone well beyond the rudimentary framework of Euclidian zoning. Euclidian zoning includes three key features: it is cumulative, it establishes a hierarchy of uses, and it is "as of right."[60] Cumulative zoning establishes specific use zones in different locations across a community. These use zones are all organized with respect to a hierarchy of desirability in terms of favoring low-density residential uses. Thus, the highest use is typically designated as single-family residential. A typical zoning code works down the hierarchy of uses by moving to various forms of multifamily housing, professional offices, retail, commercial, light industrial, heavy industrial, and so on. Under Euclidian zoning, a lower-ranked use cannot be in a zone designated for a higher-ranked use, but a higher-ranked use can be located in a lower-ranked zone. Thus, a factory could not locate in a zone designated for single-family residential housing, but a single-family residence could be located in a zone designated for industrial uses. Therefore, under traditional Euclidian zoning, there is generally only one zone with an exclusive use, and that is the single-family residential zone (the use given the highest ranking under the zoning code in question). In contrast, modern zoning law provides for many zones that are exclusively limited to the specific uses identified in the code as appropriate for the given zone.

Euclidian zoning is also said to be zoning, "as of right." This means that a property owner has a legal right to use her property for any purpose consistent with the uses permitted in a given zone. This contrasts with many modern

---

[59] JUERGENSMEYER & ROBERTS, *supra* note 2, §§ 4:1–4:3; MANDELKER, *supra* note 9, § 5.02.
[60] JUERGENSMEYER & ROBERTS, *supra* note 2, § 4:3; MANDELKER, *supra* note 9, § 6.01.

zoning practices that oftentimes make even permitted uses conditional on meeting certain criteria or on obtaining specific approvals that might rationally be denied. Moreover, we now use multiple devices that make little sense under a traditional Euclidian approach because they provide for flexibility and variation within and among zones in a way that was impermissible in the Euclid context.

Modern zoning codes are not cumulative, do not necessarily establish one clear hierarchy of use, and do not necessarily permit a use "as of right." Land use regulations now include such devices as performance zoning, floating zones, planned unit developments, mixed-use zones, transferable development rights (TDRs), linkage programs, environmental conservation easements, transect zoning, and a variety of other approaches that all make property development a much more complex process.[61] In general, however, all of these approaches are focused on the coordination of land development pursuant to the police power. Consequently, modern planning and zoning involves a highly negotiated process between property owners, members of the public, and regulatory officials.

2.3 RELATIONSHIP BETWEEN PLANNING AND ZONING

Planning and zoning are two distinct functions in the regulation of property development and land use.[62] They are supposed to work together in advancing the public interest with respect to land use regulation. Traditionally, zoning set out the regulations as to the types of uses permitted within certain districts or zones within a community. As in *Euclid*, the effort is to separate incompatible uses and to coordinate development so as to promote the public health, safety, welfare, and morals. The code is usually accompanied by a map indicating exactly where each district or zone is located. The zoning code is to be designed to implement a comprehensive plan for an entire community. In other words, a zoning code is not to be done piecemeal, nor is it to be done by focusing on a particular property or property owner. The zoning code is supposed to be enacted pursuant to a comprehensive plan based on public

---

[61] JUERGENSMEYER & ROBERTS, *supra* note 2, §§ 4:16, 4:19, 7:17–7:22, 9:9–9:10, 13:12; MANDELKER, *supra* note 9, §§ 5.41, 6.60, 6.61, 7.28, 9.01, 9.23, 9.24, 11.38.

[62] JUERGENSMEYER & ROBERTS, *supra* note 2, §§ 2:7–2:8. *See also id.* §§ 7:3–7:4. Some useful planning books include JOHN RADCLIFFE, MICHAEL STUBS, & MILES KEEPING, URBAN PLANNING AND REAL ESTATE DEVELOPMENT (3rd. ed., 2009); JAMES A. LAGRO, JR., SITE ANALYSIS: A CONTEXTUAL APPROACH TO SUSTAINABLE LAND PLANNING AND SITE DESIGN (2008); PHILIP R. BERKE, DAVID R. GODSCHALK, EDWARD J. KAISER, & DANIEL A. RODRIGUEZ, URBAN LAND USE PLANNING (5th ed., 2006).

input and accounting for current and future needs of a community.[63] This holistic approach attempts to depersonalize the regulatory process so that equal protection and due process can be protected and so that we might avoid imposing regulatory burdens on individuals when they should rightfully be shared by many. It is also intended to reduce the risk of an individual having property zoned in a negative or a positive way as a result of personal politics.

The traditional view is that all zoning must be done in accordance with a comprehensive plan, but there have been disagreements over the years as to the need for a separate documented plan and as to the level of consistency required between the plan and the zoning code that is enacted to implement the plan.[64] The various states address the plan differently in their enabling statutes, and the courts have differed on matters of interpretation. In some instances, there is a need for a separate document designated as the comprehensive plan, and there is a requirement for careful planning focused on specific elements,

---

[63] JUERGENSMEYER & ROBERTS, *supra* note 2, § 2:7; MANDELKER, *supra* note 9, § 3.13; David L. Callies, *Land Use Controls: Of Enterprise Zones, Takings, Plans and Growth Controls*, 14 URB. L. 781 (1982); Daniel R. Mandelker, *The Role of the Comprehensive Plan in Land Use Regulation*, 74 MICH. L. REV. 900 (1976); In July 2010, I did a survey of planning and zoning statutes in 10 different states: Florida (FL); Illinois (IL); Kentucky (KY); Louisiana (LA); Maryland (MD); Mississippi (MS); New Jersey (NJ); New York (NY); Pennsylvania (PA); and Texas (TX). Of these, only FL required comprehensive planning at the local and the state level; MD required planning for "smart growth"; and the other states required or provided for local planning. With respect to consistency between the plan and the local zoning code, FL has the strictest requirement for consistency between the zoning code and the plan, and between the local plan and the state plan. IL made consistency advisory/optional; LA provided for the plan to be advisory; MS provided for general conformity between the plan and the code; TX required zoning in accordance with the plan; and MD, NJ, and NY spoke generally to the matter of planning pursuant to a plan. While each of the states provided for some form of planning to address the public health, safety, welfare, and morals, none specifically required a planning element to address mobility and accessibility for people with disability. Fla. Stat. §186.007 (FL state level comprehensive planning); Fla. State. §163.3174 (FL local level comprehensive planning); §65 ILGS 5/11-12-4 (IL Municipal Code – comprehensive planning); KRS §100.111 (KY comprehensive planning law); La.R.S. 33:101 (LA Planning Commission); La.R.S. 33:106 (LA requirements for a comprehensive plan); Md. Ann. Code art. 66B §3.10 (MD "smart growth"); Md. Ann. Code. Art. 66B §1.01 (visions for comprehensive planning); Md. Ann. Code art. 66B §1.04 (county comprehensive planning); Miss. Code Ann. §17–1–1 (MS comprehensive planning); NJ comprehensive planning law is under Title 30, Subtitle 3, Chapter 55D, Art. 1 of the NJ Annotated Statutes; N.J. Stat. Ann. §40:55D-28 sets out elements of a comprehensive plan. NY planning and zoning laws are located in Article 16 of the Town Law. PA comprehensive planning and zoning laws are found in Title 53, Part I, Chapter 30, Article 1 of the PA statutes. TX comprehensive planning laws are at Title 7, Subtitle A, Chapter 213 of the Texas Local Government Law.

[64] Iowa Coal Mining Co. v. Monroe Cnty., 494 N.W.2d 664, 669 (Iowa 1993); JUERGENSMEYER & ROBERTS, *supra* note 2, § 2:8; MANDELKER, *supra* note 9, §§ 3.14–3.18; *See, e.g., supra* note 63 and the difference between IL and FL in terms of the comprehensive plan.

such as traffic, transportation, housing, open space, schools, sanitation, jobs, and infrastructure, whereas others are less specific and indicate a willingness to find a plan expressed in a collection of notes or discussions, as long as they reflect a thoughtful and rational consideration of the community as a whole.[65] The question of consistency focuses on just how specific the plan is as to present and future land use goals and the extent to which zoning accurately reflects these details. Some states, such as Illinois, tend to treat the plan as a guideline for zoning that can be malleable as implemented, whereas other states, such as Florida, require strict compliance with the details of the plan.[66]

Somewhat related to the issue of consistency between the plan and the zoning code is the issue of the legal status of the plan. In jurisdictions that require a high level of consistency, one is more likely to find independent legal status for the plan in the sense that the passing of a plan may itself give rise to an action for a taking without having to wait for zoning to be enacted to implement the plan.[67] In other states that view the plan as more suggestive in nature, one is more likely to find that the passing of a plan does not give rise to an action for a taking until an implementing code provision is enacted.[68]

Planning and zoning are both important parts of land use regulation, and both can play an important role in making sure that our communities are accessible now and even more so in the future. Although some states require careful and detailed planning as to certain enumerated elements, there is often little or no mention of a requirement for systematic planning as to accessibility.[69] Consequently, little attention is devoted to the problems of inclusion and accessibility even as considerable attention is paid to green development, sustainability, and many other important elements. This ought to be corrected by adding a specific element to the enabling legislation requiring accessibility and inclusive design to be part of all comprehensive planning – to require a community to plan on the ways in which it can best comply with federal disability law as it experiences change over time. A complement to this requirement is, of course, to then insist on a very high level of consistency between the plan and the actual enactment and implementation of the plan.

---

[65] *See* Iowa Coal Mining Co. v. Monroe Cnty., 494 N.W.2d 664 (Iowa 1993); JUERGENSMEYER & ROBERTS, *supra* note 2, § 2:9; MANDELKER, *supra* note 9, § 3.22; Edward J. Sullivan, *The Plan as Law*, 24 URB. LAW. 881 (1992). *See* 10 state comparisons, *supra* note 63.

[66] Fla. Stat. §186.007, Fla. Stat. §163.3174; §65 ILGS 5/11–12–4 (IL municipal code).

[67] Fla. Stat. §186.007, Fla. Stat. §163.3174.   [68] *See supra* note 63.

[69] COOTER & ULEN, *supra* note 16, at 102–106; MALLOY, LAW AND MARKET ECONOMY, *supra* note 13, at 144–146; MALLOY, LAW IN A MARKET CONTEXT, *supra* note 13, at 199–203; POSNER, *supra* note 16, at 119–120.

Pinecrest Lakes, Inc. v. Shidel

795 So. 2d 191 (Fla. Dist. Ct. App. 2001)
OPINION
FARMER, J.

The ultimate issue raised in this case is unprecedented in Florida. The question is whether a trial court has the authority to order the complete demolition and removal of several multi-story buildings because the buildings are inconsistent with the County's comprehensive land use plan. We conclude that the court is so empowered and affirm the decision under review.

Some twenty years ago, a developer purchased a 500-acre parcel of land in Martin County and set out to develop it in phases. Development there is governed by the Martin County Comprehensive Plan (the Comprehensive Plan). Phase One of the property was designated under the Comprehensive Plan as "Residential Estate," meaning single-family homes on individual lots with a maximum density of 2 units per acre (UPA). The Comprehensive Plan provides that

> "where single family structures comprise the dominant structure type within these areas, new development of undeveloped abutting lands shall be required to include compatible structure types on land immediately adjacent to existing single family development."

Phases One through Nine were developed as single-family homes on individual lots in very low densities.

The subject of this litigation, Phase Ten, is a 21-acre parcel between Phase One and Jensen Beach Boulevard, a divided highway designated both as "major" and "arterial."

The County's growth management staff recommended that the County Commission approve this . . . site plan for Phase Ten. Following a hearing at which a number of people objected to the proposal, including Shidel, the County Commission approved . . . and issued a Development Order for Phase Ten permitting the construction of 19 two-story buildings.

. . . Shidel and another Phase One homeowner, one Charles Brooks, along with the Homeowners Association, then filed a verified complaint with the Martin County Commission challenging the consistency of the Development Order with the Comprehensive Plan, requesting rescission of the Development Order. In response to the verified complaint, after a hearing the County Commission confirmed its previous decision to issue the Development Order.

Shidel and Brooks then filed a civil action in the Circuit Court against Martin County . . . They alleged that the Development Order was inconsistent with the Comprehensive Plan. The developer intervened . . . the trial court found that the Development Order was consistent with the Comprehensive Plan and entered final judgment in favor of the developer.

> . . . the developer decided to commence construction, notwithstanding the pendency of an appeal. Accordingly, it applied for and received building permits for construction of . . . buildings while the case was under consideration in court . . .

Appellate review did not produce the outcome for which the developer had hoped. In 1997 we reversed the trial court's decision that the County's consistency determination complied with the Comprehensive Plan . . .

We remanded the case for a trial de novo and for any appropriate relief.

On remand, the trial judge proceeded in two stages: the first stage involved a determination whether the Development Order was consistent with the Comprehensive Plan; and the second stage, which became necessary, addressed the remedy . . . At the end of the consistency phase, the trial court entered a partial judgment finding that the Development Order was not consistent with the Comprehensive Plan. The trial de novo then proceeded to the remedy.

At the conclusion of the remedy phase, the trial court entered a Final Judgment. The court found that the Comprehensive Plan established a hierarchy of land uses, paying deference to lower density residential uses and providing protection to those areas. The "tiering policy" required that, for structures immediately adjacent to each other, any new structures to be added to the area must be both comparable and compatible to those already built and occupied. The court then found significant differences between the northern tier of Phase One and the adjacent southern tier of Phase Ten. The structures in Phase One were single level, single family residences, while the structures in Phase Ten were two-story apartment buildings with eight residential units. Therefore, the court found, the 8-residential unit, two-story, apartment buildings in Phase Ten were not compatible or comparable types of dwelling units with the single family, single level residences in Phase One; nor were they of comparable density. Consequently, the court determined, the Development Order was inconsistent with the Comprehensive Plan . . .

In granting such relief, the court found that the developer had acted in bad faith. Specifically, the court found that the developer continued construction during the pendency of the prior appeal and continued to build and lease during the trial — even after losing on the consistency issue. The court found that the developer "acted at [its] own peril in doing precisely what this lawsuit sought to prevent and now [is] subject to the power of the court to compel restoration of the status prior to construction" . . .

When the Final Judgment was entered, five of the eight-unit buildings had been constructed in Phase Ten (Buildings 8–12).

Following the entry of Final Judgment, the developer filed this timely appeal and moved for a stay pending review . . . Upon review, we affirmed the stay order. We now explain our decision on the merits.

I. The Consistency Issue

Initially the developer argues that the trial court erred in the consistency phase by failing to accord any deference to the County Commission's interpretation of its own Comprehensive Plan when the County approved the second revised site plan and its multi-story, multi-family buildings. Conceding that the proceedings are de novo and that the Development Order is subject to "strict scrutiny" under the Comprehensive Plan as to the consistency issue, the developer nevertheless argues that the court must bow to the County's interpretation of its own Comprehensive Plan and the application of its many elements to the site plan . . .

When a statute authorizes a citizen to bring an action to enjoin official conduct that is made improper by the statute, and that same statute necessitates a determination by the judge in the action as to whether the official's conduct was improper under the statute, as a general matter the requirement for a determination of the propriety of the official action should not be understood as requiring the court to defer to the official whose conduct is being judged. While the Legislature could nevertheless possibly have some reason to require some deference to the officials whose conduct was thus put in issue, we would certainly expect to see such a requirement of deference spelled out in the statute with unmistakable clarity. Here it is not a question of any lack of clarity; the statute is utterly silent on the notion of deference. It is thus apparent that the structure and text of the statute do not impliedly involve any deference to the decision of the county officials. So we necessarily presume none was intended.

Section 163.3194 requires that all development conform to the approved Comprehensive Plan, and that development orders be consistent with that Plan. The statute is framed as a rule, a command to cities and counties that they must comply with their own Comprehensive Plans after they have been approved by the State. The statute does not say that local governments shall have some discretion as to whether a proposed development should be consistent with the Comprehensive Plan. Consistency with a Comprehensive Plan is therefore not a discretionary matter. When the Legislature wants to give an agency discretion and then for the courts to defer to such discretion, it knows how to say that. Here it has not. We thus reject the developer's contention that the trial court erred in failing to defer to the County's interpretation of its own comprehensive plan . . .

We have carefully reviewed the record of the trial and the evidence presented. It is apparent that there is substantial competent evidence to support the . . . [finding of inconsistency] . . . We therefore affirm the finding of inconsistency and proceed to explain our decision on the remedy.

II. Remedy of Demolition

Developer challenges what it terms the "enormity and extremity of the injunctive remedy imposed by the trial court." It argues that the trial court's order requiring the demolition of 5 multi-family residential buildings is the most radical remedy ever mandated by a Florida court because of an inconsistency with a Comprehensive Plan. Specifically, the contention is that the trial judge failed to balance the equities between the parties and thus ignored the evidence of a $3.3 million dollar loss the developer will suffer from the demolition of the buildings. The court failed to consider alternative remedies in damages, it argues, that would have adequately remedied any harm resulting from the construction of structures inconsistent with the Comprehensive Plan . . .

Developer lays great stress on the size of the monetary loss that it claims it will suffer from demolition, as opposed to the much smaller diminution in value that the affected property owner bringing this action may have suffered. It contends that a $3.3 million loss far outweighs the evidence of diminution in the value of Shidel's property, less than $26,000. Its primary contention here is that the trial judge erred in failing to weigh these equities in its favor and deny any remedy of demolition. Instead, as developer sees it, the court should have awarded money damages to eliminate the objector's diminution in value. Developer also argued that instead of demolition it should be allowed to build environmental barriers, green areas of trees and shrubbery, between the apartment buildings and the adjoining area of single family homes.

Developer emphasizes that we deal here with an expensive development: "a high quality, up-scale project"; "forty units of high-quality, upscale apartments"; "five upscale multi-family dwellings, housing 40 garden apartments, at a value of approximately $3 million." Developer concedes that there is evidence showing that plaintiff Shidel's property is diminished by $26,000. It also concedes that the total diminution for all the homes bordering its project is just under $300,000. Developer contends, however, that the real countervailing harm to all these affected property owners in the vicinity is not any diminution in the value of their homes, but instead is merely "knowing that there is an upscale apartment building approximately a football field away, partially visible through some trees behind the house."

...We doubt that there will be many instances where the cost of the newly allowed construction will be less than any diminution resulting from an inconsistency. Entire projects of the kind permitted here will frequently far exceed the monetary harms caused to individual neighbors affected by the inconsistency. In other words, if balancing the equities – that is, weighing the loss suffered by the developer against the diminution in value of the objecting party – were required before demolition could be ordered, then demolition will never be ordered.

Moreover it is an argument that would allow those with financial resources to buy their way out of compliance with comprehensive plans. In all cases where the proposed use is for multiple acres and multiple buildings, the expenditures will be great. The greater will be its cost, and so will be a resulting loss from an after-the-fact demolition order. The more costly and elaborate the project, the greater will be the "imbalance in the equities." The more a developer is able to gild an inconsistency with nature's ornaments – trees, plants, flowers and their symbiotic fauna – the more certain under this argument will be the result that no court will enjoin an inconsistency and require its removal if already built.

In this case the alleged inequity could have been entirely avoided if developer had simply awaited the exhaustion of all legal remedies before undertaking construction . . .

It also seems quite inappropriate, if balancing of equities were truly required . . . , to focus on the relatively small financial impacts suffered by those adjoining an inconsistent land use. The real countervailing equity to any monetary loss of the developer is in the flouting of the legal requirements of the Comprehensive Plan. Every citizen in the community is intangibly harmed by a failure to comply with the Comprehensive Plan, even those whose properties may not have been directly diminished in value.

We claim to be a society of laws, not of individual eccentricities in attempting to evade the rule of law. A society of law must respect law, not its evasion. If the rule of law requires land uses to meet specific standards, then allowing those who develop land to escape its requirements by spending a project out of compliance would make the standards of growth management of little real consequence. It would allow developers such as this one to build in defiance of the limits and then escape compliance by making the cost of correction too high. That would render [the statutory requirements] meaningless and ineffectual . . .

We therefore affirm the final judgment of the trial court in all respects. GUNTHER and GROSS, JJ., concur.

The *Pinecrest* case illustrates the power of requiring comprehensive planning and of insisting on consistency between the plan and the enactment of the plan. Every community should be required to plan with respect to mobility impairment and aging in place, and their plans must be made consistent with federal disability law requirements. In addition, the zoning codes and the actual regulation of property development by local officials need to be consistent with the plans that are developed and approved, providing likewise for citizen enforcement and appropriate remedies. Requiring comprehensive planning to include provision for inclusive design consistent with the ADA and related federal disability legislation is an important way of integrating federal and national standards on accessibility into local government action pursuant to the police power.

It is important to note the remedy provided in *Pinecrest*, as well as the need for consistency. The discussion in the case reflects two competing views related to what is sometimes referred to as the "efficient breach."[70] The basic idea behind the efficient breach is that in certain situations, it may be better, from an economic efficiency perspective, to permit a breach of an undertaking rather than to enforce the obligation to perform. The evaluation of the matter turns on a comparison of costs and benefits as among the alternative remedies.[71]

In *Pinecrest*, for example, the developer expressed a willingness to pay damages to the adjoining property owners to the extent that the inconsistent nature of the new project lowered the value of their property. In other words, the developer offered to make them whole by paying damages equal to the full amount of the decrease in the value of their homes because of its failure to comply with the consistency requirement. The facts of the case tell us that the loss to adjoining property owners was much less than the cost of demolition of the newly constructed project. From an economic perspective, one should try to avoid waste and seek to resolve this dispute in a way that imposes the least cost, while making the injured parties whole. In this case, efficient breach would suggest that the developer be allowed to resolve the dispute by paying the adjoining property owners for their loss and leaving the new buildings

---

[70] Groves v. John Wunder Co., 286 N.W. 235 (Minn. 1939); Peevyhouse v. Garland Coal & Mining Co., 382 P.2d 109 (Okla. 1962).

[71] Bremner v. City & County of Honolulu, 28 P.3d 350 (Hawaii App. 2001); Frank Hardie Adv., Inc. v. City of Dubuque Zoning Bd. of Adjustment, 501 N.W.2d 521 (Iowa 1993); Palmer v. St. Louis Cnty., 591 S.W.2d 39 (Mo. App. 1980); JUERGENSMEYER & ROBERTS, *supra* note 2, § 5:33(F).

in place. The court did not take this route. It reasoned, quite properly, that performance in accordance with regulatory requirements was important even if it did cost more than the alternative. The court opined that the benefits of regulatory compliance accrue not only to the adjoining property owners but to everyone in the community, just as noncompliance imposes costs on everyone and not just the adjoining property owners. It also concluded that the nature of the violation in this case and in many cases would be such as to repeatedly favor noncompliance by developers if the efficient breach were applied to permit simple money damages as the preferred remedy. Wealthy developers and property owners would do as they please, violate the regulatory requirements, and simply buy their way out of the problem by paying damages, while pocketing large profits from having ignored the regulations.

Although efficient breach may be appropriate in some situations involving performance obligations among private parties to a contract, the court in *Pinecrest* offers the better reasoning with respect to regulatory compliance for planning and zoning regulations adopted to protect the public health, safety, welfare, and morals. Consequently, the approach taken in *Pinecrest* is the approach that courts should take in reviewing developer and property owner actions with respect to requirements for inclusive design.

Another important aspect of the *Pinecrest* case, and of the zoning and land use power more generally, is the ability of third parties to have standing to challenge local decisions. In *Pinecrest,* the local officials approved the developer's plans, but third parties with an interest in the outcome brought suit to challenge the decision.[72] Third-party vigilance and self-interest assured a review of the decision, and the review determined that local officials had not properly followed the statutory requirements. The availability of judicial review reinforced the need for consistency in *Pinecrest,* and the same protective process should be available to ensure that local planning and zoning is done properly and consistently with national standards for accessibility. The process of judicial review minimizes the sometimes overstated fear that local government officials might be overly influenced by local political pressure and make bad decisions.

2.4 LEGISLATIVE AND ADJUDICATIVE ACTIONS

In regulating land use and development, local governments can act in two different capacities: legislatively or adjudicatively.[73] This division is not based on the distinction between planning and zoning but rather on the type of action

[72] *Pinecrest,* 795 So. 2d 191; JUERGENSMEYER & ROBERTS, *supra* note 2, § 8:6; MANDELKER, *supra* note 9, § 8.15.
[73] JUERGENSMEYER & ROBERTS, *supra* note 2, § 5:3; MANDELKER, *supra* note 9, §§ 6.39–6.41.

being taken. When local government officials act to consider the coordination of property development and land use generally, and to plan and zone for the best interest of the overall community, it is legislative action. Conversely, once they have developed and approved regulations, be it as part of a comprehensive plan or as a zoning code pursuant to a plan, the application of those provisions to a particular property is generally adjudicative. Examples of adjudicative action involve such procedures as determining the applicability of an *area* or *use variance*.[74] In these situations, a property owner seeks to be excused from certain elements or requirements of the zoning code that otherwise apply to the property. Typically, a request for a variance goes to a zoning board of appeal for hearing and for a decision based on established criteria that must be weighed by the members of the board. Other adjudicative actions might include approving a conditional use or amending the code or the comprehensive plan in a piecemeal fashion, as in doing so to change the regulations relating to one or a very few individual properties. Actions that single out individual properties for regulatory treatment different from surrounding properties may violate equal protection and amount to impermissible spot zoning.[75]

The difference between legislative and adjudicative action is legally significant. When acting in a legislative capacity, local governments are given a great deal of deference as to their determinations. As a legislature, their determinations have a strong presumption of legal validity and will generally only be set aside if a reviewing court can find no rational basis for the outcome. The rational basis test is also referred to as the fairly debatable test. The standard of review is that as long as the regulation is at least fairly debatable (has a rational basis), the courts should give deference to the legislature.[76] In general, the burden of demonstrating that a land use regulation is not rational is on a challenging property owner, not the government.[77] If the government action is adjudicative, as in making a determination as to a variance, the standard of deference and standard of review change. In an adjudicative setting, a property owner has to make a prima facie showing that he has satisfied all of the criteria for a requested variance or other action, and the government has the burden of demonstrating that its decision is supported by substantial competent evidence on the record.[78] Relative to legislative action, the level of supporting evidence is higher and the burden is shifted to the government. Also, because the proceeding is itself quasi-judicial, rather than legislative, different requirements prevail, such as providing the property owner with an

---

[74] JUERGENSMEYER & ROBERTS, *supra* note 2, §§ 5:10, 10:14.
[75] *Id.*; MANDELKER, *supra* note 9, §§ 2.44, 6.28.
[76] JUERGENSMEYER & ROBERTS, *supra* note 2, § 5:37; MANDELKER, *supra* note 9, § 1.12.
[77] Sources cited *supra* note 76.
[78] JUERGENSMEYER & ROBERTS, *supra* note 2, § 5:37(B); MANDELKER, *supra* note 9, § 6.52.

opportunity to be heard, to call witnesses, to submit supporting information, and to be provided with an impartial decision maker.[79]

Fasano v. Board of County Commissioners of Washington County

507 P.2d 23 (Or. 1973)

OPINION BY: HOWELL, J.

The plaintiffs, homeowners in Washington county, unsuccessfully opposed a zone change before the Board of County Commissioners of Washington County. Plaintiffs applied for and received a writ of review of the action of the commissioners allowing the change. The trial court found in favor of plaintiffs, disallowed the zone change, and reversed the commissioners' order. The Court of Appeals affirmed, 7 Or App 176, 489 P2d 693 (1971), and this court granted review.

The defendants are the Board of County Commissioners and A.G.S. Development Company. A.G.S., the owner of 32 acres which had been zoned R-7 (Single Family Residential), applied for a zone change to P-R (Planned Residential), which allows for the construction of a mobile home park. The change failed to receive a majority vote of the Planning Commission. The Board of County Commissioners approved the change and found, among other matters, that the change allows for "increased densities and different types of housing to meet the needs of urbanization over that allowed by the existing zoning."

The trial court, relying on its interpretation of Roseta v. County of Washington, 254 Or 161, 458 P2d 405, 40 ALR3d 364 (1969), reversed the order of the commissioners because the commissioners had not shown any change in the character of the neighborhood which would justify the rezoning. The Court of Appeals affirmed for the same reason, but added the additional ground that the defendants failed to show that the change was consistent with the comprehensive plan for Washington county.

According to the briefs, the comprehensive plan of development for Washington county was adopted in 1959 and included classifications in the county for residential, neighborhood commercial, retail commercial, general commercial, industrial park and light industry, general and heavy industry, and agricultural areas.

The land in question, which was designated "residential" by the comprehensive plan, was zoned R-7, Single Family Residential.

Subsequent to the time the comprehensive plan was adopted, Washington county established a Planned Residential (P-R) zoning classification in 1963. The P-R classification was adopted by ordinance and provided that a planned

---

[79] JUERGENSMEYER & ROBERTS, *supra* note 2, § 10:13; MANDELKER, *supra* note 9, § 6.70.

residential unit development could be established and should include open space for utilities, access, and recreation; should not be less than 10 acres in size; and should be located in or adjacent to a residential zone. The P-R zone adopted by the 1963 ordinance is of the type known as a "floating zone," so-called because the ordinance creates a zone classification authorized for future use but not placed on the zoning map until its use at a particular location is approved by the governing body. The R-7 classification for the 32 acres continued until April 1970 when the classification was changed to P-R to permit the defendant A.G.S. to construct the mobile home park on the 32 acres involved.

The defendants argue that (1) the action of the county commissioners approving the change is presumptively valid, requiring plaintiffs to show that the commissioners acted arbitrarily in approving the zone change; (2) it was not necessary to show a change of conditions in the area before a zone change could be accomplished; and (3) the change from R-7 to P-R was in accordance with the Washington county comprehensive plan.

We granted review in this case to consider the questions – by what standards does a county commission exercise its authority in zoning matters; who has the burden of meeting those standards when a request for change of zone is made; and what is the scope of court review of such actions?

Any meaningful decision as to the proper scope of judicial review of a zoning decision must start with a characterization of the nature of that decision. The majority of jurisdictions state that a zoning ordinance is a legislative act and is thereby entitled to presumptive validity. This court made such a characterization of zoning decisions in Smith v. County of Washington, 241 Or 380, 406 P2d 545 (1965) . . .

The Supreme Court of Washington, in reviewing a rezoning decision, recently stated:

> "Whatever descriptive characterization may be otherwise attached to the role or function of the planning commission in zoning procedures, e.g., advisory, recommendatory, investigatory, administrative or legislative, it is manifest that it is a public agency, a principle [*sic*] and statutory duty of which is to conduct public hearings in specified planning and zoning matters, enter findings of fact – often on the basis of disputed facts – and make recommendations with reasons assigned thereto. Certainly, in its role as a hearing and fact-finding tribunal, the planning commission's function more nearly than not partakes of the nature of an administrative, quasi-judicial proceeding, . . ." Chrobuck v. Snohomish County, 78 Wash 2d 884, 480 P2d 489, 495–96 (1971).

Ordinances laying down general policies without regard to a specific piece of property are usually an exercise of legislative authority, are subject to limited review, and may only be attacked upon constitutional grounds for an arbitrary abuse of authority. On the other hand, a determination whether the permissible use of a specific piece of property should be changed is usually an exercise of judicial authority and its propriety is subject to an altogether different test. An illustration of an exercise of legislative authority is the passage of the ordinance by the Washington County Commission in 1963 which provided for the formation of a planned residential classification to be located in or adjacent to any residential zone. An exercise of judicial authority is the county commissioners' determination in this particular matter to change the classification of A.G.S. Development Company's specific piece of property...

In order to establish a standard of review, it is necessary to delineate certain basic principles relating to land use regulation.

The basic instrument for county or municipal land use planning is the "comprehensive plan"... The plan has been described as a general plan to control and direct the use and development of property in a municipality.

In Oregon the county planning commission is required by ORS 215.050 to adopt a comprehensive plan for the use of some or all of the land in the county. Under ORS 215.110(1), after the comprehensive plan has been adopted, the planning commission recommends to the governing body of the county the ordinances necessary to "carry out" the comprehensive plan. The purpose of the zoning ordinances, both under our statute and the general law of land use regulation, is to "carry out" or implement the comprehensive plan. Although we are aware of the analytical distinction between zoning and planning, it is clear that under our statutes the plan adopted by the planning commission and the zoning ordinances enacted by the county governing body are closely related; both are intended to be parts of a single integrated procedure for land use control. The plan embodies policy determinations and guiding principles; the zoning ordinances provide the detailed means of giving effect to those principles.

ORS 215.050 states county planning commissions "shall adopt and may from time to time revise a comprehensive plan"...

In addition, ORS 215.055 provides:

> "215.055 Standards for plan. (1) The plan and all legislation and regulations authorized by ORS 215.010 to 215.233 shall be designed to promote the public health, safety and general welfare and shall be based on the following considerations, among others: The various characteristics of the various areas in the county, the suitability of the areas for particular land uses and improvements, the land uses and improvements in the areas, trends in land improvement, density of development, property values, the needs of economic enterprises in the future development of the areas, needed access to particular sites in the areas, natural resources of the county and prospective needs for development

thereof, and the public need for healthful, safe, aesthetic surroundings and conditions."

We believe that the state legislature has conditioned the county's power to zone upon the prerequisite that the zoning attempt to further the general welfare of the community through consciousness, in a prospective sense, of the factors mentioned above . . .

Because the action of the commission in this instance is an exercise of judicial authority, the burden of proof should be placed, as is usual in judicial proceedings, upon the one seeking change. The more drastic the change, the greater will be the burden of showing that it is in conformance with the comprehensive plan as implemented by the ordinance, that there is a public need for the kind of change in question, and that the need is best met by the proposal under consideration. As the degree of change increases, the burden of showing that the potential impact upon the area in question was carefully considered and weighed will also increase . . .

What we have said above is necessarily general, as the approach we adopt contains no absolute standards or mechanical tests. We believe, however, that it is adequate to provide meaningful guidance for local governments making zoning decisions and for trial courts called upon to review them. With future cases in mind, it is appropriate to add some brief remarks on questions of procedure. Parties at the hearing before the county governing body are entitled to an opportunity to be heard, to an opportunity to present and rebut evidence, to a tribunal which is impartial in the matter — i.e., having had no pre-hearing or ex parte contacts concerning the question at issue — and to a record made and adequate findings executed.

When we apply the standards we have adopted to the present case, we find that the burden was not sustained before the commission. The record now before us is insufficient to ascertain whether there was a justifiable basis for the decision. The only evidence in the record, that of the staff report of the Washington County Planning Department, is too conclusory and superficial to support the zoning change. It merely states:

"The staff finds that the requested use does conform to the residential designation of the Plan of Development. It further finds that the proposed use reflects the urbanization of the County and the necessity to provide increased densities and different types of housing to meet the needs of urbanization over that allowed by the existing zoning . . ."

Such generalizations and conclusions, without any statement of the facts on which they are based, are insufficient to justify a change of use.

As there has not been an adequate showing that the change was in accord with the plan, or that the factors listed in ORS 215.055 were given proper consideration, **the judgment is affirmed**.

In the planning and zoning process, it is clear that making a community accessible and safe to navigate is within the police power of local government. Action in support of inclusive design can be taken administratively and adjunctively, and this raises some interesting opportunities for using certain elements of land use law. For example, a comprehensive plan and a zoning code could set standards and goals for inclusive design and make structures with exclusionary features and barriers nonconforming uses. As nonconforming uses, the nonconformities could be *amortized* over a set of years, permitting a reasonable return on current investments while setting a timetable for extinguishing the exclusionary design preferences.[80] In addition, the variance process could be used to deal with undue financial hardships and unique circumstances that certain inclusive design regulations might pose for particular property owners. The variance process might also be used to grant variances from current regulations, such as setbacks and lot coverage, when a property owner seeks a design change that makes a property more accessible, even when the proposed design change exceeds current minimal standards for the given use. Other possibilities for making our communities more accessible emerge when considering conditional use permits that might be used when a property owner seeks to remodel, expand, or otherwise change the improvements on the property or the use of the property in an effort to make it more accessible.

In all such cases, we must remain mindful of two temporal frames of reference. We must understand that prospective planning and zoning as to property not yet developed will be much easier to bring within inclusive design regulations than properties that already have barriers to safe and easy navigation. Prospective regulations can be calculated into the reasonable investment-backed expectations of property owners and simply be accounted for as a required part of the design approval process for new construction. A different set of considerations becomes relevant in dealing with existing properties that do not currently possess inclusionary design features. To a certain extent, we already have precedent under federal law that requires retrofitting places of public accommodation to meet minimal accessibility requirements.[81]

[80] This is similar to the Rehabilitation Act of 1973, Pub. L. No. 93-112, 87 Stat. 355 (codified as amended at 29 U.S.C. § 701 (2006)).
[81] *See* Americans with Disabilities Act of 1990, Pub. L. No. 101-336, 104 Stat. 327 (codified as amended at 42 U.S.C. § 12131 et seq. (2006)); 28 C.F.R. § 35.150 (2012); 28 C.F.R. § 36.304 (2012).

Once we accept the fact that the built environment is one seamless web of space for social interaction, we will see that the distinction between places of public accommodation and private places is somewhat artificial. Private places, such as one's home, are places where one reasonably expects privacy and a right to exclude uninvited guests, but the structure of the home itself merely expresses a design preference that ought to be safe and easily navigable by anyone invited or authorized to be in it. Individual homes are part of the national housing stock, and the homes themselves are products in a significant stream of commerce; private homes are inseparable from the networks that make up our communities and connect the various venues in which we live and experience our lives.

In planning for inclusive design communities, a number of legislative and adjudicative devices might be useful, and some of these devices are discussed in Chapter 5. There may also be a role for something that I loosely refer to as a *network zone*. A network zone would be something like a floating zone in that it would have criteria for its location, but it would not necessarily be fixed at a particular geographic location at any given time; it can be provided for and then "placed" in appropriate locations as they become identified and as community needs develop over time.[82] The network zone recognizes that communities are made up of integrated networks that work best and add the most value when properly connected. A network zone might be like developing and identifying a bike path or a location for a ribbon park.[83] As population shifts and uses change over time, local officials would look for the points and paths of connectivity among the various venues in which community life is lived and experienced. The network zone would seek to connect residential venues to work, educational, recreational, shopping, and other venues. The network zone would be flexible in terms of addressing inclusive design and might include a variety of efforts, such as locating new sidewalks, identifying curb cut opportunities, siting more and safer crosswalks, rerouting or closing streets, enhancing public spaces, and adding other accessible design features to the built environment.

2.5 LIMITATIONS ON THE POLICE POWER TO REGULATE LAND USE AND DEVELOPMENT

The police power to regulate property development and land use has limitations. As already mentioned, there must be a proper delegation of the police

---

[82] Fasano v. Board of Cnty. Comm'rs, 507 P.2d 23 (Or. 1973); JUERGENSMEYER & ROBERTS, *supra* note 2, § 5:9; MANDELKER, *supra* note 9, § 6.26.

[83] MANDELKER, *supra* note 9, § 5.38; A "ribbon park" is a name sometimes used to describe a park that is more like a walking path, a trail, or a bike path that narrowly winds through an area. This may be the case of a park that follows the edges of a river, for example.

power from the state to local government, and thus, local governments must act within the limitations established by their enabling legislation. In addition, there are constraints imposed by requirements for due process, for equal protection, and by a need to accommodate other fundamental constitutional rights and values that may be in tension with the exercise of the police power in effectuating particular approaches to planning and zoning. These conflicting constitutional rights and values may arise, for example, in relationship to the First Amendment rights of freedom of speech, religion, and association; the rights of people with disabilities under the ADA and related legislation; and the right to property as protected by the Fifth Amendment prohibition against takings (be they physical invasions or regulatory in nature).[84] In this part of the chapter, attention focuses on the relationship between disability rights and the police power with respect to limitations on the authority to regulate land use.

Planning and zoning professionals understand that multiple values come into play when thinking carefully about land use regulation. The fact that people have a First Amendment right to provide and consume adult entertainment does not mean that local communities can exercise no planning authority over the location of such activity;[85] and the fact that people have a right to advertise their business does not mean that local communities cannot regulate signs and billboards.[86] Likewise, the protection of religion does not mean that communities cannot regulate ancillary uses on religious property or that they cannot regulate traffic flow and site planning to ensure that a religious use is conducted in a way that protects the public health, safety, welfare, and morals.[87] Communities may also regulate the number of people occupying a single-family residential home, even though there are restrictions on the ability to define or interfere with the definition and meaning of a family.[88] In other words, the mere fact that constraints and limitations prevent local governments from doing whatever they may want in regulating property development and land use does not mean that they can do nothing. In areas where the tension among competing fundamental rights and deeply held values is great, the regulations must be carefully tailored to accomplish a substantial state interest,

---

[84] JUERGENSMEYER & ROBERTS, *supra* note 2, §§ 4:7, 10:3–10:4, 10:15; MANDELKER, *supra* note 9, §§ 2.01, 2.50, 5.16.

[85] City of Renton v. Playtime Theatres, Inc., 475 U.S. 41 (1986).

[86] JUERGENSMEYER & ROBERTS, *supra* note 2, § 10:17; MANDELKER, *supra* note 9, § 11.06.

[87] JUERGENSMEYER & ROBERTS, *supra* note 2, § 10:19; MANDELKER, *supra* note 9, §§ 5.19, 6.57.

[88] Village of Belle Terre v. Boraas, 416 U.S. 1 (1974); Zavala v. City of Denver, 759 P.2d 664 (Colo. 1988); State v. Champoux, 566 N.W.2d 763 (Neb. 1997); Farley v. Zoning Hearing Bd., 636 A.2d 1232 (Pa. Commw. Ct. 1994).

and in a way that is least restrictive. In addition, when the people exercising certain rights that come into tension with the police power are from a suspect category (a protected class), the standard of judicial review may be higher than that of a rational basis or a rational basis supported by substantial competent evidence on the record; it may rise to intermediate or strict scrutiny.[89] The difficulty arises in knowing what groups are included in a suspect category.

In evaluating the standard of judicial review applied to local land use regulation, it is important to understand that constitutional requirements may be different from those provided in specific statutes applicable to the situation. For instance, in the area of disabilities law, the U.S. Supreme Court, in *Cleburne v. Cleburne Living Center*, has said that the standard of review is one of a rational basis, but legislation pursuant to the ADA sets other standards that may be higher.[90] This is why lawsuits are often brought as violations of the statutory requirements of federal disability law rather than as violations of the equal protection clause of the U.S. Constitution; nonetheless, it is important to understand the equal protection claim.

City of Cleburne v. Cleburne Living Center, Inc.

473 U.S. 432 (1985)

OPINION

JUSTICE WHITE delivered the opinion of the Court.

A Texas city denied a special use permit for the operation of a group home for the mentally retarded, acting pursuant to a municipal zoning ordinance requiring permits for such homes. The Court of Appeals for the Fifth Circuit held that mental retardation is a "quasi-suspect" classification and that the ordinance violated the Equal Protection Clause because it did not substantially further an important governmental purpose. We hold that a lesser standard of scrutiny is appropriate, but conclude that under that standard the ordinance is invalid as applied in this case.

In July 1980, respondent Jan Hannah purchased a building at 201 Featherston Street in the city of Cleburne, Texas, with the intention of leasing it to Cleburne Living Center, Inc. (CLC), for the operation of a group home for the mentally retarded . . .

---

[89] Vill. of Arlington Heights v. Metro. Hous. Dev. Corp., 429 U.S. 252 (1977); Wash. v. Davis, 426 U.S. 229 (1976); Contra Buchanan v. Warley, 245 U.S. 60 (1917); Scott v. Greenville Cnty., 716 F.2d 1409 (4th Cir. 1985); Daily v. City of Lawton, 425 F.2d 1037 (10th Cir. 1970); MANDELKER, *supra* note 9, § 2.36.

[90] *See* Kenneth Allen Greene, *Burdens of Proving Handicap Discrimination Using Federal Employment Discrimination Law: Rational Basis or Undue Burden?*, 1989 DET. C.L. REV. 1053 (1989).

The city informed CLC that a special use permit would be required for the operation of a group home at the site, and CLC accordingly submitted a permit application. In response to a subsequent inquiry from CLC, the city explained that under the zoning regulations applicable to the site, a special use permit, renewable annually, was required for the construction of "[hospitals] for the insane or feeble-minded, or alcoholic [*sic*] or drug addicts, or penal or correctional institutions." The city had determined that the proposed group home should be classified as a "hospital for the feebleminded." After holding a public hearing on CLC's application, the City Council voted 3 to 1 to deny a special use permit.

CLC then filed suit in Federal District Court against the city and a number of its officials, alleging, inter alia, that the zoning ordinance was invalid on its face and as applied because it discriminated against the mentally retarded in violation of the equal protection rights of CLC and its potential residents. The District Court . . . deemed the ordinance, as written and applied, to be rationally related to the city's legitimate interests in "the legal responsibility of CLC and its residents, . . . the safety and fears of residents in the adjoining neighborhood," and the number of people to be housed in the home.

The Court of Appeals for the Fifth Circuit reversed, determining that mental retardation was a quasi-suspect classification and that it should assess the validity of the ordinance under intermediate-level scrutiny. 726 F.2d 191 (1984) . . . The Court of Appeals went on to hold that the ordinance was also invalid as applied. Rehearing en banc was denied with six judges dissenting in an opinion urging en banc consideration of the panel's adoption of a heightened standard of review. We granted certiorari, 469 U.S. 1016 (1984) . . .

The Equal Protection Clause of the Fourteenth Amendment commands that no State shall "deny to any person within its jurisdiction the equal protection of the laws," which is essentially a direction that all persons similarly situated should be treated alike. Plyler v. Doe, 457 U.S. 202, 216 (1982). Section 5 of the Amendment empowers Congress to enforce this mandate, but absent controlling congressional direction, the courts have themselves devised standards for determining the validity of state legislation or other official action that is challenged as denying equal protection. The general rule is that legislation is presumed to be valid and will be sustained if the classification drawn by the statute is rationally related to a legitimate state interest. When social or economic legislation is at issue, the Equal Protection Clause allows the States wide latitude, and the Constitution presumes that even improvident decisions will eventually be rectified by the democratic processes.

The general rule gives way, however, when a statute classifies by race, alienage, or national origin. These factors are so seldom relevant to the achievement of any legitimate state interest that laws grounded in such considerations are deemed to reflect prejudice and antipathy – a view that those in the burdened class are not as worthy or deserving as others. For these reasons and because such discrimination is unlikely to be soon rectified by legislative means, these laws are subjected to strict scrutiny and will be sustained only if they are suitably tailored to serve a compelling state interest. Similar oversight by the courts is due when state laws impinge on personal rights protected by the Constitution.

Legislative classifications based on gender also call for a heightened standard of review. That factor generally provides no sensible ground for differential treatment. "[What] differentiates sex from such nonsuspect statuses as intelligence or physical disability . . . . is that the sex characteristic frequently bears no relation to ability to perform or contribute to society." Rather than resting on meaningful considerations, statutes distributing benefits and burdens between the sexes in different ways very likely reflect outmoded notions of the relative capabilities of men and women. A gender classification fails unless it is substantially related to a sufficiently important governmental interest . . .

Against this background, we conclude . . . that the Court of Appeals erred in holding mental retardation a quasi-suspect classification calling for a more exacting standard of judicial review than is normally accorded economic and social legislation . . . Heightened scrutiny inevitably involves substantive judgments about legislative decisions, and we doubt that the predicate for such judicial oversight is present where the classification deals with mental retardation . . .

Doubtless, there have been and there will continue to be instances of discrimination against the retarded that are in fact invidious, and that are properly subject to judicial correction under constitutional norms. But the appropriate method of reaching such instances is not to create a new quasi-suspect classification and subject all governmental action based on that classification to more searching evaluation. Rather, we should look to the likelihood that governmental action premised on a particular classification is valid as a general matter, not merely to the specifics of the case before us . . .

Our refusal to recognize the retarded as a quasi-suspect class does not leave them entirely unprotected from invidious discrimination. To withstand equal protection review, legislation that distinguishes between the mentally retarded and others must be rationally related to a legitimate governmental purpose. This standard, we believe, affords government the latitude necessary both to pursue policies designed to assist the retarded in realizing their full potential, and to freely and efficiently engage in activities that burden the retarded in what is essentially an incidental manner. The State may not rely on a classification whose relationship to an asserted goal is so attenuated as to render the distinction arbitrary or irrational . . .

We turn to the issue of the validity of the zoning ordinance insofar as it requires a special use permit for homes for the mentally retarded. We inquire first whether requiring a special use permit for the Featherston home in the circumstances here deprives respondents of the equal protection of the laws . . .

. . . Because in our view the record does not reveal any rational basis for believing that the Featherston home would pose any special threat to the city's legitimate interests, we affirm the judgment below insofar as it holds the ordinance invalid as applied in this case . . .

The short of it is that requiring the permit in this case appears to us to rest on an irrational prejudice against the mentally retarded, including those who would occupy the Featherston facility and who would live under the closely supervised and highly regulated conditions expressly provided for by state and federal law.

The judgment of the Court of Appeals is affirmed insofar as it invalidates the zoning ordinance as applied to the Featherston home. The judgment is otherwise vacated, and the case is remanded.

It is so ordered.

Cleburne involves a cognitive disability rather than mobility impairment, but it does present us with useful information regarding the standard of review with respect to certain groups of people with particular disabilities and thus lends some guidance for mobility impairment as well. It is an interesting decision in several respects. First, it has been criticized for not having adopted a higher standard of review for this situation and for not seeing the users of the group home as a suspect or quasi-suspect class.[91] Even without raising the standard of review, however, the court invalidated the action of the local government on grounds that it was *unconstitutional as applied* because it did not meet even the lower rational basis standard.[92] This can be read as requiring a closer look at rational basis in certain situations, even though the Court does not say that is what it is doing. Second, since the time of the decision in this case (1985), we have developed a significant amount of legislation directed at accessibility for people with disabilities, and this legislation has created additional grounds on which aggrieved parties can seek legal redress – beyond that provided for on equal protection terms. This means that aggrieved parties can be successful on statutory-based claims even if perhaps not on more general

[91] JUERGENSMEYER & ROBERTS, *supra* note 2, § 10:14(E); MANDELKER, *supra* note 9, §§ 2.36, 2.01.

[92] City of Cleburne v. Cleburne Living Ctr., 473 U.S. 432 (1985).

constitutional grounds. Third, the primary focus of ADA-related legislation and policy has been on a civil rights paradigm, effectively (even if not constitutionally) shifting our social understanding of disability as belonging to a suspect class, similar to the way we understand race and gender. This undoubtedly changes the way in which cases such as *Cleburne* are viewed today. Fourth, the case, although not raising the standard of review, illustrates the important limitation of an "as applied" claim in the equal protection area.

Even where a reviewing court determines that the nature of a challenged regulation is a valid exercise of the police power, it may nonetheless determine that the regulation violates equal protection in the way it is applied in the given case. The "as applied" claim is an important one because it can effectively require the presence of careful fact finding and evidence to support distinctions in the application of an otherwise valid land use regulation. Fifth, it is important to keep in mind that *Cleburne* endorses the rational basis standard of review for the exercise of the police power, and this is all that is needed to support inclusive design regulations that are promulgated to protect and advance the health, safety, welfare, and morals of the community. Given the implications of a dramatically changing population, communities need to plan for inclusion, and it is likely to be people resisting inclusive design who will bring claims to prevent enforcement regulations designed to enhance accessibility. In resisting inclusive design regulations, they are likely to be unsuccessful under a rational basis standard.

In addition to the constraints imposed by the requirements of equal protection, the police power may also be limited by the requirements of due process. The case of *Tennessee v. Lane*[93] seems to suggest a higher standard of review than that of the rational basis test applied in *Cleburne*, in the context of disability and a due process challenge. The case is significant as it relates to access to legal proceedings and may have a bearing on requirements with respect to access to quasi-adjudicative functions of a zoning board. Review standards applied to access to the legal process, however, address a very different issue than review standards as to substantive land use and planning decisions.

Tennessee v. Lane

541 U.S. 509 (2004)
OPINION
Justice Stevens delivered the opinion of the Court.

Title II of the Americans with Disabilities Act of 1990 (ADA or Act), 104 Stat 337, 42 U.S.C. §§ 12131–12165 [42 USCS §§ 12131–12165], provides that

---

[93] *See* Tennessee v. Lane, 541 U.S. 509 (2004).

"no qualified individual with a disability shall, by reason of such disability, be excluded from participation in or be denied the benefits of the services, programs or activities of a public entity, or be subjected to discrimination by any such entity." § 12132. The question presented in this case is whether Title II exceeds Congress' power under § 5 of the Fourteenth Amendment.

I

In August 1998, respondents George Lane and Beverly Jones filed this action against the State of Tennessee and a number of Tennessee counties, alleging past and ongoing violations of Title II. Respondents, both of whom are paraplegics who use wheelchairs for mobility, claimed that they were denied access to, and the services of, the state court system by reason of their disabilities. Lane alleged that he was compelled to appear to answer a set of criminal charges on the second floor of a county courthouse that had no elevator. At his first appearance, Lane crawled up two flights of stairs to get to the courtroom. When Lane returned to the courthouse for a hearing, he refused to crawl again or to be carried by officers to the courtroom; he consequently was arrested and jailed for failure to appear. Jones, a certified court reporter, alleged that she has not been able to gain access to a number of county courthouses, and, as a result, has lost both work and an opportunity to participate in the judicial process. Respondents sought damages and equitable relief.

The State moved to dismiss the suit on the ground that it was barred by the Eleventh Amendment. The District Court denied the motion without opinion, and the State appealed. The United States intervened to defend Title II's abrogation of the States' Eleventh Amendment immunity . . .

II

The ADA was passed by large majorities in both Houses of Congress after decades of deliberation and investigation into the need for comprehensive legislation to address discrimination against persons with disabilities. In the years immediately preceding the ADA's enactment, Congress held 13 hearings and created a special task force that gathered evidence from every State in the Union. The conclusions Congress drew from this evidence are set forth in the task force and Committee Reports, described in lengthy legislative hearings, and summarized in the preamble to the statute. Central among these conclusions was Congress' finding that

> "individuals with disabilities are a discrete and insular minority who have been faced with restrictions and limitations, subjected to a history of purposeful unequal treatment, and relegated to a position of political powerlessness in our society, based on characteristics that are beyond the control of such

individuals and resulting from stereotypic assumptions not truly indicative of the individual ability of such individuals to participate in, and contribute to, society." 42 U.S.C. § 12101(a)(7) [42 USCS § 12101(a)(7)].

Invoking "the sweep of congressional authority, including the power to enforce the fourteenth amendment and to regulate commerce," the ADA is designed "to provide a clear and comprehensive national mandate for the elimination of discrimination against individuals with disabilities." §§ 12101(b)(1), (b)(4). It forbids discrimination against persons with disabilities in three major areas of public life: employment, which is covered by Title I of the statute; public services, programs, and activities, which are the subject of Title II; and public accommodations, which are covered by Title III.

Title II, §§ 12131–12134, prohibits any public entity from discriminating against "qualified" persons with disabilities in the provision or operation of public services, programs, or activities. The Act defines the term "public entity" to include state and local governments, as well as their agencies and instrumentalities. § 12131(1). Persons with disabilities are "qualified" if they, "with or without reasonable modifications to rules, policies, or practices, the removal of architectural, communication, or transportation barriers, or the provision of auxiliary aids and services, mee[t] the essential eligibility requirements for the receipt of services or the participation in programs or activities provided by a public entity." § 12131(2). Title II's enforcement provision incorporates by reference § 505 of the Rehabilitation Act of 1973, 92 Stat 2982, as added, 29 U.S.C. § 794a [29 USCS § 794a], which authorizes private citizens to bring suits for money damages. 42 U.S.C. § 12133 [42 USCS § 12133].

III

The Eleventh Amendment renders the States immune from "any suit in law or equity, commenced or prosecuted . . . by Citizens of another State, or by Citizens or Subjects of any Foreign State." Even though the Amendment "by its terms . . . applies only to suits against a State by citizens of another State," our cases have repeatedly held that this immunity also applies to unconsented suits brought by a State's own citizens. Our cases have also held that Congress may abrogate the State's Eleventh Amendment immunity. To determine whether it has done so in any given case, we "must resolve two predicate questions: first, whether Congress unequivocally expressed its intent to abrogate that immunity; and second, if it did, whether Congress acted pursuant to a valid grant of constitutional authority." Id., at 73, 145 L. Ed. 2d 522, 120 S. Ct. 631.

The first question is easily answered in this case. The Act specifically provides: "A State shall not be immune under the eleventh amendment to the Constitution of the United States from an action in Federal or State court of competent jurisdiction for a violation of this chapter." 42 U.S.C. § 12202 [42 USCS § 12202] . . . The question, then, is whether Congress had the power to give effect to its intent.

In Fitzpatrick v. Bitzer, 427 U.S. 445, 49 L. Ed. 2d 614, 96 S. Ct. 2666 (1976), we held that Congress can abrogate a State's sovereign immunity when it does so pursuant to a valid exercise of its power under § 5 of the Fourteenth Amendment to enforce the substantive guarantees of that Amendment. Id., at 456, 49 L. Ed. 2d 614, 96 S. Ct. 2666. This enforcement power, as we have often acknowledged, is a "broad power indeed" . . . When Congress seeks to remedy or prevent unconstitutional discrimination, § 5 authorizes it to enact prophylactic legislation proscribing practices that are discriminatory in effect, if not in intent, to carry out the basic objectives of the Equal Protection Clause.

Congress' § 5 power is not, however, unlimited. While Congress must have a wide berth in devising appropriate remedial and preventative measures for unconstitutional actions, those measures may not work a "substantive change in the governing law." Boerne, 521 U.S., at 519, 138 L. Ed. 2d 624, 117 S. Ct. 2157. In Boerne, we recognized that the line between remedial legislation and substantive redefinition is "not easy to discern," and that "Congress must have wide latitude in determining where it lies." Id., at 519–520, 138 L. Ed. 2d 624, 117 S. Ct. 2157. But we also confirmed that "the distinction exists and must be observed," and set forth a test for so observing it: Section 5 legislation is valid if it exhibits "a congruence and proportionality between the injury to be prevented or remedied and the means adopted to that end." Id., at 520, 138 L. Ed. 2d 624, 117 S. Ct. 2157 . . .

IV

The first step of the Boerne inquiry requires us to identify the constitutional right or rights that Congress sought to enforce when it enacted Title II. Garrett, 531 U.S., at 365, 148 L. Ed. 2d 866, 121 S. Ct. 955. In Garrett we identified Title I's purpose as enforcement of the Fourteenth Amendment's command that "all persons similarly situated should be treated alike." Cleburne v. Cleburne Living Center, Inc., 473 U.S. 432, 439, 87 L. Ed. 2d 313, 105 S. Ct. 3249 (1985). As we observed, classifications based on disability violate that constitutional command if they lack a rational relationship to a legitimate governmental purpose. Garrett, 531 U.S., at 366, 148 L. Ed. 866, 121 S. Ct. 955 (citing Cleburne, 473 U.S., at 446, 87 L. Ed. 2d 313, 105 S. Ct. 3249).

Title II, like Title I, seeks to enforce this prohibition on irrational disability discrimination. But it also seeks to enforce a variety of other basic constitutional guarantees, infringements of which are subject to more searching judicial review. These rights include some, like the right of access to the courts at issue in this case, that are protected by the Due Process Clause of the Fourteenth Amendment. The Due Process Clause and the Confrontation Clause of the Sixth Amendment, as applied to the States via the Fourteenth Amendment, both guarantee to a criminal defendant such as respondent Lane the "right to be present at all stages of the trial where his absence might frustrate the fairness of the proceedings." The Due Process Clause also requires the States to afford certain civil litigants a "meaningful opportunity to be heard" by removing obstacles to their full participation in judicial proceedings. . . . And, finally, we have recognized that members of the public have a right of access to criminal proceedings secured by the First Amendment.

Whether Title II validly enforces these constitutional rights is a question that "must be judged with reference to the historical experience which it reflects." While § 5 authorizes Congress to enact reasonably prophylactic remedial legislation, the appropriateness of the remedy depends on the gravity of the harm it seeks to prevent . . .

It is not difficult to perceive the harm that Title II is designed to address . . . [such as seeking to address] irrational discrimination in zoning decisions, Cleburne v. Cleburne Living Center, Inc., 473 U.S. 432, 87 L. Ed. 2d 313, 105 S. Ct. 3249 (1985) . . .

With respect to the particular services at issue in this case, Congress learned that many individuals, in many States across the country, were being excluded from courthouses and court proceedings by reason of their disabilities. A report before Congress showed that some 76% of public services and programs housed in state-owned buildings were inaccessible to and unusable by persons with disabilities, even taking into account the possibility that the services and programs might be restructured or relocated to other parts of the buildings. Congress itself heard testimony from persons with disabilities who described the physical inaccessibility of local courthouses. And its appointed task force heard numerous examples of the exclusion of persons with disabilities from state judicial services and programs, including exclusion of persons with visual impairments and hearing impairments from jury service, failure of state and local governments to provide interpretive services for the hearing impaired, failure to permit the testimony of adults with developmental disabilities in abuse cases, and failure to make courtrooms accessible to witnesses with physical disabilities . . .

V

. . . Title II's requirement of program accessibility, is congruent and proportional to its object of enforcing the right of access to the courts . . .

The remedy Congress chose is nevertheless a limited one. Recognizing that failure to accommodate persons with disabilities will often have the same practical effect as outright exclusion, Congress required the States to take reasonable measures to remove architectural and other barriers to accessibility. 42 U.S.C. § 12131(2) [42 USCS § 12131(2)]. But Title II does not require States to employ any and all means to make judicial services accessible to persons with disabilities, and it does not require States to compromise their essential eligibility criteria for public programs. It requires only "reasonable modifications" that would not fundamentally alter the nature of the service provided, and only when the individual seeking modification is otherwise eligible for the service. As Title II's implementing regulations make clear, the reasonable modification requirement can be satisfied in a number of ways. In the case of facilities built or altered after 1992, the regulations require compliance with specific architectural accessibility standards. 28 CFR § 35.151 (2003). But in the case of older facilities, for which structural change is likely to be more difficult, a public entity may comply with Title II by adopting a variety of less costly measures, including relocating services to alternative, accessible sites and assigning aides to assist persons with disabilities in accessing services. § 35.150(b)(1). Only if these measures are ineffective in achieving accessibility is the public entity required to make reasonable structural changes. And in no event is the entity required to undertake measures that would impose an undue financial or administrative burden, threaten historic preservation interests, or effect a fundamental alteration in the nature of the service. §§ 35.150(a)(2), (a)(3).

This duty to accommodate is perfectly consistent with the well-established due process principle that, "within the limits of practicability, a State must afford to all individuals a meaningful opportunity to be heard" in its courts . . . Title II's affirmative obligation to accommodate persons with disabilities in the administration of justice cannot be said to be "so out of proportion to a supposed remedial or preventive object that it cannot be understood as responsive to, or designed to prevent, unconstitutional behavior." It is, rather, a reasonable prophylactic measure, reasonably targeted to a legitimate end.

For these reasons, we conclude that Title II, as it applies to the class of cases implicating the fundamental right of access to the courts, constitutes a valid exercise of Congress' § 5 authority to enforce the guarantees of the Fourteenth Amendment. The judgment of the Court of Appeals is therefore affirmed.

It is so ordered.

Tennessee v. Lane indicates that in at least a narrow set of situations, involving fundamental rights, a due process challenge may require a strict scrutiny standard of review with respect to people with disabilities, and this goes beyond the standard of review applied in *Cleburne*, which was a challenge based on equal protection. It is unclear, for now, as to how this new strict scrutiny standard of review may be extended to affect local zoning and planning activities, but the case can be read narrowly and as applicable to physical access to the places where decisions are made rather than to the evaluation of the impacts of the substantive decision-making process itself. The court in *Tennessee v. Lane* focused on the fact that Congress had determined that individuals with disabilities are a discrete and insular minority and that they have been subject to a history of purposeful unequal treatment based on characteristics beyond their control. This heightened the standard of review. It is possible that the reasoning in this case might be extended to a broader set of circumstances and we could end up with a clear overruling of the standard set out in *Cleburne*.

Whether concerning accessibility rights or First Amendment rights, local governments have dealt with numerous tensions between fundamental rights and competing values over the years. These can be complex matters for local governments. It is important, therefore, for the local land use lawyer to understand the different standards of review applied to different types of local government action, legislative and adjudicative. It is also important to understand the different grounds on which challenges to the exercise of the police power might be made, for example, improper delegation, violation of equal protection, or violation of due process.[94]

As to the underlying rights of people with disabilities, local governments can make important contributions to improving accessibility of the built environment. Local governments are equipped to study and make decisions regarding such things as where to expand sidewalks, where to add crosswalks, how to improve transportation routes, how to integrate access among multiple venues, and the best ways to adjust for local changes in demographics and shifts in population. Local governments have a close connection to their residents and are best able to plan for inclusive design needs that go beyond federal standards of compliance and that may cover housing arrangements not currently covered by federal accessibility law. Local governments are also well positioned, where appropriate under the law, to assist in the process of determining undue hardships and the nature of reasonable accommodation under local circumstances – and they are well situated to creatively develop local

---

[94] F.C.C. v. Beach Commc'ns Inc., 508 U.S. 307 (1993); Pa. Coal Co. v. Mahon, 260 U.S. 393 (1922); Honeywell, Inc. v. Minnesota Life and Health Ins. Guar. Ass'n, 110 F.3d 547, 554 (8th Cir. 1997); Moore v. City of Kirkland, 2006 WL 1993443 (W.D. Wash. 2006); Harris v. City of Akron, 20 F.3d 1396 (6th Cir. 1994).

alternatives that might enhance the goal of inclusion beyond that of minimal compliance with federal law. All of this, however, requires an understanding of mobility impairment and of declining functional mobility related to aging as a land use issue and not simply as a civil rights issue.

In considering the ability of local governments to use the police power to regulate in favor of inclusive design, another key limitation on the exercise of the police power must be considered, and this involves the potential for property owners to assert an unlawful taking of the property pursuant to the Fifth Amendment's protection of private property.[95] The assertion would be that regulatory requirements for accessibility operate to take away an owner's property rights.

This assertion is one that I know from personal experience in dealing with homeowners as a zoning official as well as from speaking with academics concerning the issue of inclusive design. Many of the homeowners I have encountered, including some who are law professors, insist that they have a constitutionally protected property right to design a home in accordance with their own personal preferences, even if that means having at least three steps leading up to the entranceway to their homes and having narrow doorways and hallways, even though these design preferences function as barriers to safe and easy access in the most simple and fundamental ways. They take this position even though they recognize that the government already regulates land use and many aspects of the building requirements for a home. They understand that building codes regulate home design and that the regulation of land use includes more than just use; it includes height, bulk, position of a house on a lot, driveways, patios, swimming pools, fences, landscaping, aesthetics, and a variety of other elements. At the same time, they insist that basic elements of inclusive design represent an unconstitutional taking of their private property rights. I think that this belief is unfounded and is influenced by a misunderstanding of inclusive design. I suspect that the underlying issue is one of reconciling the rhetoric of property in terms of the right to "exclude" and the rhetoric of disability rights as the right of "access." Rhetorically, these may seem to be in conflict, and access may seem to imply that a property owner's right to exclude is being eliminated or diminished. The misunderstanding is that inclusive design simply requires that a property be safe to enter and navigate for anyone invited or lawfully present on the land. The property owner can still choose to invite or exclude anyone he wishes. The right to

---

[95] *See e.g.* Tahoe-Sierra Pres. Council, Inc. v. Tahoe Reg'l Planning Agency, 535 U.S. 302 (2002); *Lucas*, 505 U.S. 1003; Fla. Rock Indus. v. U.S., 18 F.3d 1560 (Fed Cir. 1994); Moroney v. Mayor & City Council of Old Tappan, 633 A2d 1045 (N.J. App. Div. 1993).

exclude has nothing to do with a consumer preference for building homes with exclusionary designs that are counter to the public health, safety, welfare, and morals.

In getting a sense of the underlying issues here, of just how far the government can go in requiring inclusive design, we should start with an examination of a foundational case in the area of takings law and then briefly explain later related developments.

Penn Central Transportation Co. v. City of New York

438 U.S. 104 (1978)

OPINION

MR. JUSTICE BRENNAN delivered the opinion of the Court.

The question presented is whether a city may, as part of a comprehensive program to preserve historic landmarks and historic districts, place restrictions on the development of individual historic landmarks − in addition to those imposed by applicable zoning ordinances − without effecting a "taking" requiring the payment of "just compensation." Specifically, we must decide whether the application of New York City's Landmarks Preservation Law to the parcel of land occupied by Grand Central Terminal has "taken" its owners' property in violation of the Fifth and Fourteenth Amendments.

I

A Over the past 50 years, all 50 States and over 500 municipalities have enacted laws to encourage or require the preservation of buildings and areas with historic or aesthetic importance. These nationwide legislative efforts have been precipitated by two concerns. The first is recognition that, in recent years, large numbers of historic structures, landmarks, and areas have been destroyed without adequate consideration of either the values represented therein or the possibility of preserving the destroyed properties for use in economically productive ways. The second is a widely shared belief that structures with special historic, cultural, or architectural significance enhance the quality of life for all. Not only do these buildings and their workmanship represent the lessons of the past and embody precious features of our heritage, they serve as examples of quality for today. "[Historic] conservation is but one aspect of the much larger problem, basically an environmental one, of enhancing − or perhaps developing for the first time − the quality of life for people" . . .

The New York City law is typical of many urban landmark laws in that its primary method of achieving its goals is not by acquisitions of historic properties, but rather by involving public entities in land-use decisions affecting these properties and providing services, standards, controls, and incentives that will encourage preservation by private owners and users. While the law does place special restrictions on landmark properties as a necessary feature to the attainment of its larger objectives, the major theme of the law is to ensure the owners of any such properties both a "reasonable return" on their investments and maximum latitude to use their parcels for purposes not inconsistent with the preservation goals . . .

Final designation as a landmark results in restrictions upon the property owner's options concerning use of the landmark site. First, the law imposes a duty upon the owner to keep the exterior features of the building "in good repair" to assure that the law's objectives not be defeated by the landmark's falling into a state of irremediable disrepair. Second, the Commission must approve in advance any proposal to alter the exterior architectural features of the landmark or to construct any exterior improvement on the landmark site, thus ensuring that decisions concerning construction on the landmark site are made with due consideration of both the public interest in the maintenance of the structure and the landowner's interest in use of the property . . .

Although the designation of a landmark and landmark site restricts the owner's control over the parcel, designation also enhances the economic position of the landmark owner in one significant respect. Under New York City's zoning laws, owners of real property who have not developed their property to the full extent permitted by the applicable zoning laws are allowed to transfer development rights to contiguous parcels on the same city block . . .

B This case involves the application of New York City's Landmarks Preservation Law to Grand Central Terminal (Terminal). The Terminal, which is owned by the Penn Central Transportation Co. and its affiliates (Penn Central), is one of New York City's most famous buildings. Opened in 1913, it is regarded not only as providing an ingenious engineering solution to the problems presented by urban railroad stations, but also as a magnificent example of the French beaux-arts style.

The Terminal is located in midtown Manhattan. Its south facade faces 42d Street and that street's intersection with Park Avenue. At street level, the Terminal is bounded on the west by Vanderbilt Avenue, on the east by the Commodore Hotel, and on the north by the Pan-American Building. Although a 20-story office tower, to have been located above the Terminal, was part of the original design, the planned tower was never constructed. The Terminal itself is an eight-story structure which Penn Central uses as a railroad station and in which it rents space not needed for railroad purposes to a variety of commercial interests. The Terminal is one of a number of properties owned by appellant

Penn Central in this area of midtown Manhattan. The others include the Barclay, Biltmore, Commodore, Roosevelt, and Waldorf-Astoria Hotels, the Pan-American Building and other office buildings along Park Avenue, and the Yale Club. At least eight of these are eligible to be recipients of development rights afforded the Terminal by virtue of landmark designation.

On January 22, 1968, appellant Penn Central, to increase its income, entered into a renewable 50-year lease and sublease agreement with appellant UGP Properties, Inc. (UGP), a wholly owned subsidiary of Union General Properties, Ltd., a United Kingdom corporation. Under the terms of the agreement, UGP was to construct a multistory office building above the Terminal. UGP promised to pay Penn Central $1 million annually during construction and at least $3 million annually thereafter. The rentals would be offset in part by a loss of some $700,000 to $1 million in net rentals presently received from concessionaires displaced by the new building.

Appellants UGP and Penn Central then applied to the Commission for permission to construct an office building atop the Terminal. Two separate plans, both designed by architect Marcel Breuer and both apparently satisfying the terms of the applicable zoning ordinance, were submitted to the Commission for approval. The first, Breuer I, provided for the construction of a 55-story office building, to be cantilevered above the existing facade and to rest on the roof of the Terminal. The second, Breuer II Revised, called for tearing down a portion of the Terminal that included the 42d Street facade, stripping off some of the remaining features of the Terminal's facade, and constructing a 53-story office building . . . After four days of hearings at which over 80 witnesses testified, the Commission denied this application as to both proposals.

. . . The Commission first focused on the effect that the proposed tower would have on one desirable feature created by the present structure and its surroundings . . . the Commission stated:

> "[We have] no fixed rule against making additions to designated buildings –
> it all depends on how they are done . . . But to balance a 55-story office tower
> above a flamboyant Beaux-Arts facade seems nothing more than an aesthetic
> joke . . . Landmarks cannot be divorced from their settings – particularly when
> the setting is a dramatic and integral part of the original concept . . ."

. . . Appellees appealed, and the New York Supreme Court, Appellate Division, reversed. 50 App. Div. 2d 265, 377 N. Y. S. 2d 20 (1975). The Appellate Division held that the restrictions on the development of the Terminal site were necessary to promote the legitimate public purpose of protecting landmarks and therefore that appellants could sustain their constitutional claims only by proof that the regulation deprived them of all reasonable beneficial use of the property. The Appellate Division held that the evidence appellants introduced at trial — "Statements of Revenues and Costs," purporting to show a net operating loss for the years 1969 and 1971, which were prepared for the instant litigation — had not satisfied their burden . . . The Appellate Division concluded that all appellants had succeeded in showing was that they had been deprived of the property's most profitable use, and that this showing did not establish that appellants had been unconstitutionally deprived of their property.

The New York Court of Appeals affirmed. 42 N. Y. 2d 324, 366 N. E. 2d 1271 (1977). That court summarily rejected any claim that the Landmarks Law had "taken" property without "just compensation," id., at 329, 366 N. E. 2d, at 1274, indicating that there could be no "taking" since the law had not transferred control of the property to the city, but only restricted appellants' exploitation of it. In that circumstance, the Court of Appeals held that appellants' attack on the law could prevail only if the law deprived appellants of their property in violation of the Due Process Clause of the Fourteenth Amendment. Whether or not there was a denial of substantive due process turned on whether the restrictions deprived Penn Central of a "reasonable return" on the "privately created and privately managed ingredient" of the Terminal. Id., at 328, 366 N. E. 2d, at 1273. The Court of Appeals concluded that the Landmarks Law had not effected a denial of due process because: (1) the landmark regulation permitted the same use as had been made of the Terminal for more than half a century; (2) the appellants had failed to show that they could not earn a reasonable return on their investment in the Terminal itself; (3) even if the Terminal proper could never operate at a reasonable profit, some of the income from Penn Central's extensive real estate holdings in the area, which include hotels and office buildings, must realistically be imputed to the Terminal; and (4) the development rights above the Terminal, which had been made transferable to numerous sites in the vicinity of the Terminal, one or two of which were suitable for the construction of office buildings, were valuable to appellants and provided "significant, perhaps 'fair,' compensation for the loss of rights above the terminal itself." Id., at 333–336, 366 N. E. 2d, at 1276–1278.

II

The issues presented by appellants are (1) whether the restrictions imposed by New York City's law upon appellants' exploitation of the Terminal site effect a "taking" of appellants' property for a public use within the meaning of the Fifth Amendment, which of course is made applicable to the States through the Fourteenth Amendment, and, (2), if so, whether the transferable development rights afforded appellants constitute "just compensation" within the meaning of the Fifth Amendment . . .

A Before considering appellants' specific contentions, it will be useful to review the factors that have shaped the jurisprudence of the Fifth Amendment injunction "nor shall private property be taken for public use, without just compensation." The question of what constitutes a "taking" for purposes of the Fifth Amendment has proved to be a problem of considerable difficulty. While this Court has recognized that the "Fifth Amendment's guarantee . . . [is] designed to bar Government from forcing some people alone to bear public burdens which, in all fairness and justice, should be borne by the public as a whole," Armstrong v. United States, 364 U.S. 40, 49 (1960), this Court, quite simply, has been unable to develop any "set formula" for determining when "justice and fairness" require that economic injuries caused by public action be compensated by the government, rather than remain disproportionately concentrated on a few persons. See Goldblatt v. Hempstead, 369 U.S. 590, 594 (1962). Indeed, we have frequently observed that whether a particular restriction will be rendered invalid by the government's failure to pay for any losses proximately caused by it depends largely "upon the particular circumstances [in that] case."

In engaging in these essentially ad hoc, factual inquiries, the Court's decisions have identified several factors that have particular significance. The economic impact of the regulation on the claimant and, particularly, the extent to which the regulation has interfered with distinct investment-backed expectations are, of course, relevant considerations. See Goldblatt v. Hempstead, supra, at 594. So, too, is the character of the governmental action. A "taking" may more readily be found when the interference with property can be characterized as a physical invasion by government, see, e. g., United States v. Causby, 328 U.S. 256 (1946), than when interference arises from some public program adjusting the benefits and burdens of economic life to promote the common good.

"Government hardly could go on if to some extent values incident to property could not be diminished without paying for every such change in the general law," Pennsylvania Coal Co. v. Mahon, 260 U.S. 393, 413 (1922), and this Court has accordingly recognized, in a wide variety of contexts, that government may execute laws or programs that adversely affect recognized economic values. Exercises of the taxing power are one obvious example. A second are the decisions in which this Court has dismissed "taking" challenges on the ground that, while the challenged government action caused economic harm, it did not interfere with interests that were sufficiently bound up with the reasonable expectations of the claimant to constitute "property" for Fifth Amendment purposes . . .

More importantly for the present case, in instances in which a state tribunal reasonably concluded that "the health, safety, morals, or general welfare" would be promoted by prohibiting particular contemplated uses of land, this Court has upheld land-use regulations that destroyed or adversely affected recognized real property interests. See Nectow v. Cambridge, 277 U.S. 183, 188 (1928). Zoning laws are, of course, the classic example, see Euclid v. Ambler Realty Co., 272 U.S. 365 (1926) (prohibition of industrial use); Gorieb v. Fox, 274 U.S. 603, 608 (1927) (requirement that portions of parcels be left unbuilt); Welch v. Swasey, 214 U.S. 91 (1909) (height restriction), which have been viewed as permissible governmental action even when prohibiting the most beneficial use of the property. See Goldblatt v. Hempstead, supra, at 592–593, and cases cited; see also Eastlake v. Forest City Enterprises, Inc., 426 U.S. 668, 674 n. 8 (1976) . . .

Pennsylvania Coal Co. v. Mahon, 260 U.S. 393 (1922), is the leading case for the proposition that a state statute that substantially furthers important public policies may so frustrate distinct investment-backed expectations as to amount to a "taking." There the claimant had sold the surface rights to particular parcels of property, but expressly reserved the right to remove the coal thereunder. A Pennsylvania statute, enacted after the transactions, forbade any mining of coal that caused the subsidence of any house, unless the house was the property of the owner of the underlying coal and was more than 150 feet from the improved property of another. Because the statute made it commercially impracticable to mine the coal, id., at 414, and thus had nearly the same effect as the complete destruction of rights claimant had reserved from the owners of the surface land, see id., at 414–415, the Court held that the statute was invalid as effecting a "taking" without just compensation . . .

. . . Government actions that may be characterized as acquisitions of resources to permit or facilitate uniquely public functions have often been held to constitute "takings." United States v. Causby, 328 U.S. 256 (1946), is illustrative. In holding that direct overflights above the claimant's land, that destroyed the present use of the land as a chicken farm, constituted a "taking," Causby emphasized that Government had not "merely destroyed property [but was] using a part of it for the flight of its planes." Id., at 262–263, n. 7 . . .

B In contending that the New York City law has "taken" their property in violation of the Fifth and Fourteenth Amendments, appellants make a series of arguments, which, while tailored to the facts of this case, essentially urge that any substantial restriction imposed pursuant to a landmark law must be accompanied by just compensation if it is to be constitutional. Before considering these, we emphasize what is not in dispute. Because this Court has recognized, in a number of settings, that States and cities may enact land use restrictions or controls to enhance the quality of life by preserving the character and desirable aesthetic features of a city, see New Orleans v. Dukes, 427 U.S. 297 (1976); Young v. American Mini Theatres, Inc., 427 U.S. 50 (1976); Village of Belle Terre v. Boraas, 416 U.S. 1, 9–10 (1974); Berman v. Parker, 348 U.S. 26, 33 (1954); appellants do not contest that New York City's objective of preserving structures and areas with special historic, architectural, or cultural significance is an entirely permissible governmental goal. They also do not dispute that the restrictions imposed on its parcel are appropriate means of securing the purposes of the New York City law. Finally, appellants do not challenge any of the specific factual premises of the decision below. They accept for present purposes both that the parcel of land occupied by Grand Central Terminal must, in its present state, be regarded as capable of earning a reasonable return, and that the transferable development rights afforded appellants by virtue of the Terminal's designation as a landmark are valuable, even if not as valuable as the rights to construct above the Terminal. In appellants' view none of these factors derogate from their claim that New York City's law has effected a "taking."

They first observe that the airspace above the Terminal is a valuable property interest, citing United States v. Causby, supra. They urge that the Landmarks Law has deprived them of any gainful use of their "air rights" above the Terminal and that, irrespective of the value of the remainder of their parcel, the city has "taken" their right to this superjacent airspace, thus entitling them to "just compensation" measured by the fair market value of these air rights.

. . . "Taking" jurisprudence does not divide a single parcel into discrete segments and attempt to determine whether rights in a particular segment have been entirely abrogated. In deciding whether a particular governmental action has effected a taking, this Court focuses rather both on the character of the action and on the nature and extent of the interference with rights in the parcel as a whole . . .

Secondly, appellants, focusing on the character and impact of the New York City law, argue that it effects a "taking" because its operation has significantly diminished the value of the Terminal site. Appellants concede that the decisions sustaining other land-use regulations, which, like the New York City law, are reasonably related to the promotion of the general welfare, uniformly reject the proposition that diminution in property value, standing alone, can establish a "taking," see Euclid v. Ambler Realty Co., 272 U.S. 365 (1926) (75% diminution in value caused by zoning law); Hadacheck v. Sebastian, 239 U.S. 394 (1915) (87 ½% diminution in value), and that the "taking" issue in these contexts is resolved by focusing on the uses the regulations permit. Appellants, moreover, also do not dispute that a showing of diminution in property value would not establish a "taking" if the restriction had been imposed as a result of historic-district legislation, but appellants argue that New York City's regulation of individual landmarks is fundamentally different from zoning or from historic-district legislation because the controls imposed by New York City's law apply only to individuals who own selected properties.

. . . Agreement with this argument would, of course, invalidate not just New York City's law, but all comparable landmark legislation in the Nation. We find no merit in it.

It is true, as appellants emphasize, that both historic-district legislation and zoning laws regulate all properties within given physical communities whereas landmark laws apply only to selected parcels. But, contrary to appellants' suggestions, landmark laws are not like discriminatory, or "reverse spot," zoning: that is, a land-use decision which arbitrarily singles out a particular parcel for different, less favorable treatment than the neighboring ones. In contrast to discriminatory zoning, which is the antithesis of land-use control as part of some comprehensive plan, the New York City law embodies a comprehensive plan to preserve structures of historic or aesthetic interest wherever they might be found in the city, and as noted, over 400 landmarks and 31 historic districts have been designated pursuant to this plan.

Equally without merit is the related argument that the decision to designate a structure as a landmark "is inevitably arbitrary or at least subjective, because it is basically a matter of taste, thus unavoidably singling out individual landowners for disparate and unfair treatment . . . Appellants . . . do not . . . suggest that the Commission's decisions concerning the Terminal were in any sense arbitrary or unprincipled. But, in any event, a landmark owner has a right to judicial review of any Commission decision, and, quite simply, there is no basis whatsoever for a conclusion that courts will have any greater difficulty identifying arbitrary or discriminatory action in the context of landmark regulation than in the context of classic zoning or indeed in any other context.

Next, appellants observe that New York City's law differs from zoning laws and historic-district ordinances in that the Landmarks Law does not impose identical or similar restrictions on all structures located in particular physical communities. It follows, they argue, that New York City's law is inherently incapable of producing the fair and equitable distribution of benefits and burdens of governmental action which is characteristic of zoning laws and historic-district legislation and which they maintain is a constitutional requirement if "just compensation" is not to be afforded. It is, of course, true that the Landmarks Law has a more severe impact on some landowners than on others, but that in itself does not mean that the law effects a "taking." Legislation designed to promote the general welfare commonly burdens some more than others . . . zoning laws often affect some property owners more severely than others but have not been held to be invalid on that account. For example, the property owner in Euclid who wished to use its property for industrial purposes was affected far more severely by the ordinance than its neighbors who wished to use their land for residences.

In any event, appellants' repeated suggestions that they are solely burdened and unbenefited is factually inaccurate . . . Unless we are to reject the judgment of the New York City Council that the preservation of landmarks benefits all New York citizens and all structures, both economically and by improving the quality of life in the city as a whole — which we are unwilling to do — we cannot conclude that the owners of the Terminal have in no sense been benefited by the Landmarks Law . . .

Appellants' final broad-based attack would have us treat the law as an instance . . . in which government, acting in an enterprise capacity, has appropriated part of their property for some strictly governmental purpose . . . this New York City law has in nowise impaired the present use of the Terminal, the Landmarks Law neither exploits appellants' parcel for city purposes nor facilitates nor arises from any entrepreneurial operations of the city . . . The Landmarks Law's effect is simply to prohibit appellants or anyone else from occupying portions of the airspace above the Terminal, while permitting appellants to use the remainder of the parcel in a gainful fashion. This is no more an appropriation of property by government for its own uses than is a zoning law prohibiting, for "aesthetic" reasons, two or more adult theaters within a specified area, see Young v. American Mini Theatres, Inc., 427 U.S. 50 (1976), or a safety regulation prohibiting excavations below a certain level.

C Rejection of appellants' broad arguments is not, however, the end of our inquiry, for all we thus far have established is that the New York City law is not rendered invalid by its failure to provide "just compensation" whenever a landmark owner is restricted in the exploitation of property interests, such as air rights, to a greater extent than provided for under applicable zoning laws.

We now must consider whether the interference with appellants' property is of such a magnitude that "there must be an exercise of eminent domain and compensation to sustain [it]"...

... [T]he New York City law does not interfere in any way with the present uses of the Terminal. Its designation as a landmark not only permits but contemplates that appellants may continue to use the property precisely as it has been used for the past 65 years: as a railroad terminal containing office space and concessions. So the law does not interfere with what must be regarded as Penn Central's primary expectation concerning the use of the parcel. More importantly, on this record, we must regard the New York City law as permitting Penn Central not only to profit from the Terminal but also to obtain a "reasonable return" on its investment...

... [T]o the extent appellants have been denied the right to build above the Terminal, it is not literally accurate to say that they have been denied all use of even those pre-existing air rights. Their ability to use these rights has not been abrogated; they are made transferable to at least eight parcels in the vicinity of the Terminal, one or two of which have been found suitable for the construction of new office buildings. Although appellants and others have argued that New York City's transferable development-rights program is far from ideal, the New York courts here supportably found that, at least in the case of the Terminal, the rights afforded are valuable. While these rights may well not have constituted "just compensation" if a "taking" had occurred, the rights nevertheless undoubtedly mitigate whatever financial burdens the law has imposed on appellants and, for that reason, are to be taken into account in considering the impact of regulation.

On this record, we conclude that the application of New York City's Landmarks Law has not affected a "taking" of appellants' property. The restrictions imposed are substantially related to the promotion of the general welfare and not only permit reasonable beneficial use of the landmark site but also afford appellants opportunities further to enhance not only the Terminal site proper but also other properties.

Affirmed

The *Penn Central* case establishes a framework for thinking about the limits of lawful regulation respecting property development and land use. The basic factors to consider include balancing competing interests to prevent one property owner from carrying the full burden of benefits to be enjoyed by the public at large. In seeking this balance, one ought to consider the extent to which a reciprocal benefit is available to the property owner being regulated and the property owner's reasonable investment-backed expectations. It is permissible to impose regulations that prevent the property owner from making the highest valued use of the property or that actually diminish the value of the property, so long as the property still retains some useful economic value.[96] In making such a determination, one is to consider the "whole parcel"; that is, one is to consider the economic value of the property as a whole rather than looking at individual rights in the property and asking if one of those individual pieces has lost all of its value.[97] Thus, the air rights have to be considered as part of the full property along with the land and the building. In property law terms, we are usually asked to consider the impact on the full "bundle of sticks" that make up the entire parcel rather than looking in an isolated fashion at only one of the sticks in a multistick bundle of property rights.

Penn Central also provides some guidance for questions regarding the regulation of accessibility in that the landmark regulations upheld in this case were aesthetic and were not applied to every building in the zone, nor were they applied in the same exact way to the different properties covered by the regulation. Planning and zoning efforts to improve accessibility may need to take a similar dynamic and flexible form when applied to preexisting community landscapes.

Three additional Supreme Court opinions are also highly relevant to our inquiry. These cases are *Lucas*,[98] *Nollan*,[99] and *Dolan*.[100] *Lucas* clarified the idea that there are two categories of takings: the first involving a physical invasion of private property by the government and the second being by regulation that is so restrictive that it virtually deprives the owner of all economic value.[101] Under the facts of *Lucas*, a categorical taking occurs either when there is a physical invasion or when a regulation reduces the property to no or nominal economic value. When value is reduced but there is some value remaining as a result of regulation, one must make detailed inquiry along the lines of *Penn Central*.

Sometimes land use regulation takes the form of imposing conditions on a property owner or requiring a property owner to make payments to support a desirable public purpose to be granted a right to develop her land. In such cases, the question becomes one of determining if and when such conditions and payments violate the takings clause. In *Nollan*, the court added clarification on this point by indicating that for land use regulations involving exactions to be constitutionally valid, there must be an *essential nexus* between the regulatory requirements and the legitimate state purpose asserted to be furthered by the

---

[96] *See* Palazzolo v. Rhode Island, 533 U.S. 606 (2001); Rith Energy, Inc. v. U.S., 271 F.3d 1347 (Fed. Cir. 2001); State Dep't of Envtl. Protection v. Burgess, 772 So.2d 540 (Fla. App. 2000).
[97] *Lucas*, 505 U.S. 1003.   [98] *Id.*   [99] Nollan v. Cal. Coastal Comm'n, 438 U.S. 815 (1987).
[100] Dolan v. City of Tigard, 512 U.S. 374 (1994).   [101] *Lucas*, 505 U.S. 1003.

regulation.[102] And in *Dolan*, the court further asserted that, with respect to exactions and conditions, there must be rough proportionality between what the individual property owner is asked to contribute and the actual impacts imposed by the property owner's development project.[103] More recently, in *Koontz v. St Johns River Water Management District*, 133 S.Ct. 2586 (2013), the requirements of *Nollan* and *Dolan* were upheld and applied to a situation where Koontz, a property owner, was denied a development permit.[104] The *Koontz* case affirmed that the government may not condition a development permit on the owner's relinquishment of a portion of his property or the payment of an in lieu fee, unless there is a nexus and rough proportionality between the required condition and the effects of the proposed use. *Nollan*, *Dolan*, and *Koontz* are important because they seem to limit the ability of government to condition development approvals based on extracting exactions and fees from property owners and developers. This constrains one method of using regulation to require private parties to build and fund publicly desired improvements to accessibility of the built environment.

Notwithstanding the higher standard of having to demonstrate a nexus and rough proportionality under the circumstances of *Nollan*, *Dolan*, and *Koontz*, it is difficult to imagine that government land use regulations requiring inclusive design will violate the Fifth Amendment's prohibition on takings of private property. Inclusive design requirements are directed at regulating design for the public health, safety, welfare, and morals and not at taking away private property rights. A residential home can still be used as a residential home, for instance, even if inclusive design requirements provide that the doorways have to be 36 inches wide rather than 28 inches wide; and the property owner can still include or exclude whomever he was legally permitted to include or exclude prior to the regulations. Even if certain costs are imposed on the property owner to make the home and property more accessible, it will seldom be the case that design changes will destroy all of the economic value of the property or totally frustrate a person's reasonable investment-backed expectations with respect to the use of the property. It also seems that most inclusive design requirements will easily pass a nexus test in terms of advancing an important state interest that has been clearly identified in the federal disability laws; and in most cases, inclusive design will fall within the confines of rough proportionality. Thus, looking at inclusive design from a traditional land use perspective seems to confirm that the takings clause poses no serious inhibition on requirements for accessibility. At the same time, at

---

[102] *Nollan*, 438 U.S. 815.   [103] *Dolan*, 512 U.S. 374.
[104] Koontz v. St. John's River Water Mgmt. Dist., 133 S.Ct. 2586 (2013).

least with respect to efforts to expand inclusive design requirements beyond threshold levels of legally mandated minimal compliance, land use regulators will want to consider the relevance of the nexus and rough proportionality criteria, particularly in light of the *Koontz* case, if they seek to use exactions and in lieu fees as a way of making property owners finance higher levels of accessibility.

One case that specifically considered a takings claim with respect to inclusive design is *Pinnock v. International House of Pancakes*.[105] Although it involves a specific requirement of Title III of the ADA, its reasoning seems to be sound and relevant for most any type of inclusive design requirement, particularly given significant demographic changes in our aging population and increases in the incidence of mobility impairment across the population. For this reason, it is instructive of how the courts might deal with an inclusive design land use limitation based on a takings claim.

Pinnock v. International House of Pancakes

844 F. Supp. 574 (S.D. Cal. 1993), *cert. denied*, 512 U.S. 1228 (1994)
OPINION BY: JOHN S. RHOADES, SR.

I. Background

Plaintiff, Theodore A. Pinnock ("Pinnock") filed the complaint in this action against Defendant, Majid Zahedi, owner of an International House of Pancakes franchise ("Zahedi"). Pinnock, an attorney representing himself, is unable to walk and uses a wheelchair. Pinnock dined at the defendant's restaurant on June 21, 1992, and then attempted to use the restroom. The entrance to the restroom, however, was not wide enough to admit his wheelchair. Pinnock therefore removed himself from his wheelchair and crawled into the restroom. As a result of this encounter, Pinnock alleges nine causes of action against Zahedi . . .

Requiring Alterations to Property in Compliance with Title III of the ADA Is Not an Un-constitutional Taking Without Just Compensation

Zahedi contends that the expenditure of funds necessary to make the restrooms in his facility accessible to individuals in wheelchairs, if required under the ADA, would constitute a taking of private property "for public use, without just

---

[105] *Pinnock v. Int'l House of Pancakes*, 844 F. Supp. 574; cert denied 512 U.S. 1228 (1994). *See also* Chapter 2 *infra*.

compensation" in violation of the Fifth Amendment's Due Process Clause. In Lucas v. South Carolina Costal Council, 505 U.S. 1003 (1992); 112 S. Ct. 2886 (1992), the Supreme Court delineated three situations in which a governmental restraint is considered a taking, therefore requiring compensation. These three situations are: 1) When the regulation compels a permanent physical invasion of the property; 2) When the regulation denies an owner all economically beneficial or productive use of its land; 3) When the regulation in question does not substantially advance a legitimate governmental objective. If either of the first two situations occur, the regulation will be considered a taking regardless of whether the action achieves an important public benefit or has only minimal impact on the owner. Lucas, 112 S. Ct. at 2893. The expenditure of funds required by Title III does not constitute a taking under the Fifth Amendment as defined in Lucas.

A. REQUIRING ZAHEDI TO COMPLY WITH THE ADA DOES NOT CONSTI-TUTE A PHYSICAL INVASION [OF] HIS PROPERTY. The Fifth Amendment provides that private property may not be taken for public use without just compensation. A cornerstone of the law of takings is that if a regulation has the effect of establishing a permanent physical occupation, it will be a taking. Nollan v. California Coastal Commission, 483 U.S. 825, 831, 97 L. Ed. 2d 677, 107 S. Ct. 3141 (1987) (requiring the granting of an easement as a condition to rebuild a home is a taking). An invasion will constitute a taking even if the amount taken is insubstantial. Loretto v. Teleprompter Manhattan CATV, 458 U.S. 419, 430, 73 L. Ed. 2d 868, 102 S. Ct. 3164 (1982). The Loretto Court noted that:

> When the "character of the governmental action" is a permanent physical occupation of the property, our cases uniformly have found a taking to the extent of the occupation, without regard to whether the action achieves an important public benefit, or has only minimal economic impact on the owner.

Id. at 434. Therefore, when a law results in a permanent physical occupation of property, the government must compensate the landowner.

Zahedi argues that the remodeling required under the ADA may result in the loss of as many as 20 seating places in his restaurant. Zahedi cites Loretto in support of his argument that a regulation which requires a restaurant to widen restrooms and thereby restricts the use of part of his property, violates the Fifth Amendment. Zahedi, however, provides an inaccurate recitation of Loretto. The Supreme Court's analysis in Loretto rests on the finding that a regulation which gives an outside entity the right to physically intrude upon the property is actually the granting of an easement without compensation, which can constitute a taking. In Loretto, the Supreme Court found that a statute requiring a landlord to permit a cable television company to install cable television on his property constituted a taking. This case, however, does not involve the granting of Zahedi's property to another party for its own exclusive use and profit. Rather, the ADA merely proscribes Zahedi's use of part of his own property and it therefore could be likened to a zoning regulation. Since the ADA merely regulates the use of property and does not give anyone physical occupation of Zahedi's property, it is not within the Supreme Court's first category of takings.

B. THE ADA DOES NOT DENY ZAHEDI ALL ECONOMICALLY BENEFICIAL OR PRODUCTIVE USE OF HIS LAND. Regulations which restrict the use of property will be upheld unless the economic impact of a challenged statute is so extreme that it denies the claimant any economically viable use of the property. United States v. Riverside Bayview Homes, Inc., 474 U.S. 121, 88 L. Ed. 2d 419, 106 S. Ct. 455 (1985) (the denial of a permit to fill in a wetland does not constitute a taking); Lai v. City and County of Honolulu, 841 F.2d 301, 303 (9th Cir. 1988) (no taking found even when creation of scenic easement prevented construction of a high-rise condominium). Perhaps the Lucas Court provided the clearest justification for this rule when it stated:

> [the] total deprivation of beneficial use is, from the landowner's point of view, the equivalent of a physical appropriation.

Lucas, 112 S. Ct. at 2894. Zahedi does not, however, claim that the ADA would deny him all economic use of his property. To the contrary, Zahedi claims only that expenditures may be necessary to comply with the regulation.

Importantly, the ADA was specifically drafted to protect existing businesses from undue hardship. By adopting a "readily achievable" standard, Congress ensured that a business's obligation to remove barriers would reflect its ability to do so. As the Government states, barrier removal which would in fact have a dramatic deleterious effect on IHOP's business would not be required under the "readily achievable" standard.

The remodeling which Zahedi claims is required under the ADA regulations could result in the loss of approximately 20 seating places in his restaurant. The mere loss of approximately 20 seating places surely will not deny Zahedi all economically viable use of his property.

The Court must also consider whether the requirements of the statute frustrate the property owner's reasonable investment backed expectations. As discussed above, the ADA was specifically drafted to avoid the imposition of economic hardship upon the operators of public accommodations, particularly those running smaller operations. A showing of frustration of investment-backed expectation is a very difficult one to make, and the impact of the ADA's barrier removal requirements pales in comparison to many of the regulations which the Supreme Court has upheld. In Andrus v. Allard, 444 U.S. 51, 62 L. Ed. 2d 210, 100 S. Ct. 318 (1979), the Supreme Court held that federal laws which prohibited sale of articles made from feathers of protected birds did not violate [the] Fifth Amendment, even where laws prohibited all of the uses originally intended for the products. The Court in Andrus noted:

> loss of future profits — unaccompanied by any physical property restriction — provides a slender reed upon which to rest a takings claim . . . perhaps because of its very uncertainty, the interest in anticipated gains has traditionally been viewed as a less compelling than other property-related interests.

Andrus, 444 U.S. at 66. Regulations have been upheld even where they resulted in a complete restriction upon a specific individual's future exploitation of the property for profit. See, e.g., Keystone Bituminous Coal Ass'n v. DeBenedictis, 480 U.S. 470, 485, 94 L. Ed. 2d 472, 107 S. Ct. 1232 (1987) (restriction upon removal of coal did not completely destroy value of owner's economic interest in coal).

C. THE STATUTORY REQUIREMENTS OF TITLE III SUBSTANTIALLY ADVANCE A LEGITIMATE GOVERNMENTAL INTEREST. A taking occurs when a court finds that there is no evidence that property restrictions will further the stated rationale of a statute. Nollan, 483 U.S. at 838. In Nollan, the Court found that by requiring an owner who wished to build beach front property to grant a public easement across the property, the California Coastal Commission had taken his property without just compensation. The Court used a means/ends analysis to determine if there was a close "fit" between the restriction and the interests aimed to be advanced. Nollan, 483 U.S. at 838. The Court decided that requiring the property owner to grant an easement failed the means/ends analysis because there was no relation between the statute and its stated aim, which was to alleviate the effect the homes would have on the view of the beach from the public thoroughfare. See also Commercial Builders v. Sacramento, 941 F.2d 872 (9th Cir. 1991) (ordinance, requiring the payment of a fee before being granted a non-residential building permit was held not to be an unconstitutional taking because there was nexus between the regulation and the problem to be addressed).

In contrast, the barrier removal requirements of Title III clearly forward the stated objectives of the ADA. The ADA aims:

(1) to provide a clear and comprehensive national mandate for the elimination of discrimination against individuals with disabilities; [and]
(2) to provide clear, strong, consistent, enforceable standards addressing discrimination against individuals with disabilities;

42 U.S.C. § 12101(b)(1) & (2) (Supp. II 1990). The legislative history of the Act reflects congressional concern over the deleterious effects of discrimination against people with disabilities:

> The large majority of people with disabilities do not go to movies, do not go to the theater, do not go to see musical performances, and do not go to sports events. A substantial minority of persons with disabilities never go to a restaurant, never go to a grocery store, and never go to a church or synagogue . . . The extent of non-participation of individuals with disabilities in social and recreational activities [is] alarming.

Senate Report at 11 (citing the findings of a recent Lou Harris poll summarized by the National Council on Disability). Congress found that the exclusion of disabled individuals from public life was largely a result of the "lack of physical access to facilities." Senate Report at 11. As a result, the legislative body elected to adopt the barrier removal requirements embodied in Title III. These requirements directly address and remedy the problems which the Act aims to redress.

Zahedi argues that the ADA constitutes a "national building code" which trespasses the regulatory area reserved to the states by the Tenth Amendment. It was once contended that the federal government had no police power, as such, except in the District of Columbia. It is now the law, however, that the federal government's implied powers under the "necessary and proper clause" of the Constitution (Art. I, § 8) provide for the passage of laws similar to legislation enacted by a state under its police power. Hence, it is recognized today that "in the exercise of its control over interstate commerce, the means employed by the Congress may have the quality of police regulations." Kentucky Whip & Collar Co. v. Illinois Cen. R. Co, 299 U.S. 334, 81 L. Ed. 270, 57 S. Ct. 277 (1936).

The Tenth Amendment does not insulate states from federal regulation simply because the regulation affects an area traditionally subject to state control. Garcia v. San Antonio Metropolitan Transit Authority, 469 U.S. 528,

83 L. Ed. 2d 1016, 105 S. Ct. 1005 (1985). Rather, the Court has held that neither the Tenth Amendment nor the structure of the federal system justifies restriction of Congress's power to apply otherwise valid commercial regulation to state or local governments . . .

. . . Title III's statutory scheme does not displace local building codes. It is a federal civil rights act that sets forth accessibility standards that places of public accommodation and commercial facilities must follow. Departures from the ADA Standards are expressly permitted where "alternative designs and technologies used will provide substantially equivalent or greater access to and usability of the facility." 28 C.F.R. pt. 36, app. A, § 2.2, at 482 (1991). State and local building codes remain in effect to be enforced by state officials. State officials are not required to adopt or enforce the ADA Standards for Accessible Design.

VIII. CONCLUSION . . .   . . . Having carefully considered each of Zahedi's constitutional challenges, it is clear that none of these challenges can prevail.

Admittedly, the *Pinnock* case may be viewed narrowly on its facts as a case involving a place of public accommodation, but the better view is one of acknowledging that a takings claim directed at the regulation of design preferences in the built environment is not likely to rise to the level of violating the takings clause of the U.S. Constitution, particularly as long as it is compliance based and narrowly tailored to meet the civil rights of people with disabilities. Although the scope and extent of design regulation may need to be greater in public places and places of public accommodation relative to private residences, the primary focus of the police power is on making the built environment safe and easy to navigate so that all people may meaningfully participate in the activities of everyday life.

Developing comprehensive planning and zoning to effectuate the goals and requirements of the ADA and related legislation is a valid exercise of the police power. Moreover, regulation of design preferences and land uses that promote inclusion and the ability to safely and easily age in place do not typically involve physical invasions of the property by government. Furthermore, inclusive design does not prevent the primary use of the property, nor does it eliminate all of the economic value of the property. In fact, the preference for particular design choices, such as narrow doorways and hallways, is probably not even a property right in the first instance; it is simply a consumer preference. Even if design preferences are property rights or affect property rights, the interference with these preferences by the requirements of inclusive design is not likely to rise to the level of an unlawful taking under the current state of the law, and no compensation is likely to be required.

2.6 CONCLUSION

It seems clear that inclusive design regulations are within the police power authority of local government. The ADA establishes accessibility as an important civil right and social value, and this combined with changing demographics supports the need for inclusive design regulation as a way of advancing and protecting the public health, safety, welfare, and morals. Although there are limitations on the exercise of the police powers, the regulation of design preferences and land uses with respect to the built environment is not likely to be legally problematic. Local planning and land use professionals should understand mobility impairment as a land use issue and become more actively engaged in developing strategies for making local communities better suited for easy and safe navigation – and for aging in place.

3

Regulating inclusive design

When we look around our communities, we see roads, sidewalks, houses, office buildings, shopping centers, parks, power plants, manufacturing facilities, agricultural operations, and all sorts of other intrusions on the natural landscape. Thus, we are surrounded by, and embedded in, the built environment, sometimes forgetting that our intentional design choices are neither altogether natural nor predetermined. Making things even more complicated, this environment is woven with technology and other infrastructure that is oftentimes not even visible to the casual observer. The coordination of all of these complex land uses within a dynamic community requires careful planning, and an important element of such planning involves compliance with current regulations on accessibility.

This chapter summarizes the primary requirements for accessibility under federal law, recognizing that many states have similar provisions and that the U.S. framework developed in furtherance of the ADA has been a model for global accessibility policies in many other countries.[1] The goal is to provide

---

[1] *See, e.g.*, Ariz. Rev. Stat. Ann. § 41–1401 et seq. (2010); Cal. Code. Regs. tit. 24 § 5–101 et seq. (2011); Md. Code Ann., State Gov't § 20–601 et seq. (West 2013); Md. Code Ann., Health-Gen § 7–101 et seq. (2009); N.Y. Exec. Law § 290 et seq. (McKinney **year**). *See also* Convention on the Rights of Persons with Disabilities, G.A. Res. 61/106, U.N. Doc. A/RES/61/106 (Dec. 13, 2006); *Disability Discrimination Act 1992* (Cth) (Austl.); Canjiren Baozhang Fa [Law on the Protection of Disabled Persons] (promulgated by the Standing Comm. Nat'l People's Cong., Dec. 28, 1990, effective May 15, 1991) 1990–1992 Falü Quanshu 1268 (China), *translated in* 14 P.R.C. Laws and Regs V-03-00-101; Behindertengleichstellungsgesetz [BGG] [Equal Opportunities for Disabled People Act], May 1, 2002, BGBl. I. at 1467 (Ger.), *available at* www.gesetze-im-internet.de; 7600, Igualdad de Oportunidades para las personas con Discapacidad en Costa Rica [Equal Opportunities for Persons with Disabilities] May 29, 1996, La Gaceta, 2000, sec. 2 (Costa Rica); Canadian Human Rights Act, R.S.C. 1985, c. H-6; Equality Act, 2010, c. 15 (U.K.); Equal Opportunity, Non-Discrimination and Universal Accessibility for People with Disabilities (B.O.E. 2003, 289) (Spain).

an overview of federal disability law and its relationship to local land use regulation; as such, the chapter proceeds in several steps. First, it provides additional demographic information on mobility impairment and our aging population to develop a more complete context for understanding the current regulations governing accessibility. Second, it provides an overview of the current federal regulations applicable to inclusive design with reference to distinctions made for different categories of property, including public property, places of public accommodation, multifamily housing, single-family housing, affordable housing, and places that are otherwise distinguished in terms of the need for enhanced accessibility. The focus is on outlining the basic legal categories rather than going into the details of actual design requirements because the design requirements are more properly understood as technical construction and building code issues. There are guides and handbooks addressing the technical requirements of construction design, and these requirements are not at issue in this book. This book is focused on the legal and policy issues related to understanding mobility impairment and aging in place as land use problems rather than as simply civil rights concerns. In addressing mobility impairment and aging in place as land use problems, the third part of this chapter discusses the legal relationship between local land use regulation and federal disability rights law.

3.1 DEVELOPING THE CONTEXT

At the time of the 2000 census, the total number of families in the United States was 72.3 million.[2] Of this number, approximately 20.9 million families had at least one member with a disability,[3] and of this group, more than 12 million had at least one member with a *physical* disability.[4] For these purposes, a physical disability was defined as "a condition that substantially limited one or more basic physical activities such as walking, climbing stairs, reaching, lifting, or carrying."[5] Thus, when we stop thinking in terms of atomistic individuals with discrete mobility impairment problems, we see that 16.6 percent (or approximately 17 percent) of families in the United States include a person with some form of mobility impairment and are potentially affected by exclusionary design in our built environment. When we think in broader terms, including social networks of friends and colleagues, we begin to appreciate

---

[2] QI WANG, U.S. DEP'T OF COM., REPORT NO. CENSR-23, DISABILITY AND AMERICAN FAMILIES: 2000 (2005), *available at* www.census.gov/prod/2005pubs/censr-23.pdf.
[3] *Id.* [4] *Id.*
[5] *Id.* This definition referred to "substantial" limitations and did not include lesser physical limitations, so the number could be higher.

that perhaps 20 percent of American families are potentially touched by issues
of concern to people with mobility impairment. Therefore, the appropriate
way of understanding the impact of exclusionary design of the built environment is not simply by counting the number of discrete individuals with
mobility impairment, because for every individual with mobility impairment,
several people and multiple social networks are affected.

In considering the nature of mobility impairment, we find that almost
7 million Americans living outside of institutions use mobility assistive
devices.[6] This amounts to 2.6 percent of our total U.S. population, with the rate
of use for the specific group of people aged 65 years and older being 14 percent.[7]
In addition to age, use of mobility devices varies by gender (women use them
at a higher rate than men), income (less use as income rises), education (less
use as years of formal education increases), and by race and ethnicity (within
each population, use among African Americans at 3.1 percent, whites at 2.6
percent, Native Americans at 3.4 percent, and Pacific Islanders at 1 percent).[8]
The percentage of disability within the population also varies slightly by region
of the country, with the lowest percentage rate in the Midwest and the highest
rate in the South.[9]

Mobility impairment results in a person having difficulty navigating the
built environment, and although this may not require use of assistive technology, it can frequently lead to the need for a variety of support devices,
including canes, crutches, walkers, wheelchairs, and scooters.[10] Birth defects,
accidents, disease, combat injuries, obesity, surgery, and aging all contribute
to the potential for any person, and any family, to experience a need to address
mobility impairment issues.[11] Furthermore, tens of thousands of Americans

---

[6] *See* H. STEPHEN KAYE ET AL., U.S. DEP'T OF EDUC., DISABILITY STATISTICS CTS.,
REPORT NO. 14, MOBILITY DEVICE USE IN THE UNITED STATES 7–8 (2000), *available at*
http://dsc.ucsf.edu/pub_listing.php (the study expressly excludes people living in institutions
(nursing homes, prisons, etc.), thus it underreports the total number of seniors actually using
such devices. *Id.* at 5).

[7] *Id.*   [8] *Id.* at 7–12.

[9] WANG, *supra* note 2. The percentage of people with disabilities does vary slightly by region,
although not significantly. The lowest percentage of disability was in the Midwest, where 26.5
percent of people had a disability. *Id.* The highest percentage of disability was in the South,
where 30.8 percent of people had a disability. *Id.* The Northeast and West fell in between the
percentages of the Midwest and the South. *Id.*

[10] It should be noted that use of mobility devices has grown with a doubling in the use of
wheelchairs and walkers between 1980 and 1990. KAYE ET AL., *supra* note 6, at 1. During this
time period, the use of crutches increased by 14 percent and canes by 53 percent. *Id.* It is likely
that some of this growth is due to the improved survival rate of trauma patients as well as to
the improved design, function, and image of such devices. *Id.*

[11] For example, about 1.7 million Americans are living with limb loss, and the Amputee Coali-
tion of America warns that the number could rise because of the nation's skyrocketing

experience temporary periods of mobility impairment during their lifetimes, from such events as sporting, automobile, and other accidents. Developing mobility impairment can transform a current residence into a virtual prison because of poor design and make participation in neighborhood and community events difficult or impossible. Mobility impairment also severely restricts housing options for those seeking to relocate because so few single-family homes are built with inclusive design features.

The network implications of mobility impairment multiply quickly. Many of the elderly have mobility impairment and become increasingly isolated because their family and friends occupy inaccessible housing that cannot be easily and safely visited and because getting to and from different locations is often difficult. Many elderly adults become unable to safely operate an automobile, and oftentimes there are few alternatives to having an automobile for transportation. In addition, walking may be difficult because streets are often wide and busy with fast-moving traffic, and sidewalks are often nonexistent or in disrepair. Many of these difficulties arise from the failure of communities to think of inclusive design as an integrating element across the full spectrum of the built environment.

As our population ages, we can expect the elderly to join forces with the broader population of people dealing with mobility impairment in demanding increasing attention to inclusive design communities. We can see the potential for this growing demand when we consider demographic trends. For example, as of the year 2000, the total number of people in the United States aged 65 and older was 35 million.[12] This represented a 12 percent increase over the year 1990, when the number of people 65 and older totaled 31.2 million.[13] The

obesity rate and the link to diabetes-related amputations which are estimated to cost $3 billion annually. *See* NATIONAL LIMB LOSS INFORMATION CENTER (NLLIC), FACT SHEET: AMPUTATION STATISTICS BY CAUSE: LIMB LOSS IN THE UNITED STATES (revised 2008), www.amputee-coalition.org/fact_sheets/amp_stats_cause.pdf; NATIONAL LIMB LOSS INFORMATION CENTER, AMPUTEE COALITION OF AMERICA, FACT SHEET: DIABETES AND LOWER EXTREMITY AMPUTATIONS (revised 2008), www.amputee-coalition.org/fact_sheets/diabetes_leamp.html. Moreover, obesity can cause mobility impairment directly (it is difficult to move when extremely overweight) as well as indirectly, as in the case of increased risk of diabetes. The latest information indicates that 25.6 percent of adult Americans (aged older than 18) are obese, with the states of Alabama, Mississippi, and Tennessee having rates that exceed 30 percent. *See* CENTERS FOR DISEASE CONTROL AND PREVENTION (CDC), CDC FEATURES, OBESITY IN U.S. ADULTS, BRFSS, 2007: NO STATE MET THE HEALTHY PEOPLE 2010 GOAL OF 15% ADULT OBESITY, www.cdc.gov/features/dsobesity/.

[12] LISA HETZEL & ANNETTA SMITH, U.S. DEP'T OF COM., CENSUS 2000 BRIEF NO. C2KBR/01-10, THE 65 YEARS AND OVER POPULATION: 2000 (2001), *available at* www.census.gov/prod/2001pubs/c2kbr01-10.pdf.

[13] *Id.*

35 million people over age 65 represented 12.4 percent of the population in 2000.[14] Furthermore, in 2000, there were 18.4 million people aged 65–74,[15] and people aged 75–84 numbered 12.4 million.[16] In 2006, 23 percent of the U.S. population was age 65 or older.[17] Many of these Americans aged 65 and older must deal with disability. In fact, according to an American Community Survey performed by the Census Bureau, 40.5 percent of Americans 65 and older have a disability.[18] The elderly are one of the fastest-growing segments of our population, and we are just now starting to deal with the fact that there are 75–76 million baby boomers adding to their ranks.[19] The result is that people older than 65 are expected to account for 25 percent or more of the U.S. population by 2030.[20] This demographic trend places an increasing urgency on the need to develop more inclusive design communities. Moreover, as Americans are living longer, they are also spending more years dealing with chronic disability. Life expectancy at birth was 75.2 years in 1990, with 9.4 of those years typically involving chronic disability. In 2010, life expectancy increased to 78.2 years, and years with chronic disability increased to 10.1.[21]

Another important consideration in terms of dealing with an aging population is that the majority (64 percent) of people aged 50 and older wish to remain in single-family homes.[22] At the same time, 21 percent of these people anticipate a move during the next five years.[23] Thus, even as people age, they think in terms of mobility – mobility to live independently in a single-family

---

[14] *See* Jon Pynoos et al., *Aging in Place, Housing, and the Law*, 16 ELDER L. J. 77, 79 (2008).
[15] Hetzel & Smith, *supra* note 12.   [16] *Id.*
[17] CHERYL RUSSELL, DEMOGRAPHICS OF THE U.S.: TRENDS AND PROJECTIONS 361 (3d ed. 2007).
[18] UNITED STATES AND STATES: PERCENT OF PEOPLE 65 YEARS AND OVER WITH A DIS-ABILITY: 2005, U.S. CENSUS BUREAU tbl. R1803, http://factfinder.census.gov/home/saff/main.html?_lang=en&_ts= (follow "Data Sets" hyperlink; then follow "American Community Survey" hyperlink; then select "2005 American Community Survey"; then follow "Ranking Tables" hyperlink; then select R1803 under "Aging").
[19] *See* Judy Stark, *And Access for All*, ST. PETERSBURG TIMES, June 8, 2002; Pynoos, *supra* note 14, at 79 (using the number 75 million rather than 76 million and defining boomers as those born between 1946 and 1964).
[20] *See* Pynoos, *supra* note 14, at 79.   [21] WSJ 7/11/13.
[22] The demographics of the United States have an interesting relationship with housing. ERA Real Estate recently performed a survey of more than 1,000 people aged 50 and older. Of those interviewed, a vast majority (64 percent) stated that the single-family home was their residence of choice. At the same time, many of the respondents (21 percent) stated that they were considering a move in the next five years. *See* ERA FRANCHISE SYSTEMS LLC, NATIONAL SURVEY CONDUCTED BY ERA REAL ESTATE REVEALS BOOMERS STILL PRE-FER THE SINGLE-FAMILY HOME, EVEN FOR RETIREMENT: SINGLE-FAMILY HOMES HAVE GREATER APPEAL FOR TODAY'S MATURE CONSUMER, press release (Mar. 27, 2006), www.era.com/erapressreleases/32.html.
[23] *Id.*

home and mobility to freely relocate to a new house. Unfortunately, some of the anticipated need to move by the elderly is not so much desired as it is the result of a realization that their current homes will soon be difficult to navigate because of exclusionary design. Providing suitable housing and a wide set of housing options for our aging population will dictate a need to more fully standardize inclusive housing design across the entire housing stock.[24]

In considering single-family residential housing construction in relationship with an aging population, it is also important to note trends in the availability of single-story and multistory homes. As of 2011, there were a total of 132,419,000 housing units in the United States.[25] Of these units, 42,491,000 were single-story structures, leaving well over 89,928,000 units as multistory structures.[26] This difference is important to note because it is more difficult to make multistory structures as readily accessible as single-story structures. At the same time, it must be understood that merely because a structure is single story, it may not be readily accessible. In fact, many single-story homes are not readily accessible because they have step-up entrances, narrow entranceways, inaccessible bathrooms, and other assorted external and internal design barriers making it difficult to safely and easily navigate the property.

The trend in housing construction indicates a continuing movement toward an increasing number of multistory structures. This permits one to get higher-density use of a given size lot and effectively lowers the cost per housing unit because land costs per unit are reduced. This higher-density construction is also consistent with trends in sustainable development and with planning in accordance with "new urbanism," because higher density can reduce the need for infrastructure while also potentially reducing the carbon footprint. In 1973, 23 percent of homes were being built with two or more stories, 67 percent of homes were being built with one story, and an additional 10 percent were split-level.[27] By 1987, more than half the homes being built were multistory.[28]

---

[24] It is important for older people to have safe homes with supportive features. *See* Pynoos, *supra* note 14, at 81–82. Some 1 million older people have unmet needs in their current housing, and the three greatest needs include handrails or grab bars, ramps, and easy-access bathrooms. *Id.*

[25] U.S. Dep't of Hous. & Urban Dev. & U.S. Dep't of Commerce, 2011 American Housing Survey, at tbl. C-01-AH (General Housing Data–All Housing Units (NATIONAL)) (2011), *available at* http://factfinder2.census.gov/faces/tableservices/jsf/pages/productview.xhtml?pid=AHS_2011_C01AH&prodType=table.

[26] *Id.*

[27] U.S. Dep't of Hous. & Urban Dev. & U.S. Dep't of Commerce, No. H150/50, American Housing Survey for the United States: 2005, at 19 tbl. 1A-2 (Height and Condition of Building–All Housing Units) (2006), *available at* www.census.gov/prod/2006pubs/h150-50.pdf.

[28] U.S. Census Bureau, Number of Stories in New One-Family Houses Completed 1, www.census.gov/const/C25Ann/sftotalstories.pdf (last visited Oct. 20, 2013).

As of 2005, the percentage of multistory homes was 56 percent, whereas single-story homes were down to 44 percent.[29] The trend toward multistory housing continues to the present time.

The preceding information is limited, but it is also illustrative of the demographic changes taking place in communities across the country. These changes require planning to meet the dynamic needs of all residents. It is important to make our housing opportunities and our communities accessible so that everyone can enjoy meaningful participation in community life. No individual or group of people wish to be involuntarily isolated; most people wish to retain connections to the broader community, and they value the ability to safely and easily age in place while fully participating in a wide range of activities.

In planning for accessibility, one must appreciate that there are several approaches to inclusive design. The two major approaches are often referred to as *universal design* and *visitability*. There can also be different levels of visitability and different degrees to which universal design is incorporated into a given building or project. Guidelines for different approaches to accessibility have been developed by several sources, and it can be helpful to refer to a specific source when trying to do construction in accordance with particular standards of accessibility. In general, however, we can briefly outline the two major categories of universal design and visitability that are typically discussed in connection with residential housing.

Universal design standards are generally quite pervasive and applied throughout an entire structure.[30] One way to quickly grasp the basic idea of universal design is that everything within a structure is designed to be readily accessible to a person in a wheelchair. Thus, doorways and hallways are wider (32 inches minimum and up to a 36 inch width recommendation)

---

[29] *Id.*

[30] *See* Jordana L. Maisel, Ctr. for Inclusive Design & Environmental Access (IDEA), Visitability as an Approach to Inclusive Housing Design and Community Development: A Look at Its Emergence, Growth, and Challenges 10–12 (2005); Selwyn Goldsmith, Universal Design 1 (2001) ("Broadly, universal design means that the products which designers design are universally accommodating, that they cater conveniently for all their users. On the route toward this goal a product that was initially designed primarily for the mass market of normal able-bodied people could have been subsequently ... modified – the effect ... being that it would suit all its other potential users as well, including people with disabilities"); *see also* Wendy A. Jordan, Universal Design for the Home: Great Looking, Great Living Design for All Ages, Abilities, and Circumstances I (2008); Universal Design Alliance (UDA) Home Page, www.universaldesign.org/ (last visited Oct. 9, 2013); Universal Home Design, Aging in Place, Housing for Adults over 50–AARP, www.aarp.org/families/home/_design/ (last visited Oct. 9, 2013) [hereinafter AARP, Universal Home Design].

and have entrances that are barrier free.[31] Bathrooms must include appropriate grab bars, are bigger in size to accommodate the turning radius of a wheelchair, and include showers designed for easy roll in and out with a wheelchair.[32] Throughout the building, light switches are placed lower and traditional round doorknobs give way to lower-positioned levers.[33] Storage shelves and cabinets are lower, and countertops are lower, with cutouts so that a wheelchair user can push close enough to have the chair frame fit under the counter, thus permitting the user to be positioned to make full use of the counter space.[34] Universal design criteria such as these would ideally be applied to every room and every element throughout a building. The universal design approach seeks to maximize and equalize accessibility throughout a system.

Visitability design standards are much less pervasive than universal design.[35] The general idea behind a visitability standard is one of making the primary social space and entertainment space of a home or building easy and safe to visit without requiring the entire building to meet universal design standards.[36] This standard is typically discussed in terms of private market single-family homes. The idea is that, if I am hosting a neighborhood party at my house, it should be possible for all of my neighbors to be included and to feel that they are full participants in the social life of the neighborhood, without regard to mobility impairment. For this to readily happen, my home would have to meet some minimal inclusive design standards. The entrance to my home would have to have a zero-step elevation through the doorway and appropriate grade of incline from the street level to the entrance.[37] My entrance doorway, hallway, and first-floor doors would have to have at least 32 inches of clearance (32–36 inches in width to be consistent with that of universal design).[38] And the main portions of my entertainment area would need to be on one level floor – no drop living rooms or raised dining rooms, for instance. In addition, for all of my guests to feel equally comfortable, I would need at

---

[31] Robin Paul Malloy, *Inclusion by Design: Accessible Housing and Mobility Impairment*, 60 HASTINGS L. J. 711 (2009); *see* sources cited *supra* note 30; *see also* AMERICANS WITH DISABILITIES ACCESSIBILITY GUIDELINES FOR BUILDINGS AND FACILITIES, 28 C.F.R. pt 36, app. A, § 4.13 (2008), *available at* www.access-board.gov/adaag/ADAAG.pdf; CTR. FOR UNIVERSAL DESIGN, UNIVERSAL DESIGN IN HOUSING 1–7 (2006), *available at* www.design.ncsu.edu/cud/pubs_p/docs/UDinHousing.pdf.

[32] Malloy, *supra* note 31, at 712.   [33] *Id.*   [34] *Id.*

[35] *Id.*; *see* MAISEL, *supra* note 30, at 10–14, 16–18; *see also* Visitability, www.visitability.org (last visited Oct. 9, 2013); Housing: Visitability, www.accessiblesociety.org/topics/housing (last visited Oct. 9, 2013); Visitability Canada, www.visitablehousingcanada.com (last visited Oct. 9, 2013).

[36] *See* sources cited *supra*, note 35.   [37] Malloy, *supra* note 31, at 712.   [38] *Id.*

least a half-bathroom on the main floor of the home, and it would need to be sized to permit entrance and appropriate turning radius for a wheelchair.[39] Ideally, the bathroom would also have to have light switches and a sink at appropriate levels (slightly lower than the traditional nonaccessible levels). Round doorknobs would be replaced with lever-style door openers placed at the appropriate height (these are easier to open for people with arthritis). The approach of visitability is one of making a system accessible so that everyone has an opportunity for meaningful participation in any activity taking place at the property, but it does not require universal and equal access to every area of a property.

3.2 REGULATORY OVERVIEW

Currently we have national regulations addressing building accessibility for a number of types of property. In general, the regulations are pervasive in terms of the rights of persons with disabilities and in terms of detailed construction guidelines for inclusive design in a variety of settings. Property owners are responsible for meeting guidelines, and the government does not certify compliance, thus, property owners must engage construction consultants or other experts to seek compliance with these detailed building codes.[40] Although the regulations are very encompassing, they also contain some limitations, particularly with respect to private single-family residences and private clubs. The least regulated category of use involves the single-family residential home, even though this type of use makes up a significant part of the land uses in many communities. In this part of the chapter, a general outline of these regulatory categories is provided. The goal is to provide a regulatory context for better understanding federal disability law as it relates to land use law and not to explain the details of technical compliance with construction design guidelines for various types of uses.

The primary sources of regulation are as follows:

- *Architectural Barriers Act of 1968.*[41] The Architectural Barriers Act (ABA) requires that buildings and facilities designed, constructed, altered, or

---

[39] *Id.*

[40] *See* 29 U.S.C. § 792 (2006). *See also* U.S. DEP'T OF HOUSING & URBAN DEV. & U.S. DEP'T OF JUSTICE, ACCESSIBILITY (DESIGN AND CONSTRUCTION) REQUIREMENTS FOR COVERED MULTIFAMILY DWELLINGS UNDER THE FAIR HOUSING ACT (2013); U.S. DEP'T OF JUSTICE, 2010 ADA STANDARDS FOR ACCESSIBLE DESIGN (2010), *available at* www.ada.gov/2010ADAstandards_index.htm.; MARCELA ABADI RHOADS, THE ADA COMPANION GUIDE: UNDERSTANDING THE AMERICANS WITH DISABILITIES ACT ACCESSIBILITY GUIDELINES (ADAAG and the Architectural Barriers Act (ABA)) (2010).

[41] Architectural Barriers Act of 1968, Pub. L. No. 90-480, 82 Stat. 718 (codified as amended at 42 U.S.C. §§ 4151–4157 (2006)). Two useful resources that one can consult on this and

leased with certain federal funds after September 1969 be accessible to and useable by people with disabilities.[42] It addresses construction-based standards of accessibility for new and renovated buildings and not the services or programs being provided in such buildings. Private market construction of single-family housing is not covered by the ABA.[43]

- *Section 504 of the Rehabilitation Act of 1973.*[44] Section 504 prohibits discrimination based on disability in any program or activity receiving federal financial assistance.[45] Reasonable accommodations must be made for employees, and this includes the physical environment.[46] New construction and alterations must be accessible. To the extent that Section 504 applies to housing, it covers housing programs receiving federal funding and not privately funded single-family residential housing.[47] As to planning and zoning, the reasonable accommodation requirement under Section 504 is similar to that of the Fair Housing Act, but Section 504 applies only to programs and activities receiving federal funds, whereas the Fair Housing Act has broader application.[48]
- *Fair Housing Amendments Act of 1988.*[49] The Fair Housing Act (FHA) prohibits discrimination in housing on the basis of race, color, religion, sex, national origin, familial status, and disability and applies to private housing as well as publicly supported housing.[50] Activities covered include selling advertising, leasing, and financing of housing.[51] Zoning can also be covered. The FHA requires owners and zoning officials to make reasonable exceptions to policies and practices to afford people with disabilities an equal opportunity to obtain housing.[52] The focus is on providing an equal opportunity to obtain housing.[53] This may require

other ADA-related regulations are BNA, Disability Law Manual, and BNA, Disability Discrimination and the Workplace.

[42] *Id.*; Peter A. Susser & Peter J. Petesch, BNA Books, Disability Discrimination and the Workplace Chapter 1 § II(A) (2d ed. 2011). *See* Laura L. Rovner, *Disability, Equality, and Identity*, 55 Ala. L. Rev. 1043, 1043–47 (2004).

[43] Pub. L. No. 90-480, 82 Stat. 718 (codified as amended at 42 U.S.C. §§ 4151–4157 (2006)); Susser & Petesch, *supra* note 42.

[44] 29 U.S.C. § 794 (2006). (*See generally* BNA sources *supra*, note 41.)

[45] 29 U.S.C. § 794; *see* Rovner, *supra* note 42; Bonnie P. Tucker, *Section 504 of the Rehabilitation Act after Ten Years of Enforcement: The Past and the Future*, 1989 U. Ill. L. Rev. 845, 845–851 (1989).

[46] *See supra*, note 45.   [47] *Id.*   [48] *See* 29 U.S.C. § 794 (2006); 42 U.S.C. § 3601 (2006).

[49] Fair Housing Amendments Act of 1988, Pub. L. No. 100-430, 102 Stat. 1619 (codified as amended at 42 U.S.C. § 3601 (2006)) (amending Civil Rights Act of 1968, Pub. L. No. 90-284, Title VIII, 82 Stat. 81 (codified as amended at 42 U.S.C. § 3601 (2006))). (*See generally* BNA sources *supra*, note 41.)

[50] *Id.*   [51] *Id.*   [52] *Id.*

[53] *Id.*; Commemorating the Anniversary of the Fair Housing Act, H.R. Res. 59, 110th Cong. (2008); 134 Cong. Rec. 15,665 (1988); 134 Cong. Rec. 19,871 (1988).

zoning officials to grant a variance or exception to a zoning requirement if the person with a disability can show that doing so is a reasonable accommodation and that it is necessary for the person to be afforded an equal opportunity to obtain housing.[54] A "but for" test is used, requiring the person seeking the accommodation to demonstrate that, without the variance or exception ("but for the variance or exception"), she will not have an equal opportunity to obtain housing.[55] The FHA may also require landlords to make reasonable accommodations, such as permitting pets in an apartment even if they have a no-pet policy, if the pet is a guide dog, for example.[56] The FHA may also require a landlord to permit a tenant to make modifications to a structure for it to be reasonably accessible, even if the landlord's lease otherwise prohibits structural modifications.[57] It also provides mandates for all new multifamily housing to meet specific inclusive design standards, including guidelines for common areas, entranceways, hallways, light switches, grab bars, spacing to accommodate use of a wheelchair, and other design elements.[58] The Department of Housing and Urban Development (HUD) and the Department of Justice issue guidance on Design and Construction Requirements.[59] Failure to make multifamily dwellings accessible in compliance with these guidelines violates the FHA.[60] The regulations include definition criteria for "dwellings" covered by the FHA (for example, a hotel room is not typically considered a dwelling).[61] Single-family residential units are covered by FHA if they are in buildings of four or more units (condominiums, for example).[62] In general, the design and construction regulations do not apply to single-family residences, even though the antidiscrimination

[54] *See* Forest City Daly Hous., Inc. v. Town of North Hempstead, 175 F.3d 144 (2d Cir. 1999); Innovative Health Sys., Inc. v. City of White Plains, 931 F. Supp. 222 (S.D.N.Y. 1996), *aff'd* 117 F.3d 37 (2d Cir. 1997).

[55] *See* Lapid-Laurel, L.L.C. v. Zoning Bd. of Adjustment of the Township of Scotch Plains, 284 F.3d 442 (3d Cir. 2002); Smith & Lee Assocs., Inc. v. City of Taylor, Mich., 102 F.3d 781 (6th Cir. 1996); Sharpvisions, Inc. v. Borough of Plum, 475 F. Supp. 2d 514 (W.D. Pa. 2007).

[56] 24 C.F.R. § 100.204(b) (2013). *See* Bronk v. Ineichen, 54 F.3d 425 (7th Cir. 1995).

[57] 24 C.F.R. § 100.203(c) (2013). *See* SUSSER & PETESCH, *supra* note 42, at § II(F); Bachman v. Swan Harbour Assoc., 653 N.W.2d 415 (Mich. Ct. App. 2002).

[58] 42 U.S.C. § 3604(f)(3)(C).

[59] U.S. DEP'T OF HOUSING & URBAN DEV. & U.S. DEP'T OF JUSTICE, ACCESSIBILITY (DESIGN AND CONSTRUCTION) REQUIREMENTS FOR COVERED MULTIFAMILY DWELLINGS UNDER THE FAIR HOUSING ACT (2013); U.S. DEP'T OF JUSTICE, 2010 ADA STANDARDS FOR ACCESSIBLE DESIGN (2010), *available at* www.ada.gov/2010ADAstandards_index.htm.

[60] *See* Indep. Living Res. v. Or. Arena Corp., 1 F. Supp. 2d 1124 (D. Or. 1998).

[61] 42 U.S.C. § 3602 (defining dwelling).   [62] 24 C.F.R. § 100.25(d) ex. 1 (2008).

provisions do.[63] Single-family residences funded with public resources or operated by governmental entities may be covered under other elements of federal disability law.

- *The Americans with Disabilities Act of 1990 (ADA).*[64] The ADA pro-hibits discrimination against people with disabilities in employment, state and local government services, public accommodation, and telecommunications.[65] The ADA was enacted in 1990 and signed into law by President George H. W. Bush,[66] and in 2008, President George W. Bush signed the ADA Amendment Act.[67] The ADA requires acces-sibility, with accessibility guidelines published by the U.S. Access Board and published as the AMERICANS WITH DISABILITIES ACT ACCESSIBIL-ITY GUIDELINES (ADAAG).[68] The ADAAG guidelines have been revised and updated since their original development and have now been made consistent with guidelines for federal facilities covered by the ABA.[69] The ADAAG guidelines have also been made consistent with the model requirements of the International Building Code.[70] The Department of Justice also has a detailed publication as to the 2010 ADA Standards for Accessible Design.[71]

  Title I *Title I of the American with Disabilities Act of 1990.*[72] Under Title I, employers must provide "reasonable" accommoda-tions to qualified employees with a disability.[73] The reasonable accommodations do not require the employer to take overly costly actions, but the employer must take reasonable steps, and this may be something that is difficult to calculate precisely.[74] This includes adjusting the physical work environment of a building or property.[75] The test is one of undue hardship, which

---

[63] SUSSER & PETESCH, *supra* note 42, at § II(F).

[64] Americans with Disabilities Act of 1990, Pub. L. No. 101-336, 104 Stat. 327 (codified as amended at 42 U.S.C. § 12101–12213 (2006)). (*See generally* BNA sources *supra*, note 41.)

[65] *Id.* § 12101.

[66] 136 Cong. Rec. S16,826–04 (daily ed. Oct. 23, 1990) (Presidential Approvals).

[67] ADA Amendments Act of 2008, Pub. L. No. 110-325, 122 Stat. 3554 (codified as amended at 42 U.S.C. § 12101 et seq. (2006)).

[68] U.S. ACCESS BD., AMERICANS WITH DISABILITIES ACT ACCESSIBILITY GUIDELINES (2002), *available at* www.access-board.gov/guidelines-and-standards/buildings-and-sites/about-the-ada-standards/background/adaag#2.

[69] *Id.; see also* 42 U.S.C. §§ 4151–4157 (2013).   [70] Int'l Bldg. Code (2012).

[71] U.S. DEP'T OF JUSTICE, 2010 ADA STANDARDS FOR ACCESSIBLE DESIGN (2010), *available at* www.ada.gov/2010ADAstandards_index.htm.

[72] Americans with Disabilities Act of 1990, Pub. L. No. 101-336, 104 stat. 327 (codified as amended at 42 U.S.C. § 12111–12117 (2006)).

[73] *Id.*   [74] *Id.*   [75] 42 U.S.C. § 12111(9).

requires a showing of significant difficulty or expense.[76] It is not an easy standard to meet.

If a building or facility where an accommodation is requested was constructed, altered, renovated, or otherwise built while covered by ADA design guidelines, then these guidelines need to have been followed.[77] If the guidelines were not followed, and later there is a request for an adjustment to accommodate the needs of an employee, the adjustment would not fall within the scope of a reasonable accommodation because it was required in the first instance. This means that the cost limitation of reasonable accommodation would not be applicable to such a change to the building or property, and the employer would simply be responsible for not having complied with the requirements of federal disability law.

Title II   *Title II of the Americans with Disabilities Act of 1990.*[78] Title II prohibits discrimination based on disability in programs, services, and activities provided or made available by public entities.[79] It is designed to ensure that qualified individuals with disabilities have access to programs, services, and activities of state and local government on a basis that is equal to that of people without disability.[80] Part A of Title II covers a general range of programs, services, and activities, whereas Part B focuses on public transportation.[81] HUD enforces Title II when it relates to state and local public housing, housing assistance, and housing referrals.[82] Title II sets standards of accessibility for public facilities and programs, not for private single-family residential housing.

Title III   *Title III of the Americans with Disabilities Act of 1990.*[83] Title III prohibits discrimination based on disability in the provision of goods, services, facilities, privileges, advantages, or accommodations of any place of public accommodation by any person owning, leasing, or operating a place of public accommodation.[84]

---

[76] *Id.* § 12111(10).   [77] *Id.* § 12183.

[78] Americans with Disabilities Act of 1990, Pub. L. No. 101-336, 104 Stat. 327, 337–353 (codified as amended at 42 U.S.C. §§ 12131–12161 (2006)).

[79] *Id.*   [80] 42 U.S.C. § 12101 (2009).   [81] *Id.* §§ 12131–12134; 12141–12150, 12151–12165.

[82] *Id.* §§ 12131–12161.

[83] Americans with Disabilities Act of 1990, Pub. L. No. 101-336, 104 Stat. 327, 353–365 (codified as amended at 42 U.S.C. §§ 12181–12189 (2006)).

[84] *Id.*

Title III defines public accommodation and provides a list of examples. Private entities and property owners are considered to be operating places of public accommodation when they are open to the public.[85] Places of public accommodation are not government owned or operated as publicly operated facilities and services are covered under Title II. A partial list of examples of places of public accommodation, for illustrative purposes, includes hotels, restaurants. auditoriums, shopping malls, concert halls, retail centers, and banks.[86] Various commercial facilities are also covered under Title III. Commercial facilities are slightly different from places of public accommodation, and whereas they must comply with the new construction and alteration requirements, they do not come within the barrier removal requirements.[87] A commercial facility might be a factory or an office building where the employees are the only people allowed in the facility, but if the facility offers tours to the public or to the extent it has areas open to accommodate a range of people, it will then be subject to the full requirements of a place of public accommodation.[88] Private clubs are not covered by Title III, unless the club makes its facilities available to nonmembers.[89] A single-family residential house is not considered a place of public accommodation, but if there is a business operating out of part of the house, that part of the building is covered by Title III.[90] A mixed-use hotel development project with an area devoted to residential housing and an area with rooms let out as hotel rooms is subject to Title II with respect to the hotel rooms but subject to the FHA with respect to the residences.[91] A church-run day care center or senior facility is covered by Title III, but the actual church itself has a religious exemption.[92]

Title IV *Title IV of the Americans with Disabilities Act.*[93] This title covers equal access to telecommunications systems.[94] It may have

---

[85] *Id.* § 12181(7) (defining public accommodations).   [86] *Id.* § 12181(7)(a)–(b), (d)–(e).

[87] *Id.* §§ 12182–12183.   [88] 28 C.F.R. §36 app. C (1991).   [89] 28 C.F.R. § 36.102(e) (2013).

[90] *Id.* § 36.207. Bloomberg BNA Disability Manual, Introduction to Title III, Adam 30:3.

[91] 28 C.F.R. § 36 app. C; BNA, Adam 30:3, *supra* note 90.

[92] *Id.*; BNA, Adam 30:3, *supra* note 90.

[93] Americans with Disabilities Act of 1990, Pub. L. No. 101-336, 104 Stat. 327, 365 (codified as amended at 42 U.S.C. §§ 12181–12189 (2006)).

[94] *Id.*

implications for interconnectivity with respect to communications among various property locations but does not focus on
physical mobility, so it is mentioned only in passing.
- *Executive Order 13217*.[95] Executive Order 13217 requires federal agencies to evaluate their policies and programs to determine if any can
be revised or modified to improve the availability of community-based
living arrangements for persons with disabilities.[96] Community-based living might include senior housing, group homes, provision of clinical or
health services, and other types of arrangements that facilitate integrating
people with disability into the broader community rather than isolating
them in institutions.

As the preceding regulations indicate, the reach of federal disability law is
great, but at the same time, it touches only lightly on single-family residential
uses. Even when dealing with multifamily housing covered by more extensive
inclusive design regulations, there are limits on the extent to which units
have to meet extensive universal design requirements. For example, under
regulations related to HUD, only 5 percent of qualifying public housing units
must be fully accessible in terms of universal design.[97]

The low level of inclusive design in residential housing ignores network
effects by failing to address the inability of mobility-impaired people to safely
and easily socialize and participate in many locations that are important to
community life. Even if their own housing units are accessible, the housing
units of family, friends, and colleagues may not be, and getting from a residence

[95] Exec. Order No. 13,217, 3 C.F.R. 774 (2002), *reprinted in* 42 U.S.C. § 12131 (2006).
[96] *Id.*; *see* U.S. Dep't of Hous. & Urban Dev., Delivering on the Promise: U.S. Department of Housing and Urban Development Self Evaluation to Promote Community for People Living with Disabilities, Report to the President on Executive Order 13217 (2002), *available at* www.hud.gov/offices/fheo/images/DPromise.pdf.
[97] There is a standard of 5 percent or a minimum of at least one dwelling unit that must meet mobility impairment regulations for all projects receiving federal financial assistance, including section 202/811 capital advances, section 8 project-based assistance, newly constructed public housing projects, or public housing projects undergoing rehabilitation financed by Comprehensive Improvement Assistance Program (CIAP) funds; *see* U.S. Dep't of Hous. & Urban Dev., Mark-to-Market Program Operating Procedures Guide, app. 1 (2004), *available at* www.hud.gov/offices/hsg/omhar/readingrm/appendix/appiattb/pdf. This appendix also references, for further definitions, "New Construction (24 C.F.R. § 8.23(b))," "Substantial Alteration (24 C.F.R. § 8.23(a))," and "Other Alterations/Clarifications (24 C.F.R. § 8.23(b))." *Id.* at B-2. Guidelines for meeting mobility-impaired regulations are also outlined and are similar to what one might expect from a form of universal design. *Id.* at B-3. *See generally* Accessibility Requirements for Buildings–HUD, www.hud.gov/offices/fheo/disabilities/accessibilityR.cfm (last visited Oct. 9, 2013).

to other locations may be difficult. In excluding single-family residential uses from reasonable inclusive design requirements (such as meeting a visitability standard of accessibility), a significant part of a community's land uses may continue to have barriers to inclusion. Thus, we need to think in broader terms concerning the need for inclusive design housing, and we must recognize the public interest in making both publicly and privately funded units, and multifamily and single-family units, able to be safely and easily navigated by people with low and declining functional mobility.

A common thread running through each of the previously identified categories of regulations is one of predicating the extent of inclusive design requirements on the public character of the property in question. The greater the perceived "publicness" of the place, the more extensive is the design requirement. As mentioned in Chapter 1, this distinction between public and private seems to be in large part based on similar distinctions made in other areas of civil rights law. The federal government may prevent people from discriminating against people with disability in terms of access to the local courthouse or coffee shop, but it does not prohibit individuals from discriminating against them with respect to whom they invite into their private homes. To a certain extent, this is because of a concern for protecting an individual's rights of privacy and association.[98] When dealing with the built environment, however, all structures have some impact on the overall environment, and no one is forcing people to invite unwanted guests onto private property. The issue for planners is one of making sure that all places are capable of safe and easy navigation so that differently enabled people can enjoy meaningful participation in all of the activities, and at all of the venues, in which life is lived out.

The public–private distinction is also somewhat artificial because of the way that government and government-related entities interact to facilitate private, single-family homeownership. As is explained in Chapter 4, even private, single-family residential housing is infused with a strong public interest via publicly supported financial networks and programs in support of home-ownership. The failure to appreciate the public aspects of privately funded single-family housing amplifies the misconception that such places should be of minimal or no concern when addressing the needs for inclusive design.

---

[98] *See* Jennifer Jolly-Ryan, *Chipping Away at Discrimination at the Country Club*, 25 PEPP. L. REV. 495 (1997); Cynthia A. Leiferman, *Private Clubs: A Sanctuary for Discrimination?*, 40 BAYLOR L. REV. 71 (1988); Thomas W. Merrill, *Property and the Right to Exclude*, 77 NEB. L. REV. 730 (1998); Lior Jacob Strahilevitz, *Information Asymmetries and the Rights to Exclude*, 104 MICH. L. REV. 1835 (2006).

Some people assert that their home is their "castle," and no one should tell them how to build or design it. Of course, we all know that there are numerous restrictions on building and construction and that the public does have a right to enforce regulations on private housing despite this emotional commitment to the "castle metaphor."[99]

The key is to focus on inclusive design across the built environment. Planning should address the need for safe and easy navigation so that everyone can enjoy meaningful access to all the venues in which life is experienced. Consequently, less emphasis should be given to distinctions between public and private, while greater attention is directed at sustainable intergenerational mobility.

3.3 RELATIONSHIP BETWEEN LAND USE AND FEDERAL DISABILITY LAW

This part of the chapter addresses the relationship between land use law and disability rights with respect to local planning for inclusive design. It considers the extent to which planning and zoning actions come within federal regulations supporting disability rights, and it addresses the limits of these regulations. The first two cases in this section examine the planning and zoning process to consider the extent to which they are activities covered by federal disability law. While they indicate that planning and zoning are functions covered by the ADA and related legislation, they also affirm the continuing role of local planning in improving inclusive design in our communities. After these two cases, the next case examines local government's ability to impose inclusive design requirements on developers and property owners that go beyond those required under federal law. The case supports efforts at the local level to plan for inclusive design. This discussion is followed by two cases that explore local government obligations with respect to connective mobility infrastructure, such as sidewalks, and finally, a last case explores the tension between requiring universally equal access across the built environment and the limits of finite resources. In all of this, the focus is on identifying the "space" available for local land use planning and zoning in promoting inclusive design and not on the details of design code requirements for construction on specific properties.

---

[99] Eric R. Claeys, *Kelo, the Castle, and Natural Property Rights* 36–55 in PRIVATE PROPERTY, COMMUNITY, AND EMINENT DOMAIN (Robin Paul Malloy ed. 2008); Michael Allan Wolf, *Hysteria v. History: Public Use in the Public Eye*, in PRIVATE PROPERTY, COMMUNITY, AND EMINENT DOMAIN (Robin Paul Malloy ed. 2008).

Innovative Health Systems v. City of White Plains

117 F.3d 37 (2d Cir. 1997)

OPINION

HEANEY, Senior Circuit Judge:

In December 1992, plaintiff-appellee Innovative Health Systems, Inc. ("IHS"), an outpatient drug and alcohol rehabilitation treatment center, began efforts to relocate to a building in downtown White Plains. After over a year of seeking permission from the city, IHS was ultimately denied the necessary building permit by the White Plains Zoning Board of Appeals ("ZBA"). On November 14, 1995, plaintiffs-appellees, IHS and five individual clients, initiated this action against the City of White Plains; Mayor S.J. Schulmann; the ZBA; Chair of the ZBA, Terrence Guerrier; the White Plains Planning Board; and Chair of the Planning Board, Mary Cavallero, (collectively, "the City"), alleging that the ZBA's zoning decision violated both Title II of the Americans with Disabilities Act, 42 U.S.C. §§ 12131–12165 (1994), and section 504 of the Rehabilitation Act of 1973, 29 U.S.C. § 794 (1994). The plaintiffs-appellees moved for a preliminary injunction to prevent the City from interfering with IHS's occupation of the new site. The City cross-moved to dismiss the complaint. In a detailed and thorough opinion, the United States District Court for the Southern District of New York (Barrington D. Parker, Jr., Judge) granted the preliminary injunction and denied the motion to dismiss, except with respect to Mayor Schulmann. *Innovative Health Sys. v. City of White Plains*, 931 F. Supp. 222 (S.D.N.Y. 1996). The remaining defendants appeal. We affirm . . .

Background

In 1992, Dr. Ross Fishman, Executive Director of IHS, decided that the program should move from its current facility to a building located in downtown White Plains. The new site was more than five times as large as the current site and was closer to a bus line and to other service providers that IHS clients frequently visit. Dr. Fishman planned to expand the services offered by IHS at the new site to include a program for children of chemically dependent persons. Therefore, IHS predicted an increase in the number of clients it would serve.

In December 1992, the Deputy Commissioner of Building for the City of White Plains informed IHS that its proposed use of the downtown site – counseling offices with no physicians on staff for physical examinations or dispensing of medication – qualified as a business or professional office under White Plains' zoning ordinance and thus would be permissible in the zoning district. In January 1994, Dr. Fishman signed a lease for the new space. IHS paid a monthly rent of $8,500 from July 1, 1994 to June 30, 1995 and has paid $6,000 per month since July 1995. The leased space includes a section that formerly had been used as retail space. Dr. Fishman initially intended to renovate the former retail space for the treatment program and sublease the remaining space, which had previously been used as an office. In April 1994, IHS filed an application with the White Plains Department of Building for a building permit. Because the application requested a change of use from "retail" to "office," the Commissioner of Building ("Commissioner") referred it to the Planning Board for approval as required by the local zoning ordinance.

The application provoked tremendous opposition from the surrounding community, including Cameo House Owners, Inc. ("Cameo House"), a co-operative association representing resident-owners who lived in the remainder of the downtown building in which IHS sought to relocate, and Fashion Mall Partners, L.P. ("Fashion Mall"), the owner of a shopping mall located near the proposed IHS site. The Planning Board held two public meetings on the proposed use at which the opponents expressed their concern about the condition and appearance of people who attend alcohol and drug dependence treatment programs and the effect such a program would have on property values. Opponents also argued that the proposed use constituted a "clinic" and that, therefore, under the zoning ordinance, the use was a "hospital or sanitarium," an impermissible use in the zoning district. In response to this argument, at the Planning Board's request, the Commissioner reconsidered and reaffirmed his previous determination that the proposed site constituted permitted "office" use.

Because continued opposition caused delay and additional costs, IHS withdrew its application from the Planning Board. It instead applied to the Commissioner for a permit to renovate the former retail section of the downtown site, which did not involve a change of use or the Planning Board's approval. Again, however, the application was vehemently opposed by members of the surrounding community.

To resolve the dispute, the Commissioner sought review of his decision by the White Plains Corporation Counsel. In his written opinion, the Corporation Counsel stated that, absent compelling authority to the contrary, the Commissioner's decision should stand. The Corporation Counsel considered the opponents' argument under the zoning ordinance and concluded that the Commissioner's interpretation was correct. Accordingly, the Commissioner issued his final determination that the use was permitted and the Department of Building issued the building permit to IHS.

Cameo House and Fashion Mall immediately appealed the Commissioner's decision to the ZBA, requesting an interpretation of the zoning ordinance that an alcohol-treatment facility is not permitted in the relevant zoning district. The ZBA conducted a two-day public hearing on the matter, at which community members continued to voice strong opposition to having a drug and alcohol dependency treatment center in the downtown location. They again focused largely on fears of jeopardized safety and falling property values. The opposition also pressed the same zoning arguments rejected by the Commissioner and the Corporation Counsel. IHS relied on the reasoning of the previous decisions and urged the ZBA to consider their consistency with already-permitted uses in the same zoning district. Specifically, IHS reminded the board that the zoning district of its former location also excludes "hospitals and sanitaria" and that several other mental health professionals and social workers practiced in the district of the proposed site.

On July 5, 1995, the ZBA voted four-to-one to reverse the Commissioner's decision. The Board did not issue a written resolution, as required by the zoning ordinance, but rather stated on the record that, based on its understanding of the services IHS provides, it is better classified as a clinic than an office. Absent in their discussion, however, was any reference to the zoning ordinance or the Commissioner's interpretation.

IHS and five individual clients initiated this action against the City, alleging that the revocation of the building permit constituted discrimination and differential treatment based on a disability as against both the individual clients and the program that assisted them. They also claimed that even if the zoning decision was not discriminatory, the City should have permitted the relocation as a reasonable accommodation. In February 1996, they moved for a preliminary injunction against the City to prevent it from interfering with the occupation of the downtown site.

The City opposed the motion and moved for dismissal, arguing: (1) zoning decisions do not fall within the scope of the ADA or the Rehabilitation Act, (2) the appellees lack standing under the ADA, (3) the federal statutes do not accord preferential treatment to persons with disabilities, and (4) neither IHS nor the individual clients have demonstrated irreparable harm or a likelihood of success on the merits. The district court granted the preliminary injunction and denied the motion to dismiss, except as against the Mayor. The City now appeals, raising essentially the same arguments.

. . . The district court found, as is required for the grant of a preliminary injunction, that the appellees demonstrated that they would suffer irreparable harm absent the injunction and that they are likely to succeed on the merits of their discrimination claim . . .

A. IRREPARABLE HARM In determining whether the appellees demonstrated irreparable harm absent injunctive relief, the district court relied heavily on the affidavits of Dr. Fishman and Maria B., a current IHS client. Dr. Fishman testified that clients have dropped out or missed critical therapy sessions because of the size and location of the current site and that the new space would permit IHS to better serve its current clients and to expand its services . . .

. . . [W]e agree with the district court that the appellees have demonstrated that they would suffer irreparable harm, absent injunctive relief.

B. LIKELIHOOD OF SUCCESS ON THE MERITS The City also challenges the district court's determination that the appellees have demonstrated a likelihood of success on the merits, arguing primarily: (1) neither the ADA nor the Rehabilitation Act covers zoning decisions, (2) the appellees lack standing under both the ADA and the Rehabilitation Act, and (3) appellees have not stated a claim under either statute. We address each argument in turn.

1. APPLICATION OF DISCRIMINATION STATUTES TO ZONING Both Title II of the ADA and section 508 of the Rehabilitation Act prohibit discrimination based on a disability by a public entity. The ADA provides:

> No qualified individual with a disability shall, by reason of such disability, be excluded from participation in or be denied the benefits of the services, programs, or activities of a public entity, or be subjected to discrimination by any such entity.

42 U.S.C. § 12132 (1994). The Rehabilitation Act contains the following similar prohibition:

> No otherwise qualified individual with a disability . . . shall, solely by reason of her or his disability, be excluded from the participation in, be denied the benefits of, or be subjected to discrimination under any program or activity receiving Federal financial assistance . . .

29 U.S.C. § 794(a) (1994). It is undisputed that both anti-discrimination provisions govern the City. What the City contests is the application of either statute to its zoning decisions because it contends that zoning does not constitute a "service, program, or activity." We disagree.

The ADA does not explicitly define "services, programs, or activities." Section 508 of the Rehabilitation Act, however, defines "program or activity" as "all of the operations" of specific entities, including "a department, agency, special purpose district, or other instrumentality of a State or of a local government." 29 U.S.C. § 794(b)(1)(A) (1994). Further, as the district court recognized, the plain meaning of "activity" is a "natural or normal function or operation." Thus, as the district court held, both the ADA and the Rehabilitation Act

clearly encompass zoning decisions by the City because making such decisions is a normal function of a governmental entity. Moreover, as the district
court also noted, the language of Title II's anti-discrimination provision does
not limit the ADA's coverage to conduct that occurs in the "programs, services, or activities" of the City. Rather, it is a catch-all phrase that prohibits all
discrimination by a public entity, regardless of the context, and that should
avoid the very type of hair-splitting arguments the City attempts to make here.

In its analysis, the district court also looked to the ADA's legislative history
and the Department of Justice's regulations and Technical Assistance Manual, all of which support the court's interpretation of the plain language of
the statute. With respect to Title II of the ADA, the House Committee on
Education and Labor stated:

> The Committee has chosen not to list all the types of actions that are included
> within the term "discrimination," as was done in titles I and III, because this
> title essentially simply extends the anti-discrimination prohibition embodied
> in section 504 to all actions of state and local governments . . .

> Title II of the bill makes all activities of State and local governments subject to
> the types of prohibitions against discrimination against a qualified individual
> with a disability included in section 504 (nondiscrimination).

As the preamble to the Department of Justice regulations explains, "Title II
applies to anything a public entity does . . . All governmental activities of public entities are covered." The Department of Justice's Technical Assistance
Manual, which interprets its regulations, specifically refers to zoning as an
example of a public entity's obligation to modify its policies, []practices, and
procedures to avoid discrimination . . .

3. APPELLEES' DISCRIMINATION CLAIMS Assuming that the discrimination
statutes apply to zoning decisions and that the appellees have standing, the
City contends that the district court erred in concluding the appellees will
likely be successful on the merits of their discrimination claims. The City
argues that the appellees' claims will fail because (1) IHS's clients are not
"qualified individuals with a disability" because they are not drug-free, (2) the
appellees were not denied the benefits of the City's zoning activity, and (3) the
City's zoning decision was not based on bias against chemically-dependent
persons. We address each argument in turn.

The City claims that IHS has admitted that some of its clients are not drug-
free and that therefore, under either statute the clients are excluded from the
definition of "qualified individuals with a disability." Although, we are not

convinced that IHS has admitted that its clients are not drug-free, the program indisputably does not tolerate drug use by its participants. An inevitable, small percentage of failures should not defeat the rights of the majority of participants in the rehabilitation program who are drug-free and therefore disabled under both statutes. See 42 U.S.C. § 12210(b)(2); 29 U.S.C. § 706(8)(C)(ii)(II).

The City also argues that the appellees have not been denied the benefits of the City's zoning activity because they were able to participate in every step of the process: They were given full consideration by the Commissioner, the Corporation Counsel, the Planning Board, and the ZBA. In so arguing, the City has misconstrued the nature of the appellees' complaint. The appellees' claim is not premised on the denial of the right to participate in the zoning approval process. Rather, they allege that they have been denied the benefit of having the City make a zoning decision without regard to the disabilities of IHS's clients. They have therefore made a claim cognizable under both statutes of discrimination. The City additionally contends that the appellees have not produced any evidence of the City's discriminatory motives in denying the building permit to IHS. There is little evidence in the record to support the ZBA's decision on any ground other than the need to alleviate the intense political pressure from the surrounding community brought on by the prospect of drug- and alcohol-addicted neighbors. The public hearings and submitted letters were replete with discriminatory comments about drug and alcohol dependent persons based on stereotypes and general, unsupported fears. Although the City certainly may consider legitimate safety concerns in its zoning decisions, it may not base its decisions on the perceived harm from such stereotypes and generalized fears. As the district court found, a decision made in the context of strong, discriminatory opposition becomes tainted with discriminatory intent even if the decision makers personally have no strong views on the matter . . .

We also find the ZBA's decision to be highly suspect in light of the requirements set forth in the zoning ordinance. The Commissioner and the Corporation Counsel carefully reviewed IHS's application and gave detailed explanations for their approval. The Corporation Counsel analyzed the definition of "hospital or sanitaria" and concluded that because IHS was not an "institution for the purpose of serving general medical, surgical, psychiatric, physical therapy and rehabilitation purposes," it did not fall under this classification. The ZBA, on the other hand, simply stated, without explanation, that IHS was a clinic and thus an impermissible use in the downtown site. The ZBA ignored the requirements of the "hospital or sanitaria" classification and did not explain why it declined to follow the Corporation Counsel's straightforward analysis. Further, although made aware of other similar uses in the same district, the ZBA did not explain the distinction between IHS's proposed use and the other mental health professionals and social workers who do not work exclusively with chemically-dependent persons. On appeal, the City states that the ZBA's decision was "amply supported by legal arguments" without setting forth any of the supposed "legal arguments" for our consideration. The lack of a credible justification for the zoning decision raises an additional inference that the decision was based on impermissible factors, namely the chemical-dependent status of IHS's clients. Accordingly, we see no reason to disturb the district court's finding of likelihood of success on the merits...

Conclusion
Accordingly, **we affirm** the district court's grant of a preliminary injunction in favor of appellees...

Innovative Health Systems (IHS) makes it clear that the planning and zoning process is subject to the requirements of the ADA and related legislation with respect to providing any "service, program, or activity." This means that planning and zoning officials need to be mindful of ADA requirements and are constrained in their actions by requirements to protect the rights of people with disabilities. In this case, a permit request was at issue, and it required a determination as to the appropriate classification of IHS's proposed use: office, retail, hospital, or sanitarium. This is a quasi-adjudicative function rather than a legislative one and must meet the substantial competent evidence on the record standard when reviewed. This requires the zoning board to carefully gather information and to deliberate. It also requires a decision supported by substantial competent evidence on the record. Based on the court opinion, it seems clear that the zoning board failed to develop and present a file meeting the standard of review. This was particularly troublesome in light of the conflicting report of the corporate counsel supporting the application of IHS. The zoning board's lack of evidence also raised concern because it seemed to have been influenced by local opposition to the clinic and the record indicated that some comments were made that could be construed as discriminatory with respect to people with disabilities. The court faults the zoning board for failure to provide factual findings and "amply supported legal arguments" for its decision to deny IHS a permit. Thus, the court confirms that planning and zoning involve the provision of a service, program, or activity covered by the ADA and related legislation, and it clarified that the applicable standard of review for a quasi-adjudicative function had not been met in this case because the zoning board failed to develop an appropriate record in support of its decision.

Recognizing that the planning and zoning process is covered by the ADA and related legislation does not mean that local planning and zoning is prohibited, nor does it mean that the standard of review is changed. In making a quasi-adjudicative determination, a local planning and zoning board must make findings and develop a file that supports their decision; this is required in all situations and not just in an ADA-related case. Likewise, there is still a need to plan for community development, to respond to changing demographics, and to establish guidelines for integrated and sustainable networks of mobility across the entire built environment. The fact that the acts of planning and zoning are actions covered by the ADA and related legislation does not mean that they are substitutes for local planning and zoning or that they prevent local governments from engaging in planning and zoning. As has been said earlier in this book, setting standards for equal opportunity and for meaningful access under federal civil rights law is not a substitute for good planning and zoning; it is simply part of the framework in which good planning occurs.

The case that follows builds on our understanding of the standard of review applicable to planning and zoning that is suggested by *Innovative Health Systems*.

Wisconsin Community Services, Inc. v. City of Milwaukee

465 F.3d 737 (7th Cir. 2006)
OPINION
RIPPLE, Circuit Judge. Wisconsin Community Services ("WCS"), a provider of treatment to mentally ill patients, brought this action under Title II of the Americans with Disabilities Act ("ADA"), 42 U.S.C. §§ 12131–12134, and section 504 of the Rehabilitation Act of 1973, id. § 794.

The WCS sought an injunction ordering the City of Milwaukee ("the City") to issue a zoning permit that would allow it to move its mental health clinic to an area of Milwaukee, Wisconsin, where health clinics are permitted only on a case-by-case basis. The district court granted partial summary judgment to WCS, concluding that the ADA and the Rehabilitation Act obligated the City to accommodate the disabilities of WCS' patients by allowing WCS to move to its desired location. For the reasons set forth in this opinion, we reverse the judgment of the district court and remand for proceedings consistent with this opinion.

I

BACKGROUND

A. WISCONSIN COMMUNITY SERVICES WCS is a private, non-profit organization that provides a variety of inpatient and outpatient services to individuals afflicted with severe mental illnesses. WCS provides patients, who cannot live alone without substantial assistance, with psychiatric treatment, counseling, medication monitoring, transportation and help in finding housing and employment. A number of WCS' patients have a history of substance abuse, and a majority have had previous run-ins with the criminal justice system; WCS often accepts patient referrals from court-related agencies such as the United States Probation Service. Although WCS staff sometimes will treat patients in their homes, most of WCS' services are administered in a 7,500 square-foot mental health clinic located at 2023 West Wisconsin Avenue in the City of Milwaukee. Originally, WCS shared this facility with other non-profit organizations, but, as its clientele grew, WCS expanded to occupy the entire building. In 1994, at the time of this initial expansion, WCS employed twenty full-time employees and served 250 patients.

By 1998, the staff at WCS' 2023 West Wisconsin Avenue facility had grown to approximately forty full-time employees serving approximately 400 patients. This increase in clients, services and personnel had caused a shortage in space available for employee parking, client treatment, group therapy sessions and other services. Faced with the shortage, WCS at first considered remodeling, but finally concluded that such a project would be too costly and would interfere with client care. WCS then began searching for a new building. Despite having a limited budget, WCS needed a facility that was located in a safe neighborhood and had adequate floor space, parking and access to public transit. After searching for three years, WCS was able to find two buildings that met its criteria. Neither property, unfortunately, was located in a neighborhood zoned for health clinics. Both were in areas where health clinics are permitted only as "special uses" that require issuance of a permit by the Milwaukee zoning authorities.

WCS previously had received this type of special use permit for some of its other facilities. It therefore made an offer of purchase for one of the properties, contingent on obtaining the necessary special use permit from the Milwaukee zoning board. The seller of this property, concerned about this contingency, declined to accept the offer. WCS then abandoned its efforts to purchase that property and instead made a similar contingent offer on the other identified property. This facility was an 81,000 square-foot building located about one mile from its current facility at 3716 West Wisconsin Avenue. The larger facility is located in an area zoned as a "local business district." Milwaukee, Wis. Code § 295-703-1. According to the City Code's "use table," health care clinics, except for nursing homes, are deemed "special uses" for this zone. § 295-603-1. Incidentally, the same zone allows foster homes, shelter care facilities, community living arrangements and animal hospitals either as "permitted" or "limited" (no special approval required) uses. The seller accepted WCS' offer.

B. THE FIRST PROCEEDING BEFORE THE BOARD OF ZONING APPEALS
[BOZA] Milwaukee's City Code defines "special use" as "[a] use which is
generally acceptable in a particular zoning district but which, because of its
characteristics and the characteristics of the zoning district in which it would
be located, requires review on a case by case basis to determine whether it
should be permitted, conditionally permitted, or denied." Milwaukee, Wis.
Code § 295-7-166. Special use designations are instruments of municipal
planning that allow city officials to retain review power over land uses that,
although presumptively allowed, may pose special problems or hazards to a
neighborhood.

In Milwaukee, an applicant for a special use permit must present its plans to
the Department of City Development ("the DCD"), where they are reviewed
by a plan examiner. If the DCD denies the special use application, the applicant may appeal the decision to the Milwaukee Board of Zoning Appeals
("BOZA"), where the application is reviewed, a public hearing is held and
evidence is heard. Consistent with this procedure, WCS submitted a plan
to DCD, outlining its intent to relocate the mental health clinic and several
of its administrative offices to the new building. The plan stated that WCS
would occupy 32,000 out of the 81,000 square feet of space in the building. An
additional 12,000 square feet, according to the plan, would be occupied by two
existing tenants, a Walgreens pharmacy and an office of the Social Security
Administration. The remaining 37,000 square feet, the plan stated, would be
rented out for use as office space or for other commercial purposes.

Under Wisconsin law, in deciding whether to issue a special use permit,
the City's zoning officials are guided by four statutory considerations: (1) protection of public health, safety and welfare; (2) protection of the use, value
and enjoyment of other property in the neighborhood; (3) traffic and pedestrian safety; and (4) consistency with the City's comprehensive plan. After
reviewing WCS' plan, DCD concluded that these criteria had not been met.
Specifically, DCD expressed concern over the second factor, protection of
neighboring property value. It stated that use of the property as a mental health
clinic would jeopardize the commercial revitalization that the neighborhood
currently was undergoing. WCS, availing itself of its right to administrative
review, then appealed the DCD's decision to Milwaukee's BOZA.

On March 22, 2001, BOZA held a hearing on WCS' appeal. At the outset,
WCS argued that, even if its proposal did not meet the special-use criteria,
the ADA required BOZA to modify these criteria so that WCS would have the
same opportunity to obtain a permit as would a clinic serving non-disabled
individuals. BOZA denied this request because it did not believe that it had
the authority to deviate from the City's zoning code. Indeed, BOZA prohibited

WCS from introducing evidence on the issue. Confined to making its case under the unmodified special use considerations, WCS presented evidence in an effort to refute the perception that the mental health clinic posed a safety threat and would discourage businesses from locating in the neighborhood. This evidence included testimony from a security official who told BOZA that, based on his own investigation, WCS' patients had not been the source of any safety problems in WCS' current neighborhood. WCS also presented letters from its current neighbors to the same effect. Finally, WCS submitted evidence of an award it had received from the National Institute of Justice for exemplary care of previously institutionalized individuals with mental health needs. BOZA then heard testimony in opposition to the permit. An attorney representing several area businesses testified that opening a mental health clinic that serves a large number of young, unemployed males with histories of mental illness and illegal behavior substantially increases the chance of crime and anti-social behavior in the neighborhood. In a similar vein, a nearby high school voiced its fear that WCS' clients would be riding public transit alongside its "young and vulnerable" students. Additionally, a neighborhood organization encouraged residents to object to WCS' request; it circulated leaflets that argued that the clustering of WCS' clientele "in one location on a daily basis raises a serious risk for the health and well being of people living and working in surrounding neighborhoods."

On May 9, 2001, BOZA voted unanimously to deny WCS' application for a special use permit. The accompanying written decision said only that the proposed use was inconsistent with the considerations set forth in the zoning code. However, several board members orally announced the reasoning behind their decision. One member noted that the "overwhelming" opposition from neighborhood residents convinced him that the WCS clinic would have "a damaging effect upon neighboring business." Another member stated that WCS' clientele, with its large number of convicted criminals, raised "red flags" for local residents. These board members did not think that BOZA had the duty to question the "perceptions" of local residents regarding the possible dangers presented by WCS' patients.

C. THE FIRST FEDERAL COURT PROCEEDING Although Wisconsin law allows for direct review by a Wisconsin state court of adverse BOZA decisions, WCS instead filed the present action in the United States District Court for the Eastern District of Wisconsin, see Wisconsin Corr. Serv. v. City of Milwaukee, 173 F. Supp. 2d. 842 (E.D. Wis. 2001) ("WCS I"). Its complaint alleged that BOZA had violated the ADA and the Rehabilitation Act by failing to make reasonable modifications to its methods for determining whether to issue a special use permit. The complaint also requested an injunction directing Milwaukee to issue the desired permit.

The district court held that BOZA had violated the federal disability laws when it failed even to consider making a reasonable modification to its policies to accommodate WCS' request. The court began its analysis by noting the basic Supremacy Clause principle that federal laws are superior to conflicting local laws. See U.S. Const. art. VI, cl. 2. The court noted that invocation of this basic principle did not necessarily mean that WCS was entitled to a special use permit as an accommodation under the ADA. BOZA's failure even to consider WCS' accommodation request, however, had deprived the court of a sufficient factual record on which to determine whether WCS had a right to such an accommodation. The court directed that BOZA hear evidence on WCS' accommodation claim and determine: (1) whether WCS' patients are "disabled"; (2) whether the requested accommodation is "reasonable" and "necessary"; and (3) whether the requested relief would work a "fundamental change" to the services being rendered.

D. THE SECOND PROCEEDING BEFORE THE BOARD OF ZONING APPEALS On September 12, 2002, BOZA reconvened a public hearing to decide whether, and to what extent, the ADA and the Rehabilitation Act required it to modify its zoning policies in considering WCS' application for a special use permit. BOZA heard testimony regarding the necessity of a modification, whether such modification was a reasonable accommodation and whether it might work any fundamental change on the City's zoning practices...

On December 22, 2002, BOZA issued a written decision denying the special use permit to WCS. It concluded that WCS' claim for an accommodation under the disabilities laws failed because such an accommodation was neither reasonable nor necessary. On the question of necessity, BOZA framed the inquiry as "whether the requested accommodation will ameliorate, that is, directly improve the burden of the mental illnesses from which [WCS' patients] suffer." Concluding that WCS had not satisfied its burden on this issue, BOZA noted that mental illness, unlike a physical impairment, "is not a one size fits all handicap or disability within the ADA." Rather, in BOZA's view, the mental disabilities suffered by WCS' patients were likely to vary dramatically across the patient population. It was therefore, according to BOZA, a "gross overgeneralization and speculation" for WCS to contend that each of its patients would respond favorably to treatment in the new, larger facility. Moreover, in BOZA's estimation, the factors considered by WCS in seeking out a new facility were not linked to its patients' disabilities. According to BOZA, "[t]he WCS search criteria resemble those of many other commercial businesses, profit or non profit, which have outgrown their physical premises and want to move into a larger setting."

BOZA concluded that, in addition to being unnecessary, the requested accommodation also was unreasonable. In making this determination, BOZA stressed that the relocation of WCS' clinic to its proposed site would "place an undue financial burden on the district," threatening "the economic survival [of] this already shaky neighborhood." According to BOZA, these costs to the City were not outweighed by the needs of WCS because WCS apparently had other relocation options available in other neighborhoods.

Finally, BOZA determined that the requested accommodation, in addition to being unreasonable and unnecessary, fundamentally would alter the City's zoning scheme:

> Every time a social service agency, AA club, homeless shelter serving mentally ill homeless people; hospital, psychologists or psychiatrists [*sic*] office, thera- pists' office, etc. wanted to locate their business in a zoning district requiring a special use to do so, the City or this Board would have to automatically consider giving them an accommodation under ADA regardless of the special use criteria in the City's ordinance.

E. THE SECOND FEDERAL COURT PROCEEDING On January 24, 2003, WCS reinstated its action in federal court challenging the second BOZA ruling. It alleged that the City's refusal to grant WCS a special use permit violated the ADA and the Rehabilitation Act. In determining the standard that it ought to employ in assessing WCS' accommodation claim, the district court declined, despite the parties' recommendation, to apply the test that governs cases arising under the Fair Housing Amendments Act of 1988 ("FHAA"). The FHAA requires a reasonable accommodation to zoning rules when necessary to afford a handicapped person the "equal opportunity" to obtain housing. 42 U.S.C. § 3604(f)(3)(B). In the district court's view, this standard did not apply to the present case because WCS sought its accommodation not to obtain housing but to provide mental health services to its patients. Moreover, the court continued, "unlike housing, the general public does not require mental health services; thus, in the present case, it makes little sense to inquire whether the disabled are entitled to equal opportunity to such services."

Instead, relying upon our decision in Oconomowoc Residential Programs, Inc. v. City of Milwaukee, 300 F.3d 775 (7th Cir. 2002), the court held that, to satisfy its initial burden, WCS must show that its requested accommodation is (1) reasonable and (2) necessary to enhance affirmatively its disabled patients' "'quality of life by ameliorating the effects of the disability.'" Once WCS had made this showing, according to the district court, the City then must "demon- strate unreasonableness or undue hardship in the particular circumstances."

Applying this framework, the court first assessed the accommodation's reasonableness by weighing the benefits to WCS' clients against the potential cost to the City of issuing the special use permit. In the court's view, WCS had presented convincing evidence that overcrowding was a real problem at its current facility and one that both aggravated the effects of its clients' disabilities and impaired WCS' ability to provide services that ameliorate such effects. The new, larger facility, the court stated, would solve this overcrowding problem and benefit WCS' patients substantially. Against this benefit, the court weighed the costs purportedly incurred by the City in undermining its zoning code, interfering with the revitalization of a business district and losing potential tax revenue. The court did not find these costs significant enough to outweigh the clear benefit that the special use permit would provide WCS...

The court next considered whether WCS had established that its requested accommodation was necessary. First, the court concluded that, for reasons it already had described in its reasonableness assessment, the proposed facility would ameliorate some of the effects of WCS' patients' disabilities. Second, the court rejected the City's argument that WCS could have moved its clinic to another location where a mental health clinic would not have required a special use permit. Under the court's view of the evidence, this option was too costly for WCS. Although recognizing that WCS perhaps could have searched for available properties more effectively, the court held that necessity may be established simply by evidence of a good-faith, albeit failed, attempt to find an alternative to the accommodation requested.

II

DISCUSSION

A. The legal question before us is whether, and to what extent, a city must modify its zoning standards to prevent them from discriminating against the disabled. The statutes relevant to answering that question are three separate but interrelated federal laws that protect persons with disabilities from discrimination. The first two laws chronologically were the Rehabilitation Act of 1973 and the FHAA. Enactment of the ADA followed in 1990. All three statutory schemes embrace the concept that, in certain instances, the policies and practices of covered entities must be modified to accommodate the needs of the disabled. We now shall examine each statute's accommodation requirement in detail.

1. THE REHABILITATION ACT OF 1973 The Rehabilitation Act, 29 U.S.C. § 701 et seq., applies to federal government agencies as well as organizations

that receive federal funds. The parties in this case stipulated that the City receives federal funding and is therefore covered by the Rehabilitation Act. Much of the Rehabilitation Act focuses on employment, but section 504 broadly covers other types of programs and activities as well. Section 504(a) provides that "[n]o otherwise qualified individual with a disability in the United States . . . shall, solely by reason of her or his disability, be excluded from the participation in, be denied the benefits of, or be subjected to discrimination under any program or activity receiving Federal financial assistance . . ." 29 U.S.C. § 794(a).

The Rehabilitation Act does not contain a general accommodation requirement. Rather, in implementing the Rehabilitation Act, the Department of Health and Human Services ("HHS") promulgated several regulations that specifically require reasonable accommodations. See Traynor v. Turnage, 485 U.S 535, 550 n.10, 108 S. Ct. 1372, 99 L. Ed. 2d 618 (1988) (observing that these regulations "were drafted with the oversight and approval of Congress and therefore constitute an important source of guidance on the meaning of § 504"). The most pertinent of these regulations requires recipients of federal funds to "make reasonable accommodation to the known physical or mental limitations of an otherwise qualified handicapped applicant or employee unless the recipient can demonstrate that the accommodation would impose an undue hardship on the operation of its program." 28 C.F.R. § 41.53. The regulation's use of the terms "applicant or employee" suggests that it pertains most directly to workplace accommodation, rather than to the modification of a city's zoning practices.

Nevertheless, the Supreme Court has located a duty to accommodate in the statute generally. In Alexander v. Choate, 469 U.S. 287, 105 S. Ct. 712, 83 L. Ed. 2d 661 (1985), handicapped individuals challenged a proposal by the State of Tennessee to reduce the number of inpatient hospital days that the state Medicaid program would pay hospitals on behalf of Medicaid recipients. Because handicapped individuals spend more time in hospitals, on average, than the non-disabled, the plaintiffs argued that Tennessee's proposal had a disproportionate effect on the disabled and hence was discriminatory in violation of section 504 of the Rehabilitation Act. After rejecting Tennessee's argument that federal law prohibits only intentional discrimination against the handicapped, the Court explained that "'a refusal to modify an existing program might become unreasonable and discriminatory.'" The Rehabilitation Act's promise of "meaningful access" to state benefits, according to the Court, means that "reasonable accommodations in the grantee's program or benefit may have to be made."

However, in applying this principle, the Court in Choate held that Tennessee's proposal, in fact, did not deny the plaintiffs "meaningful access" to

Medicaid services. This was because "[t]he new limitation [did] not invoke criteria that have a particular exclusionary effect on the handicapped; the reduction, neutral on its face, [did] not distinguish between those whose coverage will be reduced and those whose coverage will not on the basis of any test, judgment, or trait that the handicapped as a class are less capable of meeting or less likely of having" . . . Following Choate, several courts of appeals have adopted the view that the Rehabilitation Act requires public entities to modify federally assisted programs if such a modification is necessary to ensure that the disabled have equal access to the benefits of that program. See, e.g., Henrietta D. v. Bloomberg, 331 F.3d 261, 274–75 (2d Cir. 2003). These circuits, including ours, also follow the corollary principle implicit in the Choate decision that the Rehabilitation Act helps disabled individuals obtain access to benefits only when they would have difficulty obtaining those benefits "by reason of" their disabilities, and not because of some quality that they share generally with the public. See, e.g., id. at 276–79 (acknowledging "that the ADA and the Rehabilitation Act are addressed to rules that hurt people with disabilities by reason of their handicap, rather than that hurt them solely by virtue of what they have in common with other people" . . .

2. THE FAIR HOUSING AMENDMENTS ACT The duty to accommodate imposed by the FHAA, 42 U.S.C. § 3601 et seq., mirrors in large part the modification obligations under the Rehabilitation Act. Enacted in 1988, the FHAA extended the scope of other federal housing laws to cover persons with disabilities. Under these amendments, disabled individuals may not be prevented from buying or renting private housing because of their disabilities. See id. § 3604. They also must be provided reasonable "accommodation in rules, policies, practices, or services when such accommodation may be necessary to afford [them] equal opportunity to use and enjoy a dwelling." Id. § 3604(f)(3)(B).

The legislative history of the Fair Housing Amendments Act explains:

> The Committee intends that the prohibition against discrimination against those with handicaps apply to zoning decisions and practices. The Act is intended to prohibit the application of special requirements through land use regulations, restrictive covenants, and conditional or special use permits that have the effect of limiting the ability of such individuals to live in the residence of their choice in the community.

H.R. Rep. No. 100–711, at 24 (1988), reprinted in 1988 U.S.C.C.A.N. 2173, 2185.

Although the plain language of the FHAA provides little guidance concerning the reach of its accommodation requirement, the contours of the obligation have been given substantial elaboration by this court and other courts of appeals. The basic elements of an FHAA accommodation claim are well-settled. First, the requested accommodation must be reasonable, which, as we have stated, is a "highly fact-specific inquiry and requires balancing the needs of the parties. An accommodation is reasonable if it is both efficacious and proportional to the costs to implement it." In the zoning context, a municipality may show that a modification to its policy is "unreasonable if it is so at odds with the purpose behind the rule that it would be a fundamental and unreasonable change."

Second, the requested accommodation must be "necessary," meaning that, without the accommodation, the plaintiff will be denied an equal opportunity to obtain the housing of her choice. This has been described by courts essentially as a causation inquiry.

In addition, the FHAA links the term "necessary" to the goal of "equal opportunity." 42 U.S.C. § 3604(f)(3)(B). The "equal opportunity" element limits the accommodation duty so that not every rule that creates a general inconvenience or expense to the disabled needs to be modified. Instead, the statute requires only accommodations necessary to ameliorate the effect of the plaintiff's disability so that she may compete equally with the non-disabled in the housing market. We have enforced this limitation by asking whether the rule in question, if left unmodified, hurts "handicapped people by reason of their handicap, rather than . . . by virtue of what they have in common with other people, such as a limited amount of money to spend on housing."

Most recently, we considered the "equal opportunity" limitation in deciding an FHAA claim brought by a group home challenging a city's ad hoc decision to shut off the water supply to the group home's land. Rejecting the group home's claim that the city had to modify its decision because shutting off its water harmed its disabled residents by preventing them from living in group homes, we stated that "[c]utting off the water prevents anyone from living in a dwelling, not just handicapped people." Put differently, the plaintiff's accommodation claim failed because the disability suffered by the group home's residents did not deny them an equal opportunity to obtain housing.

3. TITLE II OF THE AMERICANS WITH DISABILITIES ACT The ADA was built on the Rehabilitation Act and the FHAA, but extends the reach of those laws substantially. Invoking "the sweep of congressional authority, including the power to enforce the fourteenth amendment and to regulate commerce," the ADA was designed "to provide a clear and comprehensive national

mandate for the elimination of discrimination against individuals with disabilities." 42 U.S.C. § 12101(b)(1), (b)(4). It forbids discrimination against persons with disabilities in three major areas of public life: (1) employment, which is covered by Title I of the statute, id. § 12111–12117; (2) public services, programs and activities, which are the subjects of Title II, id. § 12131–12165; and (3) public and private lodging, which is covered by Title III, id. § 12181–12189. See generally, Tennessee v. Lane, 541 U.S. 509, 516–17, 124 S. Ct. 1978, 158 L. Ed. 2d 820 (2004).

This case concerns Title II, commonly referred to as the public services portion of the ADA. Title II provides that "no qualified individual with a disability shall, by reason of such disability, be excluded from participation in or be denied the benefits of the services, programs, or activities of a public entity." 42 U.S.C. § 12132.

As courts have held, municipal zoning qualifies as a public "program" or "service," as those terms are employed in the ADA, and the enforcement of those rules is an "activity" of a local government. 6 Section 12131(2) goes on to define "qualified individual with a disability" as

> an individual with a disability who, with or without reasonable modifications to rules, policies, or practices, the removal of architectural, communication, or transportation barriers, or the provision of auxiliary aids and services, meets the essential eligibility requirements for the receipt of services or the participation in programs or activities provided by a public entity.

Unlike Title I and Title III, Title II of the ADA does not contain a specific accommodation requirement. Instead, the Attorney General, at the instruction of Congress, has issued an implementing regulation that outlines the duty of a public entity to accommodate reasonably the needs of the disabled. The Title II regulation reads:

> A public entity shall make reasonable modifications in policies, practices, or procedures when the modifications are necessary to avoid discrimination on the basis of disability, unless the public entity can demonstrate that making the modifications would fundamentally alter the nature of the service, program, or activity.

28 C.F.R. § 35.130(b)(7).
Before proceeding with an assessment of the case before us, we pause for a closer examination of the regulation promulgated under the ADA because the text of this regulation gives us several important guideposts for the resolution of this case. First, as our cases already hold, failure to accommodate is an independent basis for liability under the ADA. Second, the plain language

of the regulation also makes clear that an accommodation only is required when necessary to avoid discrimination on the basis of a disability. Third, the regulation states, in its plain language, that any accommodation must be a reasonable one. We shall now examine each of these features of the regulation, keeping in mind that Congress has expressed its desire that interpretation of the ADA be compatible with interpretation of the other federal disability statutes, a point also made clear in several holdings of the Supreme Court.

Under the Title II regulation, a modification must be "necessary to avoid discrimination on the basis of disability." In this way, the regulation differs slightly from the accommodation regulation promulgated under the Rehabilitation Act, which does not contain any express language regarding necessity. See id. § 41.53. However, as we noted earlier, *Choate* seems to read the Rehabilitation Act as containing a necessity requirement.

Similarly, there is a minor difference between the Title II regulation and the FHAA's accommodation provision. Although the FHAA's accommodation provision does contain an express necessity requirement, the text is different from the ADA regulation. The FHAA version reads "necessary to afford . . . equal opportunity," 42 U.S.C. § 3604(f)(3)(B); by contrast, the ADA version reads "necessary to avoid discrimination on the basis of disability," 28 C.F.R. § 35.130(b)(7). Nevertheless, as we have interpreted it, the Title II regulation, like the FHAA provision, links necessity to a causation inquiry. In the context of the FHAA, we have enforced this limitation by asking whether the rule in question, if left unmodified, hurts "handicapped people by reason of their handicap, rather than . . . by virtue of what they have in common with other people, such as a limited amount of money to spend on housing" . . . Moreover, Title II's necessity component mirrors the judicial gloss afforded to the Rehabilitation Act in *Choate*. As in *Choate*, a plaintiff invoking Title II's modification requirement must show that his disability is what causes his deprivation of the services or benefits desired. In short, each of these provisions requires the plaintiff to satisfy the "necessary" element by showing that the reason for his deprivation is his disability.

The regulation also requires that any accommodation be a reasonable one. In the context of the FHAA, we have interpreted this requirement to mandate an inquiry into whether the accommodation is "both efficacious and proportional to the costs to implement it." In the zoning context, a municipality may show that a modification to its policy is "unreasonable if it is so at odds with the purpose behind the rule that it would be a fundamental and unreasonable change." This assessment is "a highly fact-specific inquiry and requires balancing the needs of both parties." In this regard, we think it is important to note that, in undertaking this highly fact-specific assessment, it is necessary that the court take into consideration all of the costs to both parties. Some of these costs may be objective and easily ascertainable. Others may be more subjective and require that the court demonstrate a good deal of wisdom in appreciating the intangible but very real human costs associated with the disability in question. On the other side of the equation, some governmental costs associated with the specific program at issue may be a matter of simply looking at a balance sheet. Others, however, may be those intangible values of community life that are very important if that community is to thrive and is to address the needs of its citizenry.

We pause to emphasize one other important feature of the Title II regulation. We think that the regulation makes clear that the duty to accommodate is an independent basis of liability under the ADA. The language of the regulation itself certainly supports this view. By requiring measures that are "necessary to avoid discrimination on the basis of disability," 28 C.F.R. § 35.130(b)(7), the regulation clearly contemplates that prophylactic steps must be taken to avoid discrimination . . .

Under the law of this circuit, a plaintiff need not allege either disparate treatment or disparate impact in order to state a reasonable accommodation claim under Title II of the ADA . . . In sum, a Title II claim under the ADA "may be established by evidence that (1) the defendant intentionally acted on the basis of the disability, (2) the defendant refused to provide a reasonable modification, or (3) the defendant's rule disproportionally impacts disabled people." The district court resolved WCS' claim employing the second approach, and our case law provides support for such a cause of action.

B. With the key legislative provisions in full view, we turn now to the task of applying them to the case before us. In essence, we must decide whether, and to what extent, the Rehabilitation Act and Title II require the City to modify its zoning practices in order to accommodate the needs of the disabled individuals served by WCS.

WCS submits that the City must waive application of its normal special use criteria for WCS because it has shown that granting the permit will ameliorate overcrowding, a condition that particularly affects its disabled clients. Before accepting this position, however, we must ask whether WCS has satisfied the "necessity" element contained in the Rehabilitation Act as interpreted by *Choate* and in the Title II regulation, see 28 C.F.R. § 35.130(b)(7). WCS contends that the necessity element is satisfied simply when a modification helps the disabled, regardless of whether it is necessary to alleviate discrimination. Implicit in this position is that the federal accommodation obligation reaches not only rules that create barriers "on the basis of" a person's disability, but also rules that are not disability-based and create obstacles to persons because of some factor unrelated to disability.

As we already have discussed, with respect to the Rehabilitation Act, *Choate* held that a modification is "necessary" only when it allows the disabled to obtain benefits that they ordinarily could not have by reason of their disabilities, and not because of some quality that they share with the public generally. See Choate, 469 U.S. at 302. The inquiry is the same under the ADA regulation, which asks whether a modification is "necessary to avoid discrimination on the basis of disability." 28 C.F.R. § 35.130(b)(7). Framed by our cases as a causation inquiry, the element is satisfied only when the plaintiff shows that, "but for" his disability, he would have been able to access the services or benefits desired.

On the present record, WCS' inability to meet the City's special use criteria appears due not to its client's disabilities but to its plan to open a non-profit health clinic in a location where the City desired a commercial, taxpaying tenant instead. As far as this record indicates, the City would have rejected similar proposals from non-profit health clinics serving the non-disabled. WCS contends that Title II's accommodation requirement calls, in such a situation, for "'preferential' treatment and 'is not limited only to lowering barriers created by the disability itself.'" WCS' view, however, is inconsistent with the "necessity" element as it has been defined under the Rehabilitation Act, the FHAA and Title II of the ADA. On this record, because the mental illness of WCS' patients is not the cause-in-fact of WCS' inability to obtain a suitable facility, the program that it seeks modified does not hurt persons with disabilities "by reason of their handicap" . . .

The district court assumed that the proposed modification could be deemed "necessary" even if the disabilities suffered by WCS' patients were not the cause-in-fact of its inability to find a larger building. The district court failed to apply a "but for" causation standard in determining the necessity element of WCS' accommodation claim. Choosing this course was error in light of the prevailing standards under our case law.

Conclusion

For the foregoing reasons, we reverse the judgment of the district court and remand for proceedings consistent with this opinion. The City may recover its costs in this court.

REVERSED and REMANDED

_____

As in the *IHS* case, WCS involved a quasi-adjudicative function of the zoning board. Here the WCS sought approval of a special use permit to operate a clinic in a downtown business district.[100] Significantly, as the opinion points out, there were four state-required criteria to be considered in making a decision on a special use permit.[101] Consequently, the zoning board must develop substantial competent evidence on the record relative to the stated criteria and its thinking on the denial or approval of a special use permit from any applicant. Moreover, on the assertion by WCS that it is entitled to a special use permit as an accommodation under federal disability laws, the zoning board must develop supporting evidence relative to the applicability of such laws. In doing this, it must determine the reasonableness and the necessity of the asserted accommodation. In evaluating the reasonableness of an accommodation, the court indicates that an assessment of costs and benefits for each party is appropriate and that there should be some proportionality in this regard. There is also a need for WCS to demonstrate that the disability of its clients *was the cause* of its inability to locate a larger building for its clinic. The court stresses at several points that the requested accommodation by WCS is only *"necessary when it allows the disabled to obtain benefits that they ordinarily could not by reason of their disabilities, and not because of some quality that they share with the public generally."* The record in this case indicates that WCS experienced difficulty in locating larger space for the same types of reasons that a number of other businesses and organizations do, and not because its clients were people with disabilities. Moreover, the city had developed a comprehensive plan with criteria for revitalizing this downtown business area, and the intended use by WCS could be found to be inconsistent with the plan in a way that is applicable to many other potential applicants. With an appropriately developed record, the denial of the special use permit by the zoning board could be upheld. The important points are that planning and zoning are subject to the laws enacted to protect people with disability, and local zoning officials have an obligation to evaluate the request for a reasonable accommodation independent of the specific requirements of the zoning code.

In addition to the WCS and IHS cases, a number of other cases help to clarify the constraints imposed on the exercise of the police power with respect to assertions made against a zoning board on grounds that the board failed to comply with the law protecting rights of a person with a disability, thus potentially violating the ADA, the FHA, and the Rehabilitation Act (RA).[102]

---

[100] Wis. Cmty. Servs., Inc. v. City of Milwaukee, 465 F. 3d 737 (7th Cir. 2006).
[101] The city's zoning officials are guided by four statutory considerations: (1) protection of public health, safety, and welfare; (2) protection of the use, value, and enjoyment of other property in the neighborhood; (3) traffic and pedestrian safety; and (4) consistency with the city's comprehensive plan. *Id.*
[102] *See, e.g.,* Cinnamon Hills Youth Crisis Centers, Inc. v. Saint George City, 685 F. 3d 917 (10th Cir., 2012); Candlehouse, Inc. v. Town of Vestal, NY, 2013 WL 1867114 (N.D. NY, May, 3,

These assertions usually arise in response to the denial of an application to locate a use in a particular zone. The denial may be based on an interpretation of use categories in the code, or it may be based on the denial of a request for a special or conditional use permit or on a denial of an application for a variance. Without regard to the specific type of request being denied, the denial may be challenged on three grounds. The three common challenges under the ADA, FHA, and RA include assertions of inappropriate action by zoning officials based on (1) intentional discrimination against people with disability, (2) engaging in conduct that has an unlawful disparate impact on people with disability, and (3) failure to provide a reasonable accommodation for people with disability. The courts have generally considered the proof of these assertions to be similar under each of the ADA, FHA, and RA. Thus, the court opinions in these cases typically provide a unitary discussion of each of these claims to the extent that they are at issue under any one of the three statutory schemes.[103]

Considering the WCS and *IHS* cases along with other cases, it is possible to outline guidelines for understanding the nature of each of the three common challenges to zoning under the ADA, FHA, and RA. First, the ADA, FHA, and RA all apply to local planning and zoning. Under Title II of the ADA, it is unlawful for public entities to discriminate on the basis of disability in the provision of benefits and services. Under the FHA, it is unlawful "to discriminate in the sale or rental, or to otherwise make unavailable or deny a dwelling to any buyer or renter because of a handicap" (42 USC sec. 3604(f)(1)). Discrimination under the FHA includes "a refusal to make reasonable accommodations in rules, policies, practices, or services, when such accommodations may be necessary to afford a person equal opportunity to use and enjoy a dwelling" (42 USC sec. 3604(f)(3)(b)). Under the RA, "no qualified individual with a disability . . . shall, solely by reason of her or his disability, be excluded from the participation in, be denied the benefits of, or be subjected to discrimination under any program or activity receiving Federal financial assistance" (29 USC sec. 794). An action based on an allegation of discrimination under the ADA, FHA, and RA may be pursuant to one or more of the three theories set out earlier: intentional discrimination, disparate impact, and failure to make a reasonable accommodation. To succeed on any theory, a claimant must first establish that she has a disability. This requires a showing of (1) a physical or mental impairment which substantially limits one or more major

---

2013); Nikolich v. Village of Arlington Heights, Ill., 870 F.Supp 2d 556 (N.D. Ill, 2012); Rise, Inc. v. Malheur County, 2012 WL 1085501 (D. Oregon, Feb. 13, 2012); 10th Street Partners, LL.C. v. County Commission for Sarasota, Florida, 2012 WL 4328655 (M.D. Fla., Sept. 20, 2012); U.S. v. City of Baltimore, 2012 WL 662172 (D. Md., Feb. 29, 2012).

[103] 10th Street Partners, *supra* note 102.

life activity, (2) a record of having such impairment, or (3) that she is regarded as having such impairment.[104]

The three major theories are explained in the following:

Intentional Discrimination[105]

> Claims of intentional discrimination are properly analyzed utilizing the familiar, burden shifting model developed by the courts for use in employment discrimination settings dating back to the Supreme Court's decision in McDonnell Douglas Corp. v. Green, 411 U.S. 792, 93 S.Ct. 1817, 36 L.Ed.2d 668 (1973). Under that analysis, a plaintiff must first establish a prima facie case of intentional discrimination . . . by "present[ing] evidence that animus against the protected group was a significant factor in the position taken by the municipal decision-makers themselves or by those to whom the decision makers were knowingly responsive." Once a plaintiff makes out its prima facie case, "the burden of production shifts to the defendants to provide a legitimate, nondiscriminatory reason for their decision." "The plaintiff must then prove that the defendants intentionally discriminated against them on a prohibited ground." The fact-finder is permitted "to infer the ultimate fact of discrimination" if the plaintiff has made "a substantial showing that the defendants' proffered explanation was false."

> The key inquiry in the intentional discrimination analysis is whether discriminatory animus was a motivating factor behind the decision at issue. The Second Circuit has identified the following five factors a fact-finder may consider in evaluating a claim of intentional discrimination:

>> (1) the the discriminatory impact of the governmental decision; (2) the decision's historical background; (3) the specific sequence of events leading up to the challenged decision; (4) departures from the normal procedural sequences; and (5) departures from normal substantive criteria.

Disparate Impact[106]

> "To establish a prima facie case under this theory, the plaintiff must show: (1) the occurrence of certain outwardly neutral practices, and

---

[104] Candlehouse, *supra* note 102.   [105] *Id. See also* cases cited in *supra* note 102.

[106] *Id. See also* cases cited in *supra* note 102. Note that at the time of this writing, the use of disparate impact analysis under the FHA is being contested, and we will have to await a Supreme Court decision to settle the matter. Disparate treatment may be the more appropriate standard based on the actual language of the legislation and because observing a different relative impact may not clarify the reason for the outcomes observed – with the possibility that some explanations do not involve illegal discrimination.

(2) a significantly adverse or disproportionate impact on persons
of a particular type produced by the defendant's facially neutral
acts or practices." "A plaintiff need not show the defendant's action
was based on any discriminatory intent." To prove that a neutral
practice has a significantly adverse or disproportionate impact "on
a protected group, a plaintiff must prove the practice actually or
predictably results in discrimination." In addition, a plaintiff must
prove "a causal connection between the facially neutral policy and
the alleged discriminatory effect." Once a plaintiff establishes its
prima facie case, "the burden shifts to the defendant to prove that
its actions furthered, in theory and in practice, a legitimate, bona
fide governmental interest and that no alternative would serve that
interest with less discriminatory effect."

"The basis for a successful disparate impact claim involves a comparison between two groups – those affected and those unaffected by the
facially neutral policy. This comparison must reveal that although
neutral, the policy in question imposes a significantly adverse or
disproportionate impact on a protected group of individuals."

"Statistical evidence is . . . normally used in cases involving fair housing
disparate impact claims." "Although there may be cases where statistics are not necessary, there must be some analytical mechanism to
determine disproportionate impact."

Reasonable Accommodation[107]

A claim for reasonable accommodation . . . does not require the plaintiff to prove that the challenged policy intended to discriminate or
that in effect it works systematically to exclude the disabled. Instead,
in the words of the FHA, a reasonable accommodation is required
whenever it "may be necessary to afford [a disabled] person equal
opportunity to use and enjoy a dwelling." 42 U.S.C. § 3604(f)(3)(B).

What does it mean to be "necessary"? The word implies more than
something merely helpful or conducive. It suggests instead something "indispensable," "essential," something that "cannot be done
without" . . . What's more, the FHA's necessity requirement doesn't
appear in a statutory vacuum, but is expressly linked to the goal of
"afford[ing] . . . equal opportunity to use and enjoy a dwelling." 42
U.S.C. § 3604(f) (3)(B). And this makes clear that the object of the
statute's necessity requirement is a level playing field in housing
for the disabled. Put simply, the statute requires accommodations

[107] Cinnamon Hills, *supra* note 102.

that are necessary (or indispensable or essential) to achieving the objective of equal housing opportunities between those with disabilities and those without. See Bryant Woods Inn, Inc. v. Howard County, Md., 124 F.3d 597, 605 (4th Cir. 1997); Schwarz, 544 F.3d at 1227.

Of course, in some sense all reasonable accommodations treat the disabled not just equally but preferentially. Think of the blind woman who obtains an exemption from a "no pets" policy for her seeing eye dog, or the paraplegic granted special permission to live on a first floor apartment because he cannot climb the stairs. But without an accommodation, those individuals cannot take advantage of the opportunity (available to those without disabilities) to live in those housing facilities. And they cannot because of conditions created by their disabilities . . .

But while the FHA requires accommodations necessary to ensure the disabled receive the same housing opportunities as everybody else, it does not require more or better opportunities. The law requires accommodations overcoming barriers, imposed by the disability, that prevent the disabled from obtaining a housing opportunity others can access. But when there is no comparable housing opportunity for non-disabled people, the failure to create an opportunity for disabled people cannot be called necessary to achieve equality of opportunity in any sense. So, for example, a city need not allow the construction of a group home for the disabled in a commercial area where nobody, disabled or otherwise, is allowed to live.

Requesting a reasonable accommodation for financial feasibility reasons does not qualify as a necessary accommodation.[108] The fact that a person with a disability may prefer to conduct a use of property in a less costly way, or that a given project would be more economically feasible if done on a larger scale, does not make the use necessary for FHA purposes. Thus, the use need not be approved by local zoning officials who are otherwise validly acting in accordance with the police power. At the same time, local zoning officials must show a willingness to take modest steps to accommodate a person with disability as long as the steps do not pose an undue hardship or a substantial burden on the exercise of their planning and zoning authority.[109]

From the cases, one can identify six key elements that local zoning and planning officials will need to keep in mind when they address matters at the

[108] Nikolich, *supra* note 102.   [109] Candlehouse, *supra* note 102.

intersection of land use law and the law related to people with disability. By following these six steps, the local zoning and planning officials will enhance their ability to act without violating the requirements of the ADA, FHA, and RA. These elements are as follows:

1. Have a well-developed, comprehensive plan for the present and future needs of the community; including accessibility needs; and acting in ways that are consistent with the plan. In taking action and making decisions, there should be an explanation of the way that the action taken is deemed to advance the plan.
2. Establish rules and criteria in the zoning code for implementation of the plan. For example, if there are provisions for floating zones and for conditional and special use permits, there should be clear criteria on granting an application for such a use, and these criteria need to be rationally and fairly applied.
3. When dealing with matters that raise potential disability law issues, be certain to account for federal disability law requirements under the ADA, FHA, RA, and related legislation. In evaluating the application of the zoning code to a particular case, for example, engage in fact finding as to (1) the reasonableness of a requested accommodation, (2) the necessity for an accommodation, (3) the extent that an asserted difficulty with the code is different in kind from that experienced by the public generally, and (4) with respect to housing, the ability of the property owner to obtain an equal opportunity to obtain housing in the absence of an accommodation ("but for" the accommodation the person with a disability would not have an equal opportunity to obtain housing).
4. In rendering a decision, make specific fact-based findings as to listed criteria, including the requirements of federal disability law. Quasi-adjudicative decisions, as in those made by a zoning board of appeal, must be supported by substantial competent evidence on the record; thus, be certain to document the fact finding and the rationale for supporting a decision. (Legislative acts, as in developing a comprehensive plan and the zoning code, are subject to review on a rational basis standard.)
5. The record must reveal a fair and unbiased process; consequently, to the extent that public hearings produce potentially discriminatory testimony, such as in the recording of discriminatory comments made by a member of the public at a public meeting, decision makers should clarify, on the record, that their decision is in no way influenced by such impermissible comments or considerations. Decision makers in

such situations should counter any biased comments and confirm that their decisions are based on fair and complete evaluations of the full and *relevant* information on the record.

6. Planning and zoning officials should periodically review and assess the results of their decisions to ensure that their application of facially neutral criteria does not, in fact, result in disparate treatment of people with disability. A more cautious position, although perhaps not required until the standard is better clarified by the U.S. Supreme Court, would be to assess outcomes in terms of disparate impact. From a practice perspective, disparate treatment seems more consistent with a rational basis and intermediate scrutiny standard of review, whereas disparate impact analysis really amounts to more of an indirect way of imposing the equivalent of a strict scrutiny standard of review, and strict scrutiny has not been the traditional standard of review in land use planning and zoning cases.

In working with these six criteria, one must keep in mind that the courts on review seem to be taking a "hard look" at the actions of local planning and zoning boards. The hard look doctrine applied in administrative review, and frequently associated with environmental regulation, requires the government to provide satisfactory explanations for its proposed actions.[110] Generally, this means explaining, on the record, the reasons and justifications for a proposed action. This includes clarification of the method of analysis and the quality of the information used to evaluate the situation. The hard look doctrine can be applied to the rational basis standard of review to make it more rigorous and, in practice, bring it closer to an intermediate scrutiny standard of review. In advising local planning and zoning professionals, it may be prudent for them to think and act as if they will be subject to intermediate scrutiny rather than a mere rational basis test when evaluating land use regulations that are in tension with claims asserted pursuant to disability law.

The *WCS* and *IHS* cases, and related decisions, confirm that there are limits both to what local officials can do in terms of planning and zoning and to the asserted reach of the ADA and related federal legislation. Again, there is clearly a role for planning and zoning, and there is an established process with

---

[110] "The scope of review under the "arbitrary and capricious" standard is narrow, and a court is not to substitute its judgment for that of the agency. Nevertheless, the agency must examine the relevant data and articulate a satisfactory explanation for its action, including a "rational connection between the facts found and the choice made." Motor Vehicle Manufacturers Assoc. v. State Farm Mutual Ins. Co., 463 U.S. 29, 43 (1983). *See generally*, Patrick M. Gary, Judicial Review and the Hard Look Doctrine, 7, Nevada L. J. 151 (2006); Mathew C. Stephenson, A Costly Signaling Theory of "Hard Look" Judicial Review, 58 Admin. L. Rev. 753 (2006).

standards for review of local decisions. The fact that a person or an entity seeks to use property for a particular purpose that involves persons with disabilities does not mean that local governments cannot apply their planning and zoning regulations to the situation. It is not true that planning and zoning regulations that are otherwise valid must be set aside to accommodate a person with a disability simply because the person has a disability. At the same time, it is important to provide a fair process, and following the six points outlined earlier will help ensure the viability of a local zoning decision on review.

Recognizing that federal law promotes a national standard for inclusion and that it has guidelines for land use planning does not mean that there is no role for meaningful local input on developing appropriate plans for community growth and development – even when not every property owner, developer, or user can get his way in seeking permission for a particular use in a specific zone. Federal regulations respecting accessibility do not eliminate a role for local governments in addressing inclusive design, and the fundamental responsibility for coordinating local land use should remain with local rather than national government because local governments are better positioned to assess local land use and property law issues. This includes the flexibility for local governments to establish special redevelopment or other types of zones that exclude a variety of uses deemed inappropriate for the zone. As long as a proposed use is not excluded from a zone because of a user's status in terms of disability, the local regulation should be evaluated in accordance with the normal standards of review applicable to land use law and regulation. Simply asserting that an otherwise applicable regulation should be excused because a user has a disability ought not to be the basis of decision making in the area of land use – and this is particularly true when the community provides other zones where the intended use is permitted.[111]

As an everyday example, consider a simple request for a variance from a homeowner with respect to a local zoning regulation governing the installation of fencing in a yard. Assume, as is typical of many zoning codes, that the city of Sunshine has a regulation requiring property owners who place fencing on their property to place the fencing in such a way that the finished side faces outward, in the direction of adjoining properties – meaning that if there is an unfinished side, it needs to face inward. In the case of many wooden fences, the unfinished side reveals the beams and cross-supports. Now

---

[111] As long as there is a reasonable opportunity for the use to be located somewhere in the community, the local zoning officials should be able to regulate the coordination of land use. This approach would be similar to situations involving regulation of adult entertainment uses. *See, e.g.,* City of Renton v. Playtime Theatres, 475 U.S. 41 (1986).

assume that a property owner comes to the zoning board seeking a variance from this regulation to place a fence on her property with the finished side facing inward rather than outward, as required by the code, to accommodate a child living at the property. The request is based on the child having certain cognitive disabilities or being autistic with a resulting behavioral tendency of running away from home. Having the unfinished side of the fence facing outward toward adjoining property owners leaves the finished side of the fence facing inward, and this means that the fence will be more difficult for the child to climb because the finished side is smooth and there are no exposed beams and cross-supports to facilitate climbing. Having the finished side of the fence facing inward not only looks better to the property owner (who now has the attractive side of the fence facing in toward her home) but it makes it more difficult for the child to escape by climbing over the fence. The family believes that a fence will be helpful in keeping the child safely within the property limits of the home and asserts that being excused from the zoning code rule is a required accommodation for a person with a disability.

In accordance with the guidelines discussed earlier, the local zoning authority in this example should be able to enforce the requirement that a finished side of a fence face outward. Assuming the city of Sunshine has a zoning code enacted pursuant to a comprehensive plan as a valid exercise of the police power, and it follows the criteria in the code for the granting of a variance, it should be able to enforce the regulation by requiring that the property owner simply obtain a fence finished on both sides. It would need to make its determination based on the variance criteria and on a deliberative consideration of the request for an accommodation for disability-related reasons. It could, nonetheless, determine that the requested accommodation is not reasonable and that it is unnecessary, per the *IHS* and *WCS* decisions. It could do this by finding that a denial of the accommodation is simply based on a quality shared with the public generally – this being the cost of a fence finished on two sides relative to a fence finished on only one side. The board could reason that most property owners when given the choice would express a strong preference for having the finished side of a fence facing in so that they can enjoy the more aesthetic view of the fence. Many homeowners in fact request that fences be installed so that the finished side faces inward, only to be disappointed to learn that the local zoning code prevents it. At the same time, adjoining property owners tend to be supportive of the rule; basically, no one prefers looking at the unfinished side of a fence if she has a choice. The way that this problem is addressed by many homeowners is by installing fences finished on two sides, and this is the instruction given to such people when they object on learning that the local zoning code requires them to install a fence with a finished side facing outward. In this context, an exemption from the zoning rule might be granted, but it should not necessarily be a required accommodation, because the rule applies to everyone, and any issues regarding compliance are simply ones that affect the public generally. Neighbors ought not to have to look or contend with the rough and unfinished side of the fence if the community has rationally determined that the unfinished side should face inward. The applicant must show that "but for" a variance or exception from this rule, she will not have an equal opportunity to obtain housing. The zoning board might reasonably determine that a fence finished on both sides is the appropriate solution and the requested variance is not reasonable and not necessary. Moreover, to the extent that requests for this type of exemption take place over time, the process of accommodation could completely undermine the ability to regulate the look and aesthetics of a neighborhood with regard to fencing.

Fencing is not like a sidewalk or a patio because it rises six feet in height and is usually placed at or near the property line. It can have a significant impact on adjoining properties. The primary difficulty presented by the fence regulation in this example is that which confronts the public generally, the cost of obtaining quality fencing finished on both sides – and with respect to cost, just as with any property owner, the law does not guarantee a property owner a right to build things at the lowest possible cost. Similarly, issues of financial difficulty do not by themselves make an accommodation necessary under the FHA. There may also be alternative ways for the property owner to achieve her objective, as in using vinyl fencing that is finished on both sides and sometimes priced below the cost of a cedar fence. The presence of alternatives should be evaluated in determining the reasonableness of a request for any particular accommodation.

Just as a building code and fire code can raise the cost of a house, and just as accessibility requirements in accordance with the ADA can raise the cost of a house or other building, the property owner in this case should have no expectation that she should be allowed to install a fence with the unfinished side facing out just because a fence finished on both sides costs more than an alternative. This approach should also apply to such things as ramps. Permitting a ramp to be added to a front entrance of a preexisting building or home to accommodate a person with mobility impairment should not mean that the property owner can simply install any kind of a ramp. Zoning and planning officials should be able to regulate the materials, quality, style, and placement of the ramp on the property to ensure its compatibility with the character of the neighborhood. Such a view simply acknowledges a sort of reciprocity with respect to the obligation of people living in community. The regulation of land use in accordance with the police power sometimes imposes costs and restrictions on property owners, and as long as these costs and restrictions are not discriminatory or confiscatory, they should be considered legal. Moreover, in states such as New York, where the state pays for such things as fencing, ramps, and home modifications as part of its programming to assist people with disabilities,[112] it should pay for the cost of completing these modifications in compliance with local zoning and planning regulations.

Thus, we see that even with the pervasive coverage of federal disability law, there is still room for local planning and zoning with respect to accessibility. We now turn to the issue of local planning and zoning that might set higher standards for inclusive design than is required by federal disability laws. In particular, we look at a case that addresses a local requirement for all new residential housing to meet a basic visitability standard when this standard exceeds the minimum requirements under federal law.

Washburn v. Pima County

81 P.3d 1030 (Ariz. App. 2003)
OPINION
ECKERSTROM, Judge.

Appellants Steven and Jeanette Washburn, the Southern Arizona Home-builders Association (SAHBA), and Washburn Company, Inc. (collectively the Washburns), appeal from the trial court's order granting summary judgment in favor of appellee Pima County. The Washburns contend on appeal that the county lacked statutory authority to adopt an ordinance requiring builders of single-family homes to incorporate design features allowing for greater wheelchair access and that the ordinance violates the Arizona Constitution. We affirm.

Background

On appeal from a grant of summary judgment, we view the facts and all reasonable inferences in the light most favorable to the party opposing the motion. In February 2002, the Pima County Board of Supervisors adopted Ordinance 2002-2, the Inclusive Home Design Ordinance, which was

---

[112] New York State provides up to $15,000 per year for approved environmental modification services to homes and vehicles. See Environmental Modifications Services (E-mods), www. health.ny.gov.facilities/long_term_care/waiver/nhtd_manual/section (Jan. 18, 2014); *Contract and Grant Opportunities*, Office of Temp. & Disability Assistance, http://otda.ny. gov/contracts (last visited Jan. 20, 2014). *See generally*, Lisa Ann Fagan, *Funding for Home Modifications and Programs*, Nat'l Ass'n of Home Builders, www.nahb.org/generic. aspx?genericContentID=89799 (last visited Jan. 20, 2014).

apparently modified by Pima County Ordinance 2002-72. Among its other effects, the ordinance promulgated building requirements applicable to the construction of new, single-family homes in unincorporated areas of Pima County. It did so by adopting selected construction standards found in the American National Standards Institute's (ANSI) publication A117.1, Accessible and Usable Buildings and Facilities (the ANSI standards), published by the International Code Council (ICC). The adopted provisions require that newly constructed homes incorporate design features that allow people in wheelchairs to more easily enter and use the homes. These features include "doorways wide enough to permit wheelchair access, electrical outlets reachable by a wheelchair-bound person, and bathroom walls reinforced to permit installation of grab bars." The Washburns admit that requiring these features in multi-family residential facilities and places of public accommodation serves an important government interest but challenge application of the requirements to single-family homes.

The Washburns applied for a permit to build a single-family home, but the proposed design failed to comply with the ordinance, and the county denied the application. They later filed a declaratory judgment and special action complaint in which they asked the trial court to declare that the county lacked statutory authority to adopt the ordinance and that it violated both the Equal Protection and Privacy Clauses of the Arizona Constitution. Ariz. Const. art. II, §§ 8, 13 . . . The court . . . found that the ordinance was constitutional . . . Our review focuses . . . on whether the trial court properly granted summary judgment in the county's favor . . .

Statutory Interpretation

The legislature authorized counties to adopt building codes but "limited [that authority] to the [adoption of] . . . any building, electrical or mechanical code that has been promulgated by any national organization or association that is organized and conducted for the purpose of developing codes." A.R.S. § 11-861(A), (C)(1). The Washburns challenge the county's adoption of the ANSI standards, which, through mandatory language, set forth a comprehensive collection of rules for builders to facilitate building access to people confined to wheelchairs. The Washburns contend that the county could not adopt the ANSI standards under § 11-861 because ICC neither titled nor classified those standards as a "code." Whether the legislature authorized the county to adopt requirements like the ANSI standards is a question of law subject to our de novo review.

The principal goal in interpreting a statute is to ascertain and give effect to the legislature's intent. Because § 11-861 is silent as to what the legislature intended a "code" to comprise, we find the statute ambiguous and consider other factors such as the statutory scheme, the statute's subject matter, historical context, effects and consequences, and spirit and purpose . . .

. . . § 11-861 entitles counties to determine and implement policies intended to further the general health, safety, and welfare of their residents. See Village of Euclid v. Ambler Realty Co., 272 U.S. 365, 387, 47 S. Ct. 114, 118, 71 L. Ed. 303, 310 (1926); Emmett McLoughlin Realty, Inc. v. Pima County, 203 Ariz. 557, P11, 58 P.3d 39, P11 (App. 2002). Within the confines of guidelines promulgated by national associations organized and conducted for the purpose of developing codes, the legislature has enabled both counties and municipalities to determine regionally tailored building policy, to identify specific design elements that further policy objectives, and to require builders to incorporate those elements. Thus, cities' and counties' enabling statutes rest on the same underlying policy considerations . . .

The Washburns . . . assert that, because § 11-861 requires counties to adopt building "codes" promulgated by nationally recognized organizations, we should interpret the term consistently with the term's meaning within the construction industry. However, we attribute no specialized meaning to statutory language unless the legislature has clearly conveyed its intent that we do so. ("Words are to be given their usual and commonly understood meaning unless it is plain or clear that a different meaning was intended."); ("Words and phrases shall be construed according to the common and approved use of the language."). Thus, the focus of our inquiry is not whether the terms "code" and "standard" have acquired an industry-specific meaning but whether the legislature intended the term "code" within § 11-861(C)(1) to convey an industry-specific meaning. Because there is nothing in the statutory history or the statute's language in § 11-861(C)(1) suggesting the legislature intended to imbue the terms "code" and "standards" with mutually exclusive, industry-specific definitions the Washburns proffer, we cannot agree with the Washburns' suggestion. If the legislature had intended to use the word "code" as an industry-specific term of art so as to substantially limit the options of county governments in their choice of nationally promulgated building specifications, it would have articulated that intention. Certainly, the legislature could not have expected counties to divine such an intent from a mere use of the word "code" in the statute.

Nor do we find any caveat in the ANSI standards themselves indicating they could not constitute a "code" within the meaning of § 11-861(C)(1). The foreword to the ANSI standards provides in part that the standards, "when adopted as a part of a building code, would be compatible with the building code and its enforcement." According to the Washburns, this language demonstrates that the ANSI standards were not intended to stand by themselves as a "code." But the Washburns' argument presupposes that a county could never amend or augment its current building code in a minor fashion without adopting a new comprehensive building code. We find nothing in § 11-861(C)(1) that prevents the county from amending or augmenting its comprehensive building regulations with self-contained "codes," promulgated by appropriate national organizations, that address discrete components of home construction. Moreover, the above-quoted foreword to the ANSI standards demonstrates ANSI's expectation that the standards would have an equal status to other parts of a pre-existing building code once adopted.

We are also not persuaded to reach a contrary result merely because initially the ANSI standards were not applicable to single-family homes. See ANSI standards § 101 ("These criteria are intended to be consistent with the intent of only the technical requirements of the Federal Fair Housing Act Accessibility Guidelines."); 42 U.S.C. § 3603(b)(1) (Fair Housing Act does not apply to most single-family homes). Notwithstanding the original application of the ANSI standards, those standards include a provision that suggests ANSI drafted the standards to be capable of flexible application to different types of "dwelling units" in various settings. Furthermore, the foreword demonstrates that ANSI anticipated the need to be compatible with other types of building codes and drafted the standards with this in mind. Indeed, the very use of the term "standard" connotes compatibility with complementary regulations. We address the Washburns' other claims regarding the county's application of the ANSI standards to single-family homes in the context of their challenges to the ordinance's constitutionality.

We also find no policy-based explanation for why the legislature would have intended to limit the breadth of the word "code" as used in § 11-861(C)(1). Without question, counties are generally empowered to regulate the construction of homes consistent with specifications suggested by appropriate national bodies. A county's ability to do so depends upon its power to mandate the incorporation of particular design elements. The Washburns do not dispute that counties may enact guidelines regulating the construction of new homes. Although they strenuously argue that a county may only adopt a set of requirements labeled as a "code" but not a set of requirements labeled as "standards," they point to no procedural differences or differences in professional or scientific scrutiny between the manner in which ANSI promulgated the standards adopted here and the manner in which, for example, the ICC promulgates the International Building Code. Both publications define minimum design criteria to implement public policy goals in the building of structures; both anticipate that local governmental authorities will tailor the criteria to promote

regionally prioritized public policy; and, once adopted, both contain mandatory language for how the construction must occur. Thus, we are given no
plausible explanation as to why the legislature would have intended to make
the hypertechnical distinction that the Washburns now urge in challenging
the county's authority to adopt the ANSI standards as a code. To accept the
Washburns' construction of § 11-861(C) would require us to exalt form over
substance. For the foregoing reasons, we find that the county has not exceeded
its statutory authority in adopting the ANSI standards here because those col-
lected standards constitute an example of "any building . . . code that has been
promulgated by any national organization . . . that is organized for the purpose
of developing codes." § 11-861(C)(1) . . .

 . . . We therefore determine that § 11-861(C)(1) enables counties to adopt
individual building design criterion "promulgated by any national organization or association that is organized and conducted for the purpose of developing codes" that the county determines advances the general health, safety,
and welfare of its residents.

Constitutional Claims

As they did below, the Washburns next claim the ordinance violates a homeowner's right to privacy in his or her home under the Privacy Clause, article
II, § 8 of the Arizona Constitution. Although they concede that the government possesses the right to adopt building, fire, and mechanical codes that
provide for the protection of the general population, they question whether
the county can constitutionally impose costly design requirements on all new
private homeowners "that have value to less than 1% of the population." They
further assert the ordinance "deprives new home-owners and builders of the
fundamental right to design private homes . . . by imposing design criteria that
invade the exercise of personal, private, and aesthetic choices for personal
private living spaces."

Homeowners do not have "a right to be completely free from governmental
regulation of the use and occupancy of [their] real property." State v. Watson,
198 Ariz. 48, P9, 6 P.3d 752, P9 (App. 2000). Our courts have already determined
that building codes that affect the exercise of homeowners' "personal, private,
and aesthetic choices" are a proper exercise of police power. Accordingly,
we agree with the trial court that the ordinance does not unconstitutionally
infringe on a homeowner's right to privacy.

In a related argument, the Washburns contend the ordinance violates their
rights under Arizona's Equal Protection Clause, article II, § 13 of the Arizona
Constitution, because it burdens only those people constructing new homes.
The level of scrutiny we apply to a discriminatory law depends upon whether

that law affects a fundamental right or a suspect class or enacts a gender-based classification. Other than pointing to their fundamental right to privacy, the Washburns point to nothing that would subject the ordinance to heightened scrutiny. Because we have already found that the ordinance does not unconstitutionally affect the right to privacy, and because the county has not engaged in any suspect classification in burdening builders of new homes, we uphold the ordinance "so long as there is a legitimate state interest to be served and the legislative classification rationally furthers that interest." The Washburns bear the burden of establishing the unconstitutionality of the ordinance.

To the extent the Washburns argue the Board of Supervisors had no rational basis for concluding that private home designs should facilitate access to people confined to wheelchairs, we disagree. "If the court can hypothesize any rational reason why the legislative body made the choice it did, the statute or ordinance is constitutionally valid. This test validates statutes even if the legislative body did not consider the reasons articulated by the court." Haines v. City of Phoenix, 151 Ariz. 286, 290, 727 P.2d 339, 343 (App. 1986). While reasonable minds might differ over whether government should impose these types of design criteria on those building new homes, the propriety of that public policy decision must be made through the political process by duly elected officials.

The uncontested evidence established that approximately one percent of the population is confined to wheelchairs, but the county points out that a much larger percentage will suffer a disability at some point in their lives. Although all age groups are affected by disability, the county introduced evidence that approximately forty-one percent of people over the age of sixty-five have some form of disability. Disability is a growing problem both nationally and locally, and the county also introduced evidence that Arizona's population of people over the age of sixty is expected to triple by 2025. Although many of these disabled people will not be confined to wheelchairs, the county concluded from these figures that the number of people confined to wheelchairs is rising. For these reasons, the county addressed a legitimate governmental interest when it adopted a building code designed to increase the number of homes accessible to those in wheelchairs. Cf. Arizona Fence Contractors Ass'n, 7 Ariz. App. at 131–32, 436 P.2d at 642–43 (adopting building code valid exercise of municipality's police power).

The Washburns also argue that the ordinance is not rationally related to further the county's interests. Again, we disagree. "A perfect fit is not required; a statute that has a rational basis will not be overturned" merely because it is not made with "mathematical nicety, or because in practice it results in some inequality." Although it is true that not all of the people affected by disabilities will benefit from the wheelchair access provisions of the ordinance and although those conducting renovations of existing homes are not required to comply with the ordinance, a regulation may rationally advance a governmental interest despite the fact that it is underinclusive.

The Washburns lastly contend the ordinance does not rationally advance the county's interests because it places the financial design burdens on homeowners who will probably never be confined to wheelchairs. But the county submitted to the trial court the results of a study suggesting that complying with the ordinance would cost only about $100. In addition, § 103.1 of the ordinance provides that the county may waive any design requirement if a building official determines that the cost of complying with the requirement exceeds $200. Indeed, the Board of Supervisors found that the cost of including the ordinance's designs into a new home was substantially less than the cost of renovating a home to accommodate a person confined to a wheelchair. On this record, the Board of Supervisors could have rationally concluded that the benefit to the community in providing for the disabled justified the comparatively minimal cost of implementing the required design features. Although the Washburns now contest the accuracy of the county's assertions as to the costs of these renovations, they failed in the trial court to introduce controverting evidence regarding the cost of compliance. The Washburns, therefore, have failed to establish that there were genuine issues of material fact precluding summary judgment. Because the ordinance rationally advances a legitimate governmental interest, the trial court did not err in concluding that the ordinance does not violate Arizona's Equal Protection Clause.

Affirmed

The *Pima County* case illustrates one direction in local planning for inclusive design. It presents an example of a community seeking to promote inclusion in response to local concerns and demographics. Its design requirements exceeded those required under federal law while being reasonably tailored to promote a legitimate state purpose and not imposing an undue hardship on property owners. Such efforts should be permissible under local planning and zoning law.

One thing to keep in mind when considering the *Pima County* case is that local exercise of the police power is governed by the scope of the enabling provisions of state law. In Arizona, Pima County was authorized to adopt or amend building code provisions. Pima County enacted inclusive design regulations pursuant to the police power delegated to it under Arizona law. Some states, however, may restrict local exercise of the police power by providing that local building codes cannot impose higher standards than those set by a state building code.[113] Such a restriction would seem to be bad public policy if it prevents local communities from setting higher standards of inclusive design to meet local needs. Perhaps there is a distinction that can be made, however, if the regulations can be cast more as *use* requirements than as elements of a building code. For example, maybe the zoning code could simply require that all new residential properties be safe and easily useable by a person in a wheelchair, leaving the details of how this gets accomplished to those responsible for state building codes. Under this approach, buildings and properties that have barriers to safe and easy use by a person in a wheelchair might be considered as nonconforming uses. Use regulations differ from building codes because building codes are directed at how best to technically achieve certain building standards and not at coordinating land uses. In any event, the authority of a local government to promote inclusive design will depend on the state enabling law and on the way that the state defines a building code and a use.

Collectively, the preceding three cases provide some guidance as to the limits to land use planning and zoning with respect to disability rights. The next two cases focus on a different problem. These two cases address the issue of planning for mobility infrastructure needs across the built environment. Connective infrastructure is important in planning for a "complete" community, because without good connectivity between and among the places of community life, people can become isolated on properties that are nothing more than fully accessible islands or silos of truncated relationships.

Frame v. City of Arlington

657 F.3d 215 (5th Cir. 2011)
OPINION
BENAVIDES and PRADO, Circuit Judges:
Title II of the Americans with Disabilities Act (ADA), like § 504 of the Rehabilitation Act, provides that individuals with disabilities shall not "be denied the benefits of the services, programs, or activities of a public entity, or be subjected to discrimination by any such entity." For nearly two decades, Title II's implementing regulations have required cities to make newly built and altered sidewalks readily accessible to individuals with disabilities. The

---

[113] Title 19 (NYCRR), Chapter 32, Part 1202, § 1202.1. Local governments are charged with administration and enforcement of the state-passed uniform building code. If there is a practical difficulty or unnecessary hardship, a variation may be requested. Other than seeking a variation, the state code is what must be applied statewide. *See* N.Y. Lab. Law, http://code.lp.findlaw. com/nycode/LAB/2/30.

plaintiffs-appellants in this case, five individuals with disabilities, allege that defendant-appellee the City of Arlington (the City) has recently built and altered sidewalks that are not readily accessible to them. The plaintiffs brought this action for injunctive relief under Title II and § 504.

... [W]e must determine whether Title II and § 504 (and their implied private right of action) extend to newly built and altered public sidewalks . . . We hold that the plaintiffs have a private right of action to enforce Title II and § 504 with respect to newly built and altered public sidewalks, and that the right accrued at the time the plaintiffs first knew or should have known they were being denied the benefits of those sidewalks.

The plaintiffs in this case depend on motorized wheelchairs for mobility. They allege that certain inaccessible sidewalks make it dangerous, difficult, or impossible for them to travel to a variety of public and private establishments throughout the City. Most of these sidewalks allegedly were built or altered by the City after Title II became effective on January 26, 1992. The plaintiffs sued the City on July 22, 2005, claiming that the inaccessible sidewalks violate Title II of the ADA and § 504 of the Rehabilitation Act . . .

It is established that Title II of the ADA and § 504 of the Rehabilitation Act are enforceable through an implied private right of action. The issue is whether these statutes (and their established private right of action) extend to newly built and altered public sidewalks. Based on statutory text and structure, we hold that Title II and § 504 unambiguously extend to newly built and altered public sidewalks. We further hold that the plaintiffs have a private right of action to enforce Title II and § 504 to the extent they would require the City to make reasonable modifications to such sidewalks.

The ADA is a "broad mandate" of "comprehensive character" and "sweeping purpose" intended "to eliminate discrimination against disabled individuals, and to integrate them into the economic and social mainstream of American life." Title II of the ADA focuses on disability discrimination in the provision of public services. Specifically, Title II, 42 U.S.C. § 12132, provides that "no qualified individual with a disability shall, by reason of such disability, be excluded from participation in or be denied the benefits of the services, programs, or activities of a public entity, or be subjected to discrimination by any such entity."

Section 504 of the Rehabilitation Act prohibits disability discrimination by recipients of federal funding. Like Title II, § 504 provides that no qualified individual with a disability "shall, solely by reason of her or his disability, be excluded from participation in, be denied the benefits of, or be subjected to discrimination under any program or activity receiving Federal financial assistance." The ADA and the Rehabilitation Act generally are interpreted in pari materia. Indeed, Congress has instructed courts that "nothing in [the ADA] shall be construed to apply a lesser standard than the standards applied under title V [i.e., § 504] of the Rehabilitation Act . . . or the regulations issued by Federal agencies pursuant to such title." The parties have not pointed to any reason why Title II and § 504 should be interpreted differently in this case. Although we focus primarily on Title II, our analysis is informed by the Rehabilitation Act, and our holding applies to both statutes.

As mentioned, there is no question that Title II and § 504 are enforceable through an implied private right of action. Moreover, to the extent Title II's implementing regulations "simply apply" Title II's substantive ban on disability discrimination and do not prohibit conduct that Title II permits, they too are enforceable through Title II's private right of action. This is because when Congress intends a statute to be enforced through a private right of action, it also "intends the authoritative interpretation of the statute to be so enforced as well."

In interpreting the scope of Title II (and its implied private right of action), our starting point is the statute's plain meaning. In ascertaining the plain meaning of Title II, we "must look to the particular statutory language at issue, as well as the language and design of the statute as a whole."

If we determine that the plain meaning of Title II is ambiguous, we do not simply impose our own construction on the statute. When confronted with a statutory ambiguity, we refer to the responsible agency's reasonable interpretation of that statute. Here, because Congress directed the Department of Justice (DOJ) to elucidate Title II with implementing regulations, DOJ's views at least would "warrant respect" and might be entitled to even more deference . . .

We begin by determining whether the plain meaning of Title II extends to newly built and altered sidewalks. As noted, Title II provides that disabled individuals shall not be denied the "benefits of the services, programs, or activities of a public entity, or be subjected to discrimination by any such entity" . . .

The ADA does not define the "services, programs, or activities of a public entity." The Rehabilitation Act, however, defines a "program or activity" as "all of the operations of . . . a local government." As already stated, we interpret Title II and the Rehabilitation Act in pari materia. Accordingly . . . we must determine whether newly built and altered city sidewalks are benefits of "all of the operations" and "services" of a public entity within the ordinary meaning of those terms.

Before resolving this issue, however, we briefly acknowledge two different ways of framing it. Some parties urge us to consider whether building and altering sidewalks are services, programs, or activities of a public entity, and thus whether the resulting sidewalks are "benefits" of those services, programs, or activities. Other parties urge us to consider whether a city sidewalk itself is a service, program, or activity of a public entity. As discussed below, we believe this case does not turn on how we frame the issue. Either way, when a city decides to build or alter a sidewalk and makes that sidewalk inaccessible to individuals with disabilities without adequate justification, the city unnecessarily denies disabled individuals the benefits of its services in violation of Title II.

Building and altering city sidewalks unambiguously are "services" of a public entity under any reasonable understanding of that term. The Supreme Court has broadly understood a "service" to mean "the performance of work commanded or paid for by another," or "an act done for the benefit or at the command of another." Webster's Dictionary additionally defines a "service" as "the provision, organization, or apparatus for . . . meeting a general demand." For its part, Black's Law Dictionary defines a "public service" as work "provided or facilitated by the government for the general public's convenience and benefit."

Under each of these common understandings, building and altering public sidewalks unambiguously are services of a public entity. The construction or alteration of a city sidewalk is work commanded by another (i.e., voters and public officials), paid for by another (i.e., taxpayers), and done for the benefit of another (e.g., pedestrians and drivers). When a city builds or alters a sidewalk, it promotes the general public's convenience by overcoming a collective action problem and allowing citizens to focus on other ventures. Moreover, when a city builds or alters a sidewalk, it helps meet a general demand for the safe movement of people and goods. In short, in common understanding, a city provides a service to its citizens when it builds or alters a public sidewalk.

A "service" also might be defined as "[t]he duties, work, or business performed or discharged by a public official." Under this definition too, newly built and altered public sidewalks are services of a public entity. Cities, through their officials, study, debate, plan, and ultimately authorize sidewalk construction. If a city official authorizes a public sidewalk to be built in a way that is not readily accessible to disabled individuals without adequate justification, the official denies disabled individuals the benefits of that sidewalk no less than if the official poured the concrete himself.

Furthermore, building and altering public sidewalks easily are among "all of the operations" (and thus also the "programs or activities") of a public entity. Webster's Dictionary broadly defines "operations" as "the whole process of planning for and operating a business or other organized unit" and defines "operation" as "a doing or performing esp[ecially] of action." In common understanding, the operations of a public entity would include the "whole process" of "planning" and "doing" that goes into building and altering public sidewalks.

In sum, in common understanding, building and altering public sidewalks are services, programs, or activities of a public entity. When a city decides to build or alter a sidewalk and makes that sidewalk inaccessible to individuals with disabilities without adequate justification, disabled individuals are denied the benefits of that city's services, programs, or activities. Newly built and altered sidewalks thus fit squarely within the plain, unambiguous text of Title II.

Even if we focus on a public sidewalk itself, we still find that a sidewalk unambiguously is a service, program, or activity of a public entity. A city sidewalk itself facilitates the public's "convenience and benefit" by affording a means of safe transportation. A city sidewalk itself is the "apparatus" that meets the public's general demand for safe transportation. As the Supreme Court has observed, sidewalks are "general government services" "provided in common to all citizens" to protect pedestrians from the "very real hazards of traffic." The Supreme Court also has recognized that public sidewalks are "traditional public fora" that "time out of mind" have facilitated the general demand for public assembly and discourse. When a newly built or altered city sidewalk is unnecessarily made inaccessible to individuals with disabilities, those individuals are denied the benefits of safe transportation and a venerable public forum . . .

Additionally, in clarifying the requirements of Title II in the unique context of "designated public transportation services" (e.g., regular rail and bus services), Congress expressly provided that § 12132 requires new and altered "facilities" to be accessible. Although Congress did not define "facilities," the relevant Department of Transportation (DOT) regulations define the term to include, inter alia, "roads, walks, passageways, [and] parking lots." Congress's express statement that § 12132 extends to newly built and altered facilities is a good indication that Congress thought § 12132 would extend to newly built and altered sidewalks . . .

Though unnecessary to resolve this case, legislative purpose and history confirm that Congress intended Title II to extend to newly built and altered sidewalks. Congress anticipated that Title II would require local governments "to provide curb cuts on public streets" because the "employment, transportation, and public accommodation sections of [the ADA] would be meaningless if people who use wheelchairs were not afforded the opportunity to travel on and between streets." Implicit in this declaration is a premise that sidewalks are subject to Title II in the first place. Congress's specific application of Title II is consistent with its statutory findings. In enacting Title II, Congress found that individuals with disabilities suffer from "various forms of discrimination," including "isolat[ion] and segregat[ion]," and that inaccessible transportation is a "critical area[]" of discrimination. Moreover, Congress understood that accessible transportation is the "linchpin" that "promotes the self-reliance and self-sufficiency of people with disabilities." Continuing to build inaccessible sidewalks without adequate justification would unnecessarily entrench the types of discrimination Title II was designed to prohibit.

Title II does not only benefit individuals with disabilities. Congress recognized that isolating disabled individuals from the social and economic mainstream imposes tremendous costs on society. Congress specifically found that disability discrimination "costs the United States billions of dollars in unnecessary expenses resulting from dependency and nonproductivity." Congress also anticipated that "the mainstreaming of persons with disabilities will result in more persons with disabilities working, in increasing earnings, in less dependence on the Social Security system for financial support, in increased spending on consumer goods, and increased tax revenues." The Rehabilitation Act was passed with similar findings and purpose. Continuing to build inaccessible sidewalks without adequate justification would unnecessarily aggravate the social costs Congress sought to abate.

To conclude, it would have come as no surprise to the Congress that enacted the ADA that Title II and its implementing regulations were being used to regulate newly built and altered city sidewalks. Indeed, Title II unambiguously requires this result. Having considered both the statutory language of § 12132 as well as the language and design of Title II as a whole, we hold that Title II unambiguously extends to newly built and altered sidewalks. Because we interpret Title II and § 504 of the Rehabilitation Act in pari materia, we hold that § 504 extends to such sidewalks as well . . .

For the reasons stated, **we hold** that the plaintiffs have a private right of action to enforce Title II of the ADA and § 504 of the Rehabilitation Act with respect to newly built and altered sidewalks.

The *Frame* case explains the requirement for local government to provide access to programs and services and clarifies that this can include infrastructure serving the built environment and connecting the various venues in which community life is experienced. In an earlier case holding similarly, *Barden v. City of Sacramento*, 292 F.3d 1073 (9th Cir., 2002), it was pointed out that accessible sidewalks include planning with respect to the placement of signs, benches, and other potential obstacles along the route of the sidewalk.[114] In dealing with older sidewalks, accessibility refers to the overall system and not necessarily every square foot of sidewalk in a community.[115] Updating older sidewalk infrastructure may be excused to the extent that the cost of updating imposes an undue hardship, but this excuse does not apply to alteration work or to the construction of new sidewalks.[116] As confirmed in *Kinney v. Yerusalim*, 9 F.3d 1067 (3d Cir. 1993) (dealing with the resurfacing of streets in Philadelphia), alterations and new construction work must be built to accessible standards in accordance with federal guidelines, and there is no exception for cost or undue hardship.[117]

There is no obligation to build sidewalks, but if they are built, they must be compliant with federal accessibility guidelines. A question that arises concerns the obligation to keep such infrastructure in good repair and operational. The following case addresses the obligation of local government with respect to the ability to maintain continuous and unobstructed access to transportation infrastructure for people with mobility impairment.

Foley v. City of Lafayette

359 F.3d 925 (7th Cir. 2004)

OPINION

KANNE, Circuit Judge. Robert Foley alleges that the City of Lafayette violated the Americans with Disabilities Act ("ADA") and the Rehabilitation Act of 1973 by failing to provide adequate egress from the city-owned train station platform. The district court, relying on 49 C.F.R. § 37.161, concluded that the inoperable elevators and snow-covered ramp that prevented Foley from an easy exit from the platform were non-actionable isolated or temporary conditions as a matter of law. Because we agree with the district court's conclusion, we affirm the grant of summary judgment to the City of Lafayette.

I. History

Robert Foley, a lifetime resident of West Virginia, has suffered from significant pain in his legs and back since a work related injury in August of 2000. From the time of his injury, he has relied on a wheelchair because of intense pain

---

[114] Barden v. City of Sacramento, 292 F. 3d 1073 (9th Cir. 2002).
[115] *See* 28 C.F.R. § 35.150(a) (2012); Culvahouse v. City of LaPorte, 629 F. Supp. 2d 931 (N.D. Ind. 2009).
[116] *Id.*   [117] Kinney v. Yerusalim, 9 F. 3d 1067 (3d Cir. 1993).

caused by standing or walking. Robert's health problems are compounded by his morbid obesity – he weighs nearly four hundred pounds – and diabetes.

In December of 2000, Robert decided to travel to Indiana so that he could celebrate the holidays with his extended family. Robert's brother, Greg, hosting the proposed reunion at his home in Battle Ground (a town near Lafayette), made arrangements for Robert to travel from West Virginia to Indiana by train. Greg chose this means of transportation in part because the Lafayette train station is advertised by Amtrak as fully accessible to persons in wheelchairs. Joined by his teenage son, David, Robert left West Virginia on December 17 with an estimated time of arrival in Lafayette of 7:08 a.m. on Monday, December 18.

The sole Lafayette train station is owned and operated by the City of Lafayette. Amtrak, Greyhound, the city bus system, and several other organizations utilize the station as a depot and/or for office space. Fred Taylor was the only City employee assigned to the station on a regular basis during the time period in question. Taylor performed maintenance and janitorial work. He worked from 6:00 a.m. to 3:00 p.m., Monday through Friday. Bill O'Connor, an employee of the Downtown Business Center, also worked at the station. His duties mirrored those of Taylor, he often followed orders given by Taylor, and he usually started work at 2:30 p.m. and ended work around 11:30 p.m. Two passenger trains stop at the Lafayette station each day of the week; in December of 2000, the northbound train had a scheduled arrival time of 7:08 a.m., and the southbound train had a scheduled arrival time of 11:38 p.m.

The train station is located at Riehle Plaza in downtown Lafayette and is situated on the east side of the tracks. Passenger trains arriving in Lafayette unload at a ground level platform on the west side of the tracks. The facility has three levels.

In order to reach the parking lot on the east side of the tracks, passengers must go up to the third level, by way of stairs or an elevator, to a short bridge that crosses above the tracks. After crossing the short bridge, passengers can take the east-side stairs or elevator to descend to the middle or ground-floor levels of the station, where they can access the parking lot.

Alternatively, by taking either the stairs or a ramp up one level from the west-side platform, passengers can reach a pedestrian bridge and cross west over the Wabash River into the adjacent community of West Lafayette. This pedestrian bridge is large enough to be accessed by vehicles for emergency purposes from the West Lafayette side of the river.

It is undisputed that significant snowfall, up to nine inches, blanketed the Lafayette area over the weekend prior to Robert's arrival. It is also uncontested that it was extremely cold and that the wind was particularly strong on the morning of December 18. In resolving all factual disputes in favor of Robert, we assume that the bulk of the snow fell early in the weekend, but there is no dispute that blizzard-like conditions prevailed through Monday morning due to a large amount of snow on the ground and strong winds.

At 6:00 a.m. on December 18, Greg Foley set out with his brother-in-law, Mike Flagg, to pick up Robert. Although the ten-mile trip from Battle Ground usually took about twenty minutes, the harsh winter conditions led to an arrival forty-five minutes later at 6:45 a.m. When Greg arrived at the station, he discovered that neither of the elevators were working. Concerned, Greg notified Fred Taylor. Taylor was surprised and may have tried to fix the problem by switching a circuit breaker. At his deposition, Taylor recalled that the elevators were broken the previous week and stated that he had called his boss to report the problem. Taylor notified Greg that the train had been delayed for two hours, but provided no further assistance to the Foleys. Greg, believing that Taylor would take care of the necessary repairs, took his family to breakfast. Taylor, in fact, spent most of the balance of his day shoveling snow, assisting other patrons of the depot, and attending to routine duties.

Greg returned to the station at approximately 9:00 a.m., and with Taylor present, he expressed concern about the inoperable elevators to Jane Ness, an employee of the Downtown Business Center. Whereupon Ness contacted the Indianapolis branch of Montgomery Kone, a Moline, Illinois company that was the contract provider of maintenance and repair services for the elevators.

Kone's records show the phone call for service regarding the train-station elevators was received at 9:13 a.m. At 9:31 a.m., Kone dispatched a Lafayette-area repairman to the scene. He arrived at 10:00 a.m. In commencing the repairs, it was discovered that the heating elements necessary to maintain the proper temperature of the oil in the outdoor hydraulic elevators were burned out. Because of the extremely cold temperatures, the elevators were rendered inoperable. Nothing further could be done that day, however, because parts were needed. The Kone repairman left sometime before 11:30 a.m.

In the meantime, Greg received misinformation from the Amtrak hotline that led him to believe that the northbound train would now not arrive until 12:30 p.m. He returned to Battle Ground with his family. The train, in fact, arrived at approximately 11:30 a.m.

Robert and his son, David, were helped off the train by Amtrak employees but were left alone in the cold weather on the platform. Amtrak does not employ personnel at the Lafayette station and the individuals who assisted the Foleys returned to their posts on the northbound train. David searched for Greg in vain. Robert and David considered the option of going up the ramp to the pedestrian bridge. They decided that the snow, not yet removed from the ramp, made maneuvering the wheelchair up the incline too difficult and dangerous. Robert, clad in light clothing, felt he could not endure the frigid temperatures. Robert decided his best option was to slowly walk up the stairs. Bill O'Connor (the Downtown Business Center employee), called in early to help shovel snow, assisted Robert by walking alongside and supporting some of Robert's weight.

Greg arrived around noon, after discovering at 11:30 a.m. that the train was not as late as the faulty estimate had indicated. After assessing the situation, Greg and Flagg drove in Flagg's truck to the West Lafayette side and drove east on the plowed pedestrian bridge. By this point, Robert had successfully reached the top of the first flight of stairs, and everyone helped him to the truck.

The next day, Tuesday, December 19, repairs continued and one elevator was returned to service. Both elevators were made fully operational by December 22.

Robert made several trips to Lafayette's Home Hospital and visited other doctors in West Virginia. He complained of increased pain in his legs due to alleged frostbite caused by the cold air. Robert contends that the City of Lafayette discriminated against him on the basis of his disability in violation of Title II of the ADA and the Rehabilitation Act. He alleges that the lack of equal egress on the morning of December 18 constitutes a violation of these statutes. The district court granted Lafayette's motion for summary judgment and sent the state law claims to the Indiana courts.

II. Analysis . . .

The ADA seeks to "provide a clear and comprehensive national mandate for the elimination of discrimination against individuals with disabilities[.]" 42 U.S.C. § 12101(b)(1) (2003). In pursuit of this goal, Title II of the ADA requires that "no qualified individual with a disability shall, by reason of such disability, be excluded from participation in or be denied the benefits of the services . . . of a public entity, or be subjected to discrimination by any such entity." 42 U.S.C. § 12132 (2003). For summary judgment purposes, the district court found that Robert was protected by the ADA as a "qualified individual" under 42 U.S.C. § 12131(2), and this finding was not challenged on appeal. Furthermore, the City of Lafayette is clearly a "public entity" under 42 U.S.C. § 12131(1). Thus, the issue before us under the ADA is whether the district court was correct in finding that the City, as a matter of law, did not unlawfully discriminate, exclude, or deny services to Robert. "Since Rehabilitation Act claims are analyzed under the same standards as those used for ADA claims," Ozlowski v. Henderson, 237 F.3d 837, 842 (7th Cir. 2001), we will confine our analysis to the ADA.

The Lafayette train station is, in the normal course of operation, fully accessible to individuals with disabilities. The dispute in this case is whether the City of Lafayette did enough to prevent and/or remedy the elevator difficulties in December of 2000. It is in this context that the district court properly relied on a rule promulgated by the Department of Transportation ("DOT") that provides guidance on the particular issue of access to mass transit facilities. This rule states:

(a) Public and private entities providing transportation services *shall maintain in operative condition* those features of facilities and vehicles that are required to make the vehicles and facilities readily accessible to and usable by individuals with disabilities. These features include, but are not limited to . . . elevators.

(b) Accessibility features *shall be repaired promptly if they are damaged or out of order.* When an accessibility feature is out of order, the entity *shall take reasonable steps to accommodate* individuals with disabilities who would otherwise use the feature.

(c) This section does not prohibit isolated or temporary interruptions in service or access due to . . . repairs.

49 C.F.R. § 37.161 (emphasis added). Thus, Lafayette has three duties under this particular regulation: it must maintain the elevators in operative condition, it must repair the elevators promptly once an elevator malfunctions, and it must take reasonable steps to accommodate an individual who otherwise would have used the elevators when the elevators are out of order. But the regulation does not subject Lafayette to liability for isolated or temporary interruptions in service due to repairs.

The DOT provided further guidance regarding the regulations in the published commentary. On the issue of maintenance and prompt repair, the DOT noted:

The rule points out that temporary obstructions or isolated instances of mechanical failure would not be considered violations of the ADA or this rule. Repairs must be made "promptly." The rule does not, and probably could not, state a time limit for making particular repairs, given the variety of circumstances involved. However, repairing accessible features must be made a high priority. Transportation for Individuals with Disabilities, 56 Fed. Reg. 45,621 (Sept. 6, 1991) app. D, subpt. G, § 37.161.

The DOT's interpretation of its own regulation makes sense: the only way to apply 49 C.F.R. § 37.161 is to consider the unique circumstances inherent in any particular transportation service site. In other words, there are no universal definitions in the regulations for what is required to "maintain in operative condition" the accessibility features, to repair "promptly" such features, or to take "reasonable steps" to accommodate when the features are not accessible. The extent of inaccessibility covered by the terms "isolated or temporary" in 49 C.F.R. § 37.161 is likewise unclear and only determinable by considering the unique circumstances of the case.

Robert insists that Lafayette failed to maintain the elevators in operative condition. Furthermore, he argues that Lafayette did not repair the elevators promptly, and did not take reasonable steps to accommodate him – by clearing the ramp of snow, for instance. Lafayette argues that the elevator repairs, necessitated by the cold weather, led to a temporary or isolated interruption in service that should not be punished under the ADA.

Nothing in the record indicates frequent denial of access to disabled persons or a policy that neglects elevator maintenance. Lafayette has a long-term service contract with Kone, the elevator-repair company. The elevators have indeed been serviced on numerous occasions during this contractual relationship, but Robert does not attempt to show that Kone was not providing the necessary maintenance to limit extended outages of service or that any other individual had suffered harm from an elevator outage. In short, there was no evidence from which a reasonable inference could be drawn that other disabled persons were denied access because of frequent elevator breakdowns . . .

Moreover, Lafayette has provided a reasonable accommodation for temporary elevator outages in the form of the ramp. The ramp to the pedestrian bridge provides an alternative means of access and egress for an event such as this – an elevator malfunction at the same time an individual with a disability is in need of elevator service.

An issue of fact has been raised as to whether the ramp was in fact passable at the time of Robert's arrival. But even assuming, as we must, that the ramp was impassable, that too was a temporary condition. The snowfall covered the sizeable exterior area of Riehle Plaza for which Taylor was responsible for snow removal. That Taylor had four-and-a-half hours' notice that Robert was arriving but had not yet cleared the ramp by the time Robert's train arrived does not vitiate the temporary nature of the snow obstruction of the alternative accommodation – and the ADA was not violated.

In the face of the failure of both primary and alternative accommodations, O'Connor assisted Robert to his vehicle in the manner that Robert was forced to pursue – walking up the stairs. In such unusual circumstances – heavy snowfall, inoperative elevators, and frigid temperatures combining to create a difficult situation for a passenger at a station with very limited train traffic and personnel – O'Connor's actions constituted a reasonable emergency accommodation . . .

III. Conclusion

Neither the interruption of elevator service nor the alternative ramp's snow-covered condition, under the circumstances of this case, constitutes a violation of the ADA or the Rehabilitation Act of 1973. The district court's grant of summary judgment is **AFFIRMED**.

As the *Foley* case illustrates, local governments must figure out how to maintain navigable connectors for access across the built environment. Although they are not expected to accomplish superhuman outcomes, they must use appropriate care in ensuring continuous access. In another case, *Midgett v. Tri-County Metropolitan Transportation District*, 254 F. 3d 846 (9th Cir. 2001), a similar issue was raised with the same basic outcome.[118] In *Midgett*, the problem involved access to the public bus system. As in *Foley*, it was an extremely cold day when the plaintiff attempted to board a city bus while in his wheelchair. The lift system on the bus did not function properly, and the plaintiff was unable to board. This happened to the plaintiff more than once on this day, but he did end up obtaining transportation on the bus system when a functioning bus did arrive to transport him at a later time. The plaintiff sued, complaining that the bus system was not ADA compliant because of failures in its service.[119] The court reasoned that the evidence presented was sufficient to demonstrate that the bus system had a plan and a track record supporting ADA compliance, and even though the occasional failures may be frustrating to certain users, the evidence did not sustain the finding of a violation of the obligation to make the service accessible.[120]

As *Foley* and *Midgett* illustrate, it is important to plan for appropriate upkeep and maintenance of transportation systems and pathways as well as to provide them in the first instance. For some types of infrastructure, such as sidewalks, this can raise difficult cost-related questions beyond those related to paying for initial construction. In parts of the country that have significant snowfall, for example, it is important to plan for the clearing of snow on the sidewalks so that they can be used. The question is one of determining how best to pay for and manage the continuous removal of snow from sidewalks. Should the local

---

[118] Midgett v. Tri-Cnty. Metro. Transp. Dist. of Or., 254 F. 3d 846 (9th Cir. 2001).
[119] *Id.*   [120] *Id.*

government be responsible for snow removal and pay for this out of general tax revenues? Should property owners be responsible for removal of snow on sidewalks along their property, and what is to be done with respect to property owners who do not do this on a continuing basis or who fail to do an adequate job of snow removal? If a property is owned by one person or entity and leased to another, who has responsibility for any potential ADA requirement to keep the sidewalk in good repair and clear of snow and ice? The answer may be that both parties remain fully liable for ADA compliance, even if the lease is structured to put the responsibility on the tenant.[121]

In the absence of sidewalks or in the presence of sidewalks covered in snow, people will move out into the street, and pedestrians will then be competing with automobile traffic for space. The presence of high snow banks on the edges of the road will make matters even worse because the snow cuts down on visibility and oftentimes narrows the street. In many cities located in regions of high snowfall, it is not unusual to come across people in wheelchairs and motorized mobility scooters traveling in the street because of the absence of sidewalks or because the sidewalks are not easily passable. Can this type of unsafe condition be tolerated in an inclusive community?

Another consideration with respect to sidewalks relates to the design of curb cuts and the consequences of heavy rainfall. In parts of the country that get frequent and heavy rainfall, one will often notice that water accumulates at the location of curb cuts. This can result in the formation of large pools of water that make the curb cut difficult to use. This too can motivate people to circumvent the planned path of navigation and move out into the street with automobile traffic or force unsafe sidewalk crossings at points away from the curb cut. Good curb cutting clearly involves more than just cutting curbs. Careful planning must go into determining other features of the built environment in close proximity to the curb cut as well as thinking about the cut itself. Again, planning is required. Planning is also required for the location, design, and construction of safe crosswalks. Many variables need to be considered when planning crosswalks, including such things as where to place crosswalks, how wide they need to be, how much time should be allocated to cross, whether there should be a crossing light, and whether there should be a "safe pedestrian island" at the halfway point of a major street. These are all important planning questions, and it is better to think about the best solutions to these questions in the context of developing a thoughtful and comprehensive plan for the future than to be making decisions in an after-the-fact way in response to litigation.

---

[121] *See, e.g.,* 28 C.F.R. §36.201(b) (2013), providing that both remain fully liable for ADA compliance in the situation of a public accommodation.

Planning, building, and maintaining connective infrastructure can be difficult for small communities or communities lacking ample resources, and the issues to be considered may vary by geographic location and local conditions. It is therefore important to think carefully about the need for and the location of such connective infrastructure and how best to pay for it – these are also local planning matters, not simply civil rights issues.

In planning for inclusive design, cost is always a factor; and when considering costs, a distinction must be made between the actual dollars and cents of building to specific design criteria on new construction and the cost of rehabilitation work for prior existing construction.[122] From a broader policy perspective, it is also important to determine the point at which some approaches to inclusive design become cost prohibitive, or in other words, to determine the extent to which cost considerations are legally cognizable considerations in establishing compliance with the requirements for inclusive design. In many cases, cost is not a legally cognizable factor in excusing compliance with accessible design requirements, thus, communities must carefully plan the extent to which they will build infrastructure, such as sidewalks, and how they will finance the services they do provide.

The following case addresses the question of cost in the setting of an employment discrimination dispute. The legal dispute at issue involves an employment relationship and the requirement of making a reasonable accommodation for an employee in the work setting. The reasonable accommodation standard applies to adjusting the work environment given an existing work environment.[123] It is not a standard for addressing the construction requirements for new buildings or for doing alterations and remodeling, as that is covered under other regulations.[124] The discussion of cost in the Court's opinion is instructive for setting a framework with respect to the obvious problem of scarce resources confronted by many property owners and developers. While some people may consider discussions of costs and of limits to resources to be impolite conversation when it comes to matters of mobility impairment and aging in place, the reality is that resources are not unlimited and that choices have to be made. This does not mean, of course, that such decisions must be made according to a strict costs and benefits analysis or that decisions have to be based on an economist's understanding of efficiency. The extent to which costs are relevant to compliance with federal disability law requirements varies in accordance with different activities and different uses. How they are or are not accounted for under the law is really a political matter for determination by the legislature (Congress).

---

[122] Malloy, *supra* note 31, at 715–716.   [123] 42 U.S.C. § 12111(9) (2013).   [124] *Id.*

As to legal considerations of cost, however, a land use approach to disability may vary from that of a typical civil rights approach, and it is therefore important to understand the cost-related issues when seeking better communication among land use regulators and disability rights advocates. Cost and benefit analsysis is relevant to evaluating a reasonable accommodation in the planning and zoning process, as we saw in the cases of *IHS* and *WCS* discussed earlier in this chapter. Cost considerations may also be important because of the limitations on the police power imposed by the takings clause. For example, undue financial hardship may be construed as triggering a regulatory taking in some circumstances. At the same time, it should be noted that land use law is quite comfortable with regulatory outcomes that defy demand for economic efficiency and wealth maximization, and it has long been a view of land use law that a property owner is not entitled to make the highest and best use of her property. Likewise, planning and zoning regulations have been permitted to diminish property values to a considerable extent when done to protect and advance the public health, safety, welfare, and morals of the community. Consequently, the mere recognition of the fact that there are outside limits to the amount of resources that might be devoted to particular strategies for inclusive design does not mean that the quest for inclusion should be a slave to efficiency or that cost alone should be a determinate factor in providing for an inclusive design community.

Vande Zande v. Wisconsin Department of Administration

44 F.3d 538 (7th Cir. 1995)

OPINION

POSNER, Chief Judge. In 1990, Congress passed the Americans with Disabilities Act, 42 U.S.C. §§ 12101 et seq. The stated purpose is "to provide a clear and comprehensive national mandate for the elimination of discrimination against individuals with disabilities," said by Congress to be 43 million in number and growing. §§ 12101(a), (b)(1). Disability" is broadly defined. It includes not only "a physical or mental impairment that substantially limits one or more of the major life activities of [the disabled] individual," but also the state of "being regarded as having such an impairment." §§ 12102(2)(A), (C). The latter definition, although at first glance peculiar, actually makes a better fit with the elaborate preamble to the Act, in which people who have physical or mental impairments are compared to victims of racial and other invidious discrimination. Many such impairments are not in fact disabling but are believed to be so, and the people having them may be denied employment or otherwise shunned as a consequence. Such people, objectively capable of performing as well as the unimpaired, are analogous to capable workers discriminated against because of their skin color or some other vocationally irrelevant characteristic . . .

The more problematic case is that of an individual who has a vocationally relevant disability – an impairment such as blindness or paralysis that limits a major human capability, such as seeing or walking. In the common case in which such an impairment interferes with the individual's ability to perform up to the standards of the workplace, or increases the cost of employing him, hiring and firing decisions based on the impairment are not "discriminatory" in a sense closely analogous to employment discrimination on racial grounds. The draftsmen of the Act knew this. But they were unwilling to confine the concept of disability discrimination to cases in which the disability is irrelevant to the performance of the disabled person's job. Instead, they defined "discrimination" to include an employer's "not making reasonable accommodations to the known physical or mental limitations of an otherwise qualified individual with a disability who is an applicant or employee, unless . . . [the employer] can demonstrate that the accommodation would impose an undue hardship on the operation of the . . . [employer's] business." § 12112(b)(5)(A).

The term "reasonable accommodations" is not a legal novelty . . . Indeed, to a great extent the employment provisions of the . . . Act merely generalize to the economy as a whole the duties, including that of reasonable accommodation, that the regulations under the Rehabilitation Act imposed on federal agencies and federal contractors. We can therefore look to the decisions interpreting those regulations for clues to the meaning of the same terms in the new law.

It is plain enough what "accommodation" means. The employer must be willing to consider making changes in its ordinary work rules, facilities, terms, and conditions in order to enable a disabled individual to work. The difficult term is "reasonable." The plaintiff in our case, a paraplegic, argues in effect that the term just means apt or efficacious. An accommodation is reasonable, she believes, when it is tailored to the particular individual's disability. A ramp or lift is thus a reasonable accommodation for a person who like this plaintiff is confined to a wheelchair. Considerations of cost do not enter into the term as the plaintiff would have us construe it. Cost is, she argues, the domain of "undue hardship" (another term borrowed from the regulations under the Rehabilitation Act) – a safe harbor for an employer that can show that it would go broke or suffer other excruciating financial distress were it compelled to make a reasonable accommodation in the sense of one effective in enabling the disabled person to overcome the vocational effects of the disability.

These are questionable interpretations both of "reasonable" and of "undue hardship." To "accommodate" a disability is to make some change that will enable the disabled person to work. An unrelated, inefficacious change would not be an accommodation of the disability at all. So "reasonable" may be intended to qualify (in the sense of weaken) "accommodation," in just the same way that if one requires a "reasonable effort" of someone this means less than the maximum possible effort, or in law that the duty of "reasonable care," the cornerstone of the law of negligence, requires something less than the maximum possible care. It is understood in that law that in deciding what care is reasonable the court considers the cost of increased care. (This is explicit in Judge Learned Hand's famous formula for negligence. United States v. Carroll Towing Co., 159 F.2d 169, 173 (2d Cir. 1947).) Similar reasoning could be used to flesh out the meaning of the word "reasonable" in the term "reasonable accommodations." It would not follow that the costs and benefits of altering a workplace to enable a disabled person to work would always have to be quantified, or even that an accommodation would have to be deemed unreasonable if the cost exceeded the benefit however slightly. But, at the very least, the cost could not be disproportionate to the benefit. Even if an employer is so large or wealthy – or, like the principal defendant in this case, is a state, which can raise taxes in order to finance any accommodations that it must make to disabled employees – that it may not be able to plead "undue hardship," it would not be required to expend enormous sums in order to bring about a trivial improvement in the life of a disabled employee. If the nation's employers have potentially unlimited financial obligations to 43 million disabled persons, the Americans with Disabilities Act will have imposed an indirect tax potentially greater than the national debt. We do not find an intention to bring about such a radical result in either the language of the Act or its history. The preamble actually "markets" the Act as a cost saver, pointing to "billions of dollars in unnecessary expenses resulting from dependency and non-productivity." § 12101(a)(9). The savings will be illusory if employers are required to expend many more billions in accommodation than will be saved by enabling disabled people to work.

The concept of reasonable accommodation is at the heart of this case. The plaintiff sought a number of accommodations to her paraplegia that were turned down. The principal defendant as we have said is a state, which does not argue that the plaintiff's proposals were rejected because accepting them would have imposed undue hardship on the state or because they would not have done her any good. The district judge nevertheless granted summary judgment for the defendants on the ground that the evidence obtained in discovery, construed as favorably to the plaintiff as the record permitted, showed that they had gone as far to accommodate the plaintiff's demands as reasonableness, in a sense distinct from either aptness or hardship – a sense based, rather, on considerations of cost and proportionality – required. On this analysis, the function of the "undue hardship" safe harbor, like the "failing company" defense to antitrust liability (on which see International Shoe Co. v. FTC, 280 U.S. 291, 302, 74 L. Ed. 431, 50 S. Ct. 89 (1930); United States v. Greater Buffalo Press, Inc., 402 U.S. 549, 555, 29 L. Ed. 2d 170, 91 S. Ct. 1692 (1971); 4 Phillip Areeda & Donald F. Turner, Antitrust Law pp. 924–31 (1980)), is to excuse compliance by a firm that is financially distressed, even though the cost of the accommodation to the firm might be less than the benefit to disabled employees.

This interpretation of "undue hardship" is not inevitable – in fact probably is incorrect. It is a defined term in the Americans with Disabilities Act, and the definition is "an action requiring significant difficulty or expense," 42 U.S.C. § 12111(10)(A). The financial condition of the employer is only one consideration in determining whether an accommodation otherwise reasonable would impose an undue hardship. See 42 U.S.C. §§ 12111(1)(B)(ii), (iii). The legislative history equates "undue hardship" to "unduly costly." These are terms of relation. We must ask, "undue" in relation to what? Presumably (given the statutory definition and the legislative history) in relation to the benefits of the accommodation to the disabled worker as well as to the employer's resources.

So it seems that costs enter at two points in the analysis of claims to an accommodation to a disability. The employee must show that the accommodation is reasonable in the sense both of efficacious and of proportional to costs. Even if this prima facie showing is made, the employer has an opportunity to prove that upon more careful consideration the costs are excessive in relation either to the benefits of the accommodation or to the employer's financial survival or health. In a classic negligence case, the idiosyncrasies of the particular employer are irrelevant. Having above-average costs, or being in a precarious financial situation, is not a defense to negligence. One interpretation of "undue hardship" is that it permits an employer to escape liability if he can carry the burden of proving that a disability accommodation reasonable for a normal employer would break him. Barth v. Gelb, 303 U.S. App. D.C. 211, 2 F.3d 1180, 1187 (D.C. Cir. 1993).

Lori Vande Zande, aged 35, is paralyzed from the waist down as a result of a tumor of the spinal cord. Her paralysis makes her prone to develop pressure ulcers, treatment of which often requires that she stay at home for several weeks . . .

Vande Zande worked for the housing division of the state's department of administration for three years, beginning in January 1990 . . . her tasks were of a clerical, secretarial, and administrative assistant character. In order to enable her to do this work, the defendants, as she acknowledges, "made numerous accommodations relating to the plaintiff's disability." As examples, in her words, "they paid the landlord to have bathrooms modified and to have a step ramped; they bought special adjustable furniture for the plaintiff; they ordered and paid for one-half of the cost of a cot that the plaintiff needed for daily personal care at work; they sometimes adjusted the plaintiff's schedule to perform backup telephone duties to accommodate the plaintiff's medical appointments; they made changes to the plans for a locker room in the new state office building; and they agreed to provide some of the specific accommodations the plaintiff requested in her October 5, 1992 Reasonable Accommodation Request."

But she complains that the defendants did not go far enough . . .

Her . . . complaint has to do with the kitchenettes in the housing division's building, which are for the use of employees during lunch and coffee breaks. Both the sink and the counter in each of the kitchenettes were 36 inches high, which is too high for a person in a wheelchair. The building was under construction, and the kitchenettes not yet built, when the plaintiff complained about this feature of the design. But the defendants refused to alter the design to lower the sink and counter to 34 inches, the height convenient for a person in a wheelchair. Construction of the building had begun before the effective date of the Americans with Disabilities Act, and Vande Zande does not argue that the failure to include 34-inch sinks and counters in the design of the building violated the Act. She could not argue that; the Act is not retroactive. But she argues that once she brought the problem to the attention of her supervisors, they were obliged to lower the sink and counter, at least on the floor on which her office was located but possibly on the other floors in the building as well, since she might be moved to another floor. All that the defendants were willing to do was to install a shelf 34 inches high in the kitchenette area on Vande Zande's floor. That took care of the counter problem. As for the sink, the defendants took the position that since the plumbing was already in place it would be too costly to lower the sink and that the plaintiff could use the bathroom sink, which is 34 inches high.

Apparently it would have cost only about $150 to lower the sink on Vande Zande's floor; to lower it on all the floors might have cost as much as $2,000, though possibly less. Given the proximity of the bathroom sink, Vande Zande can hardly complain that the inaccessibility of the kitchenette sink interfered with her ability to work or with her physical comfort. Her argument rather is that forcing her to use the bathroom sink for activities (such as washing out her coffee cup) for which the other employees could use the kitchenette sink stigmatized her as different and inferior; she seeks an award of compensatory damages for the resulting emotional distress. We may assume without having to decide that emotional as well as physical barriers to the integration of disabled persons into the workforce are relevant in determining the reasonableness of an accommodation. But we do not think an employer has a duty to expend even modest amounts of money to bring about an absolute identity in working conditions between disabled and nondisabled workers. The creation of such a duty would be the inevitable consequence of deeming a failure to achieve identical conditions "stigmatizing." That is merely an epithet. We conclude that access to a particular sink, when access to an equivalent sink, conveniently located, is provided, is not a legal duty of an employer. The duty of reasonable accommodation is satisfied when the employer does what is necessary to enable the disabled worker to work in reasonable comfort.

AFFIRMED

Vande Zande deals with the requirement to provide a "reasonable accommodation" under Title II of the ADA. Although this case considers a different context, employment, the discussion of reasonable accommodation may be useful in working through the reasonable accommodation requirments in planning and zoning situations. Other standards are also set out under the ADA and its related legislation, such as the need to make public facilities, under Title II, accessible to the extent that compliance does not impose an "undue financial and administrative burden"[125] and, under Title III, the requirement that places of public accommodation be brought into compliance "to the maximum extent feasible."[126] Each of these standards contains a cost-limiting element: "reasonable accommodation," "undue burden," and "feasible." These are not the terms associated with a straight-up cost and benefit analysis nor with strict economic efficiency, but they are terms that acknowledge the scarcity of resources. As the court informs us in *Vande Zande*, the calculus of scarcity does not need to be exact, and the fact that costs may outweigh estimated benefits is not determinate of the limits of the legal requirements. Considering costs and thinking about the rational limits to spending to reshape the natural and built environment is not about an economist doing an economic analysis of law; rather, it is about lawyers taking recognition of the fact that law operates in a market context.[127] There are many important social values to be furthered by the law, and choices have to be made with respect to the way in which scarce private and public resources are deployed. These choices, to a large extent, are political matters to be determined by a political process of public choice.[128]

---

[125] 28 C.F.R. §35.150(a)(3) (2008).   [126] 28 C.F.R. §36.402(c) (2013).

[127] ROBIN PAUL MALLOY, LAW IN A MARKET CONTEXT: AN INTRODUCTION TO MARKET CONCEPTS AND LEGAL REASONING (2004); ROBIN PAUL MALLOY, LAW AND MARKET ECONOMY: REINTERPRETING VALUES OF LAW AND ECONOMICS (2004).

[128] MAXWELL L. STEARNS & TODD J. ZYWICKI, PUBLIC CHOICE CONCEPTS AND APPLICATIONS IN LAW (2009); DANIEL A. FARBER & PHILIP P. FRICKEY, LAW AND PUBLIC

Traditionally, the political framing of these choices has been in terms of a civil rights model based on race, but from a land use perspective, a civil rights model may be less than ideal for understanding the underlying land use issues. Mobility impairment, as the type of disability discussed in this book, is not, after all, an exact fit with some aspects of a civil rights model based on race. Mobility impairment is a medically based condition of low functional mobility, and it affects people without regard to race, religion, nationality, gender, and ethnicity. Moreover, as people age, everyone's functional mobility level declines. Mobility impairment involves gradient functionality, and addressing low functional mobility requires application of technology and the spending of scarce resources to adjust the natural environment to facilitate access for people of a wide range of abilities. In some ways, therefore, making the built environment fully accessible to everyone without regard to a person's level of functional mobility may impose costs, whereas elimination of arbitrary barriers based on race typically reduces cost.[129] Significantly, the point is not that certain actions should never be taken because of costs but that intelligent and deliberative planning should include a conversation about costs rather than simply avoiding the topic.[130]

An example of one area that may benefit from a cost-conscious approach is residential housing. As previously mentioned in this book, a police power approach should favor making all residential housing accessible for safe and

Choice: A Critical Introduction (1991); Jerry L. Mashaw, Greed, Chaos, & Government: Using Public Choice to Improve Public Law (1997); James M. Buchanan & Gordon Tullock, The Calculus of Consent: Logical Foundations of Constitutional Democracy (1962).

[129] For example, in eliminating racial discrimination, we moved from having two separate race-based drinking fountains to having just one (a cost savings). Under the ADA and related legislation, we have moved from having a single water fountain to having two positioned at different heights (an added cost).

[130] For some examples of the cost of accessible design, one can refer to a pricing guide for estimating the cost of making modifications to comply with the ADA. These sample estimates come from RSMEANS, ADA Compliance Pricing Guide (2d ed., 2004) (a collaboration between the Adaptive Environments Center and RSMEANS engineering staff). It should be noted that these pricing estimates were published in a 2004 book, and according to the Federal Reserve Bank of Minneapolis web calculator, an item costing $1.00 in 2004 would cost $1.25 in 2014. To make just two automobile parking spaces accessible in an already built surface parking lot requires four regular spaces. This reduces the number of parking spaces in the property owner's lot, and this is a cost in addition to the pricing guide cost, which focuses only on the cost of the work to convert the space. The estimated cost is $2,118 ($2,647 in 2014). *Id.* at 13. Constructing a new "switch-back" ramp at a building entranceway, $12,020 ($15,025 in 2014); a new "dog-leg" ramp, $11,445 ($14,306 in 2014). *Id.* at 44–49. Installing a single-user vertical platform lift with a maximum height not to exceed eight feet, $11,071 ($13,839 in 2014). *Id.* at 63. Modifying an existing door, $1,000 plus ($1,250 in 2014). *Id.* at 82–85. Constructing a family/single-user accessible toilet room, $9,358 ($11,697 in 2014). *Id.* at 184–187. Installing a "roll-in" home shower, $3,905 ($4,811 in 2014). *Id.* at 198–199.

easy navigation. At the same time, there are multiple levels of accessibility, including various degrees of visitability and the more pervasive standards of universal design. It seems reasonable, therefore, to approach any expansion of enhanced accessibility to residential housing with a cost-conscious consideration of the effectiveness of achieving varying levels of inclusive design and use. In other words, the desire to make residential housing more accessible in the future ought not to mean that we necessarily must make 100 percent of the housing stock achieve the highest level of universal design. Under the police power, having a range of design and use alternatives may best promote the general health, safety, welfare, and morals of the public. These determinations ought to be part of an ongoing and deliberative planning process, with an appropriate appreciation for the role of local government in regulating property development and land use.

3.4 CONCLUSION

Federal regulations on accessibility already cover many aspects of the built environment. These regulations are based on a civil rights model and seek to provide equal opportunity of access to the built environment by all Americans. Under federal law, the local activities of planning and zoning have been identified as activities and services subject to the requirements of the ADA and related legislation. This means that local planning and zoning officials need to be cognizant of the requirements regarding inclusive design. Even with extensive federal regulations, there are still important planning issues that need to be addressed by local governments, and local governments should retain the power to coordinate land uses to improve accessibility even if they chose to regulate beyond the minimal levels of compliance required by federal law. Consequently, local governments have a continuing and important role to play in coordinating land uses and advancing inclusive design to protect and advance the public health, safety, welfare, and morals.

4

The market context of inclusive design

As we look to the future and think about the demographic changes confronting the United States and other developed countries, we see a need for holistic planning capable of meeting the lifelong needs of a rapidly aging population. In the United States by the year 2030, 25 percent of the population will be age 65 or older.[1] This forecast has a dramatic impact on the kind of communities we need to be building. It impacts building design, the need for better public transit, and a variety of other lifestyle factors. These needs will coincide with greater attention to "green development," "sustainable development," and efforts to reduce our carbon footprint.[2] In one form or another, we will be rethinking many of the principles made popular by the movement to "new urbanism": making places more walkable and navigable while replicating a sense of small, identifiable neighborhoods within broader regional and urban landscapes.[3] The overall effort is one of making our communities inclusive and accessible so that everyone can easily and safely age in place without being unduly limited by low or declining mobility.

---

[1] DEP'T OF HEALTH AND HUMAN SERVS., ADMIN. ON AGING, A PROFILE OF OLDER AMERICANS: 2010, www.aoa.gov/AoARoot/Aging_Statistics/Profile/2010/4.aspx (last modified Feb. 25, 2011).

[2] See WILLIAM H. HUDNUT, III, CHANGING METROPOLITAN AMERICA: PLANNING FOR A SUSTAINABLE FUTURE (2008); Keith H. Hirokawa, *At Home with Nature: Early Reflections on Green Building Laws and the Transformation of the Built Environment*, 39 ENVTL. L. 507 (2009); Keith H. Hirokawa, *Sustaining Ecosystem Services through Local Environmental Law*, 28 PACE L. REV. 760 (2011); Sarah B. Schindler, *Following Industry's LEED®: Municipal Adoption of Private Green Building Standards*, 62 FLA. L. REV. 285 (2010).

[3] James A. Kushner, *Smart Growth, New Urbanism and Diversity: Progressive Planning Movements in America and Their Impact on Poor and Minority Ethnic Populations*, 21 UCLA J. ENVTL. L. & POL'Y 45 (2002–2003); Jeremy R. Meredith, *Sprawl and the New Urbanist Solution*, 89 VA. L. REV. 447 (2003).

In planning for greater accessibility, it is important to understand some of the market dynamics related to inclusive design and the built environment. A market-based approach to inclusive design might suggest that to the extent that inclusive design is valuable and desired by consumers, it will be provided by private market actors. In other words, in a market that values inclusive design, people should be willing to contract for, and pay for, the desired outcomes. The underlying assumption of this viewpoint is that private individuals bargaining in the marketplace can achieve results that simultaneously maximize both private and public benefits. This assumption traces its roots all the way back to Adam Smith and his famous metaphor of the invisible hand, wherein Smith suggested that private individuals acting in their own self-interest promote the public good even though it is no part of their original intention.[4] This means that private and public benefits are invariant. As we know, however, from counterexamples, such as the tragedy of the commons, the prisoner's dilemma, and the problem of transaction costs more generally, there is often variance between private and public interest.[5] Under the invariance model of the invisible hand, consumers of housing, office space, shopping centers, and other such facilities should drive the demand for inclusive design, and builders should meet the demand to satisfy consumer preferences. This outcome would reflect the direct and indirect preferences of such groups as buyers, renters, shoppers, and employees who make use of the various facilities. In this approach, inclusive design would generally be considered a private market matter subject to price driven competition to produce the products, including the uses and designs, desired by consumers. This outcome is not what we observe, however.

In Chapter 2, we discussed the traditional foundations for land regulation under the police power. That chapter focused on using land regulation to prevent a nuisance and on the use of the police power to prevent harms while addressing externalities and spillovers. We also discussed the role that transaction costs and other variables play in making it difficult for individuals to coordinate property development in an effective way that advances a property owner's self-interest while at the same time promoting the public health, safety, welfare, and morals. This chapter explores more particularized reasons

---

[4] ROBIN PAUL MALLOY, LAW AND MARKET ECONOMY: REINTERPRETING THE VALUES OF LAW AND ECONOMICS 90 (2000); ROBIN PAUL MALLOY, LAW IN A MARKET CONTEXT: AN INTRODUCTION TO MARKET CONCEPTS IN LEGAL REASONING 27–30 (2004); Robin Paul Malloy, *Adam Smith in the Courts of the United States*, 56 LOY. L. REV. 33 (2010); Robin Paul Malloy, *Mortgage Market Reform and the Fallacy of Self-Correcting Markets*, 30 PACE L. REV. 79 (2009).

[5] *See* sources cited *supra* note 4.

for public land regulation with respect to planning and zoning for accessible communities. It focuses on the public nature of property and on the network relationship among individual properties and land uses. Consequently, this chapter explores additional reasons, beyond those discussed in Chapter 2, for the public regulation of property development. The reasons offered in this chapter expand on those examined earlier with respect to the police power. The ideas presented in this chapter provide additional reasons for using the police power to make communities more accessible – even though the reasons discussed in Chapter 2 are probably sufficient on their own. In proceeding, the chapter first addresses the public nature of private property by focusing on ways in which even private residential housing markets express a public interest and a public "subsidy," thus undermining much of the force behind assertions that the public should have no say about the design and use preferences of private property owners. This also includes consideration of other ways that property markets may function to create variance between private and public interests. The second part of the chapter explores the idea that the market for inclusive design is different from that of other ordinary production goods because of the "network" nature of the built environment and should therefore not be guided by the assumption of invariance implicit in the idealized "free market" and invisible hand model. This network aspect of the built environment offers an additional rationale for land use regulation in contravention of self-interested market choice in the coordination of property development.

4.1 PUBLIC NATURE OF PRIVATE PROPERTY

Encouraging private homeownership has long been a public policy goal in the United States.[6] Adequate and affordable housing is important. Currently approximately 657 to 70 percent of Americans own their own homes.[7] This means, of course, that about 30 percent do not. For those who do not currently own a home, there may be multiple reasons. These reasons may include the voluntary choice to be a renter, or it may be that private housing is too

---

[6]   U.S. Dep't of Treas. & U.S. Dep't of Hous. & Urban Dev., Reforming America's Housing Finance Market: A Report to Congress (2011); Tim Iglesias, *A Place to Call Home? Affordable Housing Issues in America: Our Pluralist Housing Ethics and the Struggle for Affordability*, 42 Wake Forest L. Rev. 511 (2007); Julie Farrell Curtin & Lance Bocarsly, *CLTS: A Growing Trend in Affordable Home Ownership*, 17 J. Affordable Hous. & Cmty. Dev. L. 367, 368 (2008).

[7]   *See* Robin Paul Malloy & James Charles Smith, Real Estate Transactions 315–358; 375–418 (4th ed. 2013) (discussing government support for housing, mortgage markets and insurance through such things as VA and FHA loans); Grant S. Nelson & Dale A. Whitman, Real Estate Finance Law 916–1011 (5th ed. 2007).

expensive. Many people find that they are involuntary renters. They are in rental housing because they lack the income, employment history, savings, and access to credit necessary to become an owner. Even with an adequate monthly income, it is difficult for some people to save enough for the down payment and closing costs. In fact, many home buyers are people that already own a home and who are simply moving on to buy a different one. The most difficult hurdle to homeownership is, therefore, the inability to move from renting (or residing for free with a friend or family member) to owning a *first* home.

Although the average rate of homeownership in the United States is around 65–70 percent, homeownership rates differ by race, with a significant disparity between whites and Asians on the high end and blacks and Latinos on the low end.[8] Correspondingly, mortgage application approval and denial rates also reveal similar disparities, although gains in each area have been made by "people of color" over the past few years.[9]

In many instances, people may be homeowners and yet find themselves underhoused, in housing of poor quality, or located in undesirable areas (areas of urban decay or rural poverty). The overwhelming majority of housing in both the rental and ownership markets is private. In addition to the private sector, we also have a much smaller yet significant number of people living in public and publicly subsidized housing. Public housing may be directly owned, regulated, or subsidized by the government.

Although much progress has been achieved in making the built environment more accessible, particularly with respect to public or common spaces, private single-family residential housing remains largely unable to be freely and safely visited by people with mobility impairment. This is a significant problem, because private residential housing makes up a significant part of the private land uses in many communities, and because the lack of inclusive design here and on other private properties truncates the socioeconomic relationships of a large, diverse, and growing population within our community. The problem is not simply localized because barriers to inclusion exist across the built environment and impact the free and safe movement of

---

[8] U.S. Dep't of Hous. & Urban Dev. & U.S. Dep't of Commerce, No. H150/05, American Housing Survey for the United States: 2005, at 42–43, tbl. 2-1 (2006), *available at* www.census.gov/prod/2006pubs/h150-05.pdf (last visited Oct. 20, 2013) (indicating that 68.8 percent of housing units are owner occupied, per this 2005 report; the rest are renter occupied); *see also* Malloy & Smith, *supra* note 7, at 315 (indicating variance in ownerships by race, with whites having a much higher rate of ownership than other identified racial groups).

[9] Carol N. Brown, *Intent and Empirics: Race to the Subprime*, 93 Marq. L. Rev. 907 (2010).

people in interregional exchanges. For example, people with mobility impairment may have difficulty in moving from one community to another when many of the residential housing options in the new community are not readily accessible, and attendance at conferences and meetings may be limiting to some prospective participants if the venues have barriers to safe and easy navigation for those with low functional mobility. The lack of inclusive design can also raise potential difficulty in responding quickly to emergency rehousing needs in the wake of disasters such as Hurricane Katrina, Superstorm Sandy, and the Moore, Oklahoma, tornado.[10] In these situations, emergency relocation is made more difficult than it could be because so few housing structures are currently accessible to people with mobility impairment.[11] This makes it harder for families to exercise self-help, because many family members have houses without inclusive design, and their homes may pose problems for a relocated family member with mobility impairment. This means that more time and effort are required to safely rehouse people during an emergency and that the rehousing is in some ways more dependent on government rather than on individuals being able to easily help each other.

Many residential homes are poorly designed in terms of accessibility. My own tri-level home, for instance, is difficult to access and navigate, and like many people, this was not something that I noticed until I had a family member unable to easily and safely enter my home and navigate its interior. Some of the difficulties posed by my home are that every entrance into the home has a number of steps. Not only are all three entrances to my home subject to access barriers, but once a person enters my home through the main entrance, she has to deal with a sunken living room (2 steps down from the entrance hall), a 2-step rise to my dining room, a small first-floor powder

---

[10] *See* LAW AND RECOVERY FROM DISASTER: HURRICANE KATRINA (Robin Paul Malloy ed. 2009); Manuel Roig-Franzia & Spencer Hsu, *Many Evacuated, but Thousands Still Waiting*, WASH. POST (Sept. 4, 2005), www.washingtonpost.com/wp-dyn/content/article/2005/09/03/AR2005090301680_pf.html; Todd S. Purdum, *Across U.S., Outrage at Response*, N.Y. TIMES (Sept. 3, 2005), www.nytimes.com/2005/09/03/national/nationalspecial/03voices.html; Marc Santora & Benjamin Weiser, *Court Says New York Neglected Disabled in Emergencies*, N.Y. TIMES (Nov. 7, 2013), www.nytimes.com/2013/11/08/nyregion/new-yorks-emergency-plans-violate-disabilities-act-judge-says.html. *See generally* DANIEL FITZPATRICK ET AL., PROPERTY AND SOCIAL RESILIENCE IN TIMES OF CONFLICT: LAND, CUSTOM AND LAW IN EAST TIMOR (Robin Paul Malloy ed. 2012). *See generally* DISASTERS AND THE LAW: KATRINA AND BEYOND (Daniel A. Farber and Jim Chen, 2006); John A. Lovett, *Property and Radically Changed Circumstances: Hurricane Katrina and Beyond*, 74 TENN. L. REV. 463 (2007).
[11] Robin Paul Malloy, *Inclusion by Design: Accessible Housing and Mobility Impairment*, 60 HASTINGS L. J. 711, 736–737 (2009).

room with a door and interior space too narrow for a wheelchair or walker, a 7-step rise to a quasi-accessible master bathroom and all of the bedrooms, and a 14-step barrier to our lower-level family and activity room. Inaccessible bathrooms and bathrooms with bathtubs that are unable to be entered by a person with mobility impairment can make for unsanitary conditions when housing a person with low functional mobility.

Unsanitary conditions arise when bathrooms are difficult to navigate because they are too small to accommodate a wheelchair or a walker or when bathroom fixtures impose barriers to use by a person with mobility impairment (such as when a bathtub is inaccessible). In fact, these difficulties were observed when people with disability had to be rehoused in emergency shelters after Hurricane Katrina. Many of the shelters and rehousing options did not have readily accessible bathrooms, and as a result, a number of people with mobility impairment experienced great difficulty. Design difficulties of this type make such housing fall below a visitability standard, much less meeting some broader standard of universal design. They also raise concerns about the public health, safety, welfare, and morals and should be the subject of comprehensive planning to ensure greater accessibility.

Despite these general concerns about inclusive design in private housing, there is difficulty in getting some people to understand the need to deal with changing demographics and to address the needs of people with mobility impairment. In terms of residential housing, there is still a sense by some people that a private home is a person's "castle" and, as such, the owner should have complete control over design preferences, even if these preferences are exclusionary.[12] This view seems to be based on an overly idealized sense of people acquiring property without any support or infrastructure provided by the government or by the public at large. In reality, however, housing and property development markets are national in scope and heavily influenced by government policy and programming. Although we see housing units constructed on local lots, the market supporting this construction is national and international in scope. The funding for construction and for residential home mortgages is funneled through fully integrated and global financial markets. America would be greatly underhoused but for the financial resources that

[12] *See* Eric R. Claeys, *Kelo, the Castle, and Natural Property Rights*, in PRIVATE PROPERTY, COMMUNITY, AND EMINENT DOMAIN 36–55 (Robin Paul Malloy ed. 2008); Michael Allan Wolf, *Hysteria v. History: Public Use in the Public Eye*, in PRIVATE PROPERTY, COMMUNITY, AND EMINENT DOMAIN (Robin Paul Malloy ed. 2008); Jonathan L. Hafetz, *A Man's Home Is His Castle? Reflections on the Home, the Family, and Privacy during the Late Nineteenth and Early Twentieth Centuries*, 8 WM. & MARY J. WOMEN & L. 175 (2002).

are brought into local markets by complex secondary mortgage market and financial market operations, facilitated by government.[13]

Realtors and a variety of other service providers for locally built housing construction also operate on a national scale. Likewise, the production of the construction supplies and equipment needed for building residential housing is national in scope and not simply local. Moreover, government (public) support for this activity occurs at multiple levels through such things as the use of insured lending institutions; regulated financial markets created by and directly and indirectly supported by the public; tax deductions and credits; and guaranteed, insured, and subsidized mortgages for buyers.[14] Local construction activities are heavily dependent on institutions expressing strong public characteristics, such as banks, mortgage markets, and networks of interstate commerce. Government and government-related entities support mortgage markets and the development of uniform mortgage documentation.[15] The government also supports programming, such as Veterans Administration and Federal Housing Administration lending, and the government built the infrastructure needed for a strong and efficient primary and secondary mortgage market.[16] In addition, homeowners are assisted in their efforts to acquire housing by subsidies extended via the mortgage interest rate deduction on their federal income tax returns.[17] Private housing markets also benefit from government bailouts of lenders. The most recent example of this was the subprime mortgage disaster of 2008, and another not-so-distant example includes the bailout of the savings and loan industry in the 1980s.[18] All of this suggests that

[13] MALLOY & SMITH, *supra* note 7, at 400–401; Malloy, *Mortgage Market Reform, supra* note 4.
[14] *See* 26 U.S.C. § 163 (2006).
[15] Robin Paul Malloy, *The Secondary Mortgage Market: A Catalyst for Change in Real Estate Transactions*, 39 Sw. L. J. 991 (1986); David J. Reiss, *Reforming the Residential Mortgage-Backed Securities Market*, 35 HAMLINE L. REV. 475 (2012).
[16] *FHA Loan for Homeowners*, Federal Housing Administration, www.fha.com/fha_loan (last visited Oct. 21, 2013); *Single Family FHA Insured Mortgage Programs*, U.S. Department of Housing and Urban Development, http://portal.hud.gov/hudportal/HUD?src=/program_offices /housing/sfh/insured (last visited Oct. 21, 2013); *Home Loans*, Veterans Benefits Administration, www.benefits.va.gov/homeloans/ (last visited Oct. 21, 2013).
[17] *See* 26 U.S.C. § 163 (2006); INTERNAL REVENUE SERVICE, PUBLICATION 936, HOME MORTGAGE INTEREST DEDUCTION, *available at* www.irs.gov/publications/p936/ar02.html (last visited Oct. 21, 2013).
[18] *See* JAMES R. BARTH, THE GREAT SAVINGS AND LOAN DEBACLE (1991); EDWARD J. KANE, THE S&L INSURANCE MESS: HOW DID IT HAPPEN? (1989); Timothy Curry & Lynn Shibut, *The Cost of the Savings and Loan Crisis: Truth and Consequences, FDIC Banking Review*, in FDIC BANKING REVIEW (2000); *The Savings and Loan Crisis and Its Relationship to Banking, in* HISTORY OF THE EIGHTIES — LESSONS FOR THE FUTURE: AN EXAMINATION OF THE BANKING CRISES OF THE 1980S AND EARLY 1990S (1997).

the claim to complete control over housing design preferences by an individual are rather thin. A strong public element to so-called private housing in the United States makes the objection to public regulation of basic design preferences less persuasive.

Another significant consideration regarding the thinness of the private property as "my castle" claim is the fact that private housing units and structures stay in the housing stock much longer than the occupation time of a typical owner. Whereas an average homeowner may occupy a home for 7–10 years, the average age of a unit in our national housing stock is 30–40 years,[19] with some 25 percent of housing being in excess of 70 years old.[20] Thus, we see that housing units enter the market and stay in service for a long number of years. Each of these units becomes part of our national housing stock. Significantly, while individual housing units remain in the national housing stock for 20, 40, 70, or even 100 years, the typical American moves once every 7–10 years.[21] This means that an individual home buyer, contracting in his or her own self-interest with a private developer for particular design features, fails to account for the long-term social consequences of those personal design preferences. For example, assume a person acquires land and hires a builder to construct a house on the property. The property owner may instruct the builder to include steps leading to the front door and to use relatively narrow doorways and hallways, as well as keeping the first-floor bathroom small so that space can be allocated for other uses on the main floor, such as for a breakfast nook.

---

[19] Malloy, *Inclusion by Design*, *supra* note 11, at 726; How We Are Housed: Results from the 1999 American Housing Survey, www.huduser.org/periodicals/ushmc/fall00/summary-2.html (last visited Oct. 13, 2013).

[20] Malloy, *Inclusion by Design*, *supra* note 11, at 726; How We Are Housed: Results from the 1999 American Housing Survey, *supra* note 19.

[21] Malloy, *Inclusion by Design*, *supra* note 11, at 726. Mobility/moving by Americans measured in terms of percentage of people living in a new location in a five-year period indicates that 31.2 percent of owner-occupiers moved and 72 percent of renters moved at least once in the time period of 1990 to 1995. Jason P. Schachter, U.S. Census Bureau, Report No. P23-200, Geographical Mobility: Special Studies, 1990–1995, at 2 (2000), *available at* www.census.gov/prod/2000pubs/p23-200.pdf. Rate of moving varies by age with the rate of moving between the years 1995 and 2000 being at 64.9 percent for people age 25–39; 34.2 percent for those aged 40–64; and 23.3 percent for those aged 65 and older. Rachel S. Franklin, U.S. Census Bureau, Report No. CENSR-12, Migration of the Young, Single, and College Educated: 1995 to 2000, at 3 (2003), *available at* www.census.gov/prod/2003pubs/censr-12.pdf. For married and college-educated adults aged 25–39, the rate was 72.3 percent, and for single and college-educated adults in this same age group, the rate was 75 percent. *Id.* Another report puts the rate of moving at 22.8 percent for people age 65 and older during the period 1995–2000. Wan He & Jason P. Schachter, U.S. Census Bureau, Report No. CENSR-10, Internal Migration of the Older Population: 1995 to 2000, at 2 (2003), *available at* www.census.gov/prod/2003pubs/censr-10.pdf.

The owner may feel that all of these design preferences should be honored inasmuch as she is paying for the house. The problems that may arise with these preferences are threefold. First, the owner may have high functional mobility at the time of building the house and at a later date develop low functional mobility. Second, the owner may have a family member or friend that over time develops mobility impairment and then is unable to safely and easily navigate the home, becoming unable to visit. Third, the owner is only likely to occupy the house for a small portion of the useful life of the structure. When she moves out, the house continues to have exclusionary barriers to a significant and growing part of our population. Consequently, when the original owner was making decisions about design preferences, she was probably not taking fully into account the costs of those design choices over time and the implications for others who will occupy, visit, or be on the property over the many years of its useful life. This is how private parties, acting out of self-interest in the housing market, often miscalculate the costs and benefits of inclusive design housing. They are not forced to internalize the costs that will be imposed on others over time as a result of their own exclusionary design preferences, and thus they end up overproducing homes with exclusionary barriers and underproducing inclusionary houses. The results of these miscalculations cause exclusionary ripple effects across time, and this negative spillover is repeated on a large scale across the national housing stock. Therefore, we have to be mindful of the fact that accessibility is not just a question with respect to current occupants. Current occupants may not have mobility impairment, but they may have friends, relatives, grandparents, or neighbors with mobility impairment. At some point in the future, they may develop a temporary or permanent impairment as the result of an accident, aging, or other incident that puts them in a wheelchair or requires them to use a walker, crutches, or a cane. Our housing stock must, therefore, be designed and built for a dynamic and aging population over time.

In the private homeownership market, developers often build products assumed to meet the personal preferences of their buyers, and the assertion is made that to the greatest extent possible, private homes should reflect individual preferences rather than government dictates. For the most part, however, these private preferences are expressed in the context of prefabricated housing units or preconstruction design templates. In other words, people are not going into the process asking to have inaccessible doorways and homes. They are being shown inaccessible designs and housing products and are selecting based on preferences for other elements such as layout, colors, and construction materials. Only at the high end of the housing market is there any significant amount of custom design in housing construction. Thus, core

accessibility issues are driven not so much by intentional consumer preferences as by prepackaged and prefabricated housing designs.

In addition to these reasons for underproduction of inclusive design housing,
some developers just do not want to update their building work because they
are resistant to change and prefer to follow path-dependent designs of the
past rather than invest in learning about new approaches and designs. Inertia
is a powerful defender of the status quo. Inertia may also be cheaper if it
permits a builder to use prefabricated components that are mass-produced.
For example, if the standard doorway is 30 inches wide, building doorways
to a 30-inch specification is cheaper than doing a custom order based on
specifications of 36-inches. Conversely, once the industry standard is adjusted
to a new specification, such as 36 inch doorways, the economics of the situation
generally changes in favor of the new standard, which becomes prefabricated
and mass produced.

Another reason for resisting inclusive designs in residential housing has
to do with what I have referred to as "amenity pricing." Because developers
may believe that price and profit can be enhanced by allocating scarce square
footage inside the housing unit to features other than general accessibility, they
are reluctant to sign on to a national standard for inclusive design that expands
the space within the structure needed for hallways, bathrooms, and other
accessibility features. Many developers would rather offer an exclusionary
house design with one and a half bathrooms than an inclusionary one with
only one bathroom. More bathrooms add market value, whereas wider hallways
and bigger bathrooms simply allocate more precious square footage to what is
already there. When hallways and bathrooms are kept small and exclusionary,
some square footage can be reallocated to other defined amenities with higher
consumer appeal (another bathroom, a bigger kitchen with a breakfast nook,
an additional closet, etc.). After all, builders and realtors generally sell houses
by advertising amenities such as one and a half baths and not by advertising
36-inch-wide hallways. The problem with this, of course, is that self-interested
consumers are drawn to these other amenity options because they do not
absorb the full cost of adding to our exclusionary housing stock, and they do
not account for the externality of generating truncated social networks for the
mobility impaired.

Some builders and developers have opposed inclusive design standards
because they think it will drive up their costs. Of course, many building code
features can be opposed for similar reasons. Although costs are important to
keeping housing affordable, cost alone is not the only value factor to consider
when building safe and socially desirable housing. Housing costs are probably
less significant to most developers than loss of control with respect to flexible

allocation of square footage to enhance amenity pricing inside the unit. In contrast to developers who express concern about housing costs, we find that others have willingly adopted visitability standards because they have found it to be another marketing tool in some markets that may outweigh any added costs. There are other complaints about inclusionary housing standards. In addition to cost-based complaints, some developers assert that inclusionary features are impractical, go beyond the scope and purposes of building codes, and unfairly restrict consumer choice. These concerns seem to be outweighed by the negative implications of exclusionary housing and by the reality of the market imperfections on which they are based. Likewise, they underappreciate the health and safety issues of noninclusive design housing. Exclusionary designs are not costless; they impose costs on a significant number of people who are unable to safely and easily navigate them.

As to the cost of achieving a visitability standard of inclusion, there is some debate. Some of the debate likely stems from the fact that houses can be built in a variety of ways and in a number of geographically dissimilar locations. These variables obviously affect the cost. Despite these many variables, some numbers may be less difficult to determine. A paper by the Center for Inclusive Design and Environmental Access (IDEA; published in 2005) stated that a zero-step entrance would only add $150 to the cost of new construction.[22] Additionally, the cost of having wider interior doors could be as little as $50 if they are put in during construction.[23] Adding these features later on is significantly more costly. For example, the cost of having a no-step entrance added later would be around $1,000.[24] Also, the cost of widening the doors after construction could be as much as $700.[25] Adjusting these cost estimates for changes in the value of the dollar since the original publication date of the report would increase them by 20 percent in terms of 2013 dollars ($1.20 is required in 2013 to purchase what was able to be acquired for $1.00 in 2005). In addition to the IDEA report, a study in Canada indicated a higher cost for basic visitability improvements (between $2,500 and $5,000 in U.S. dollars per housing unit), but a key variable in any cost analysis will be local environmental conditions for construction (on a hillside, or on sandy soil or rocky soil, for instance). These costs, though they do not seem high, are not insignificant, because it is estimated that for every 1 percent increase in the cost of housing, 1 million

---

[22] *See* Jordana L. Maisel, Ctr. for Inclusive Design & Envtl. Access (IDEA), Visitability as an Approach to Inclusive Housing Design and Community Development: A Look at Its Emergence, Growth, and Challenges 5 (2005). *See also* note 126 of Chapter 3 for additional comparative cost information.

[23] *Id.*   [24] *Id.*   [25] *Id.*

people are potentially disqualified from buying a home.[26] Moreover, these cost increases relate to simple design changes that make a property visitable, and efforts at going beyond this basic level of accessibility may impose higher costs.

As a counterpoint to the potential costs of inclusive design, we should consider potential savings. To the extent that we can make homes more accessible, it will be possible for people to age in place for a longer period of time. This can slow down the relocation of aging Americans from private residential homes to institutional settings. This is important, because the average annual cost of being in an assisted-living facility in the United States in 2009 was $34,000, with high-cost communities, such as New York City, costing closer to $70,000.[27] Living in a nursing home is considerably more costly, at an average annual cost between $70,000 and $80,000, and as with assisted living, high-cost communities are even more expensive.[28] In 2004, $194 billion was spent on nursing home care in the United States.[29] The cost of assisted living and of nursing home care is very high, and many people relocate to these facilities when they have difficulty navigating their residential homes. Many may relocate earlier than might otherwise be required simply because of barriers to accessibility in the design and construction of their homes; this typically includes the presence of steps and unsafe bathrooms. If inclusive design standards in housing could simply keep people in their homes a year or two longer than otherwise, we would save billions of dollars nationally. When these potential savings are considered, the cost of inclusive design, be it $500 or $5,000 per housing unit, seems much less burdensome.

Even if wider hallways and larger bathrooms add no cost to new home construction, such design changes will affect the allocation of space within a structure. One home builder, for example, indicated to me that in his experience, inclusive design (as in making homes visitable) did raise the cost of construction, but the added cost for specific visitability features was not as big a contributor to the rise in overall construction price as was the fact that his customers expected to get an even bigger home out of the deal. His

[26] Nestor M. Davidson & Robin Paul Malloy, Affordable Housing and Public-Private Partnerships 215 (2009); Nat'l Ass'n of Home Builders, Households Priced Out by Higher House Prices and Interest Rates, www.nahb.org/generic. aspx?genericContentID=40372 (last visited Sept. 23, 2013).

[27] Lesley Alderman, *Making Home a Safer Place, Affordably*, N.Y. Times, July 18, 2009, at B1.

[28] Genworth Financial, Genworth Financial 2006 Cost of Care Survey: Nursing Homes, Assisted Living Facilities and Home Care Providers, *available at* http:// longtermcare.genworth.com/comweb/pdfs/long_term_care/Cost_Of_Care_Survey.pdf.

[29] Harriet L. Komisar & Lee Shirley Thompson, *National Spending for Long-Term Care*, Health Pol'y Inst. (Jan. 2007), www.ltc.georgetown.edu/pdfs/natspending2007.pdf.

customers expected to get all of the regular amenities of a standard home (in terms of number of rooms, bathrooms, etc.) while also allocating more space in the home to larger bathrooms, wider hallways, and bigger kitchens, all designed to accommodate a wheelchair user. Accounting for visitability features as added space (not being able to reallocate amenity space within the structure) translated into *adding* square footage to the structures, and thus added to the total cost of any given project. Perhaps the answer to this is that consumers need to adjust their preferences for space, especially given that the average size of the American home has gone up significantly since the 1950s, even though the average size of the typical family has substantially declined.[30]

Referring back to the case of Pima County, Arizona (discussed in Chapter 3), you will recall that before implementing its visitability ordinance, it did a study on the cost of visitability.[31] The court noted the study in its opinion. The results of the study corroborated the numbers stated in the paper by the Center for Inclusive Design and Environmental Access.[32] The study found that implementing the visitability standards (in the Pima County ordinance) would only cost about $100. Specifically, the court stated, "The Board of Supervisors could have rationally concluded that the benefit to the community in providing for the disabled justified the comparatively minimal cost of implementing the required design features." Even though these cost numbers are somewhat dated, they do suggest that making residential structures minimally visitable at the initial construction stage is relatively cheap, particularly when compared with the cost of postconstruction rehabilitation.

Given the asserted low cost of making homes visitable, it is surprising that enhanced accessibility has not seemed to have gathered as much grassroots support as "green" construction and sustainable development. A possible reason for this may be that whereas promoters of green buildings identify potential cost savings and payback periods for various energy savings improvements, there is little evidence to support direct cost savings to the typical home

---

[30] *See* MALLOY & SMITH, *supra* note 8, at 601 (citing U.S. CENSUS BUREAU, U.S. DEP'T OF COMMERCE, BRIEF NO. SB/95-18, HOME SWEET HOME — AMERICA'S HOUSING, 1973 TO 1993 (1995)); *cf.* U.S. DEP'T OF HOUS. & URBAN DEV. & U.S. DEP'T OF COMMERCE, NO. H150/05, AMERICAN HOUSING SURVEY FOR THE UNITED STATES: 2005, at 166–167 tbl. 3–18 (2006), *available at* www.census.gov/prod/2006pubs/h150–05.pdf (indicating that the median square footage of an owner-occupied single-family home was 1858 square feet (for two-person occupancy, the median is 1862 square feet)). New Construction Square Foot Costs: Home Construction Improvement, www.homeconstructionimprovement. com/2007/12/new-construction-square-foot-costs.html (last visited Oct. 13, 2013).

[31] Washburn v. Pima Cnty., 81 P. 3d 1030 (Ariz. App. 2003); *supra* Chapter 3.

[32] *See Pima Cnty.*, 81 P. 3d 1030; Maisel *supra* note 22, at 14.

buyer who invests in enhanced accessibility.[33] Although it is true that, as a society, we should be able to save money by allowing people to safely and easily age in place rather than having them prematurely relocate to higher-cost assisted-living and nursing homes, these savings are differed, difficult to quantify, and not necessarily attributed to the person making the initial investment.[34]

In the context of commercial properties, the cost of inclusive design must be considered in a slightly different way than from how it is done for residential properties. In the residential house, as we said, a large enough bathroom to accommodate a wheelchair user and having wider hallways may affect the size, shape, and number of rooms in the totality of the structure, but to a large extent, the costs are experienced on a one-shot basis; once paid for, it is done. With a commercial property, the property owner looks at the property as producing valuable income from cash flow based on such things as rent or sales per square foot. Consequently, if a person is operating a retail outlet or a restaurant, and more square feet are required for an ADA-accessible bathroom, and for space between aisles or tables capable of accommodating a wheelchair, the greater the income that will need to be generated per square foot of actual useable retail space. The commercial property owner does not have a one-time cost, as he experiences the cost of accessible construction plus an ongoing impact on the ability to generate cash flow on a useable square foot basis. In effect, the operating costs go up per square foot, in terms of opportunity costs with respect to the prior alternative uses of the space. This was the basis of the takings claim in the *Pinnock* case discussed in Chapter 2.[35] As a result of the requirement to expand the size of the bathroom in his restaurant (a place of public accommodation), Pinnock had to eliminate a number of tables and seats, and this cut into revenue.

---

[33] Dennis Kennedy, *Go Green, Save Green: 8 Ideas to Help the Planet, Your Pocketbook*, 94 A.B.A. 36 (2008); Gregory H. Kats, *Green Building Costs and Financial Benefits*, MASS. TECH. COLLABORATIVE (2003); Judith Heerwagen, *Sustainable Design Can Be an Asset to the Bottom Line*, ENVTL. DESIGN & CONSTR. (2002).

[34] If we require homes to be built to be more accessible and to be easily modified as people age, society may well reap major benefits and cost savings as people are better able to age in place rather than having to locate to higher-cost assisted-living communities. In the short run, however, young and healthy home buyers may not readily appreciate these benefits at the time they purchase a new home because they do not anticipate having mobility impairment. This is similar to the issue of getting young people to participate in the Affordable Care Act for health insurance when they feel that the cost may not be merited because they are currently young and healthy.

[35] Pinnock v. Int'l House of Pancakes, 844 F. Supp. 574 (S.D. Cal. 1993), *cert. denied*, 512 U.S. 1228 (1994); *supra* Chapter 2.

From a cost-awareness perspective, accessible design and construction costs something, and it typically requires additional costs for engagement of consultants and experts to ensure compliance with federal disability construction design guidelines. These costs are sometimes difficult to calculate and are frequently less than transparent. For example, in the case of a commercial retail establishment or restaurant, the business owner may readily appreciate the potential cost of accessibility guidelines, but his customers typically only experience a roomier and more accessible environment. To the extent that competitive pressures permit it, the business owner may pass the costs of accessibility on to customers in the form of higher prices, but even when costs are passed on, the customers are not likely to appreciate the reason for the higher prices, and in this way, the cost of accessibility is less than transparent.[36] In a similar way, the costs of accessibility to public buildings and for government services also tend to lack transparency because these costs are generally covered indirectly through tax revenues such that users of the buildings and services do not directly appreciate the cost of accessibility.

These cash flow opportunity costs, as well as the physical costs of construction, should be accounted for in planning with respect to inclusive design because the information can make for better planning and decision making. At the same time, cost alone should not drive decisions about the public health, safety, welfare, and morals. After all, a requirement for having a bathroom in the first instance, no matter how small, reduces the space available for tables and chairs, and fire codes, for example, also limit the number of people who can be invited in at any given time despite the fact that potentially greater numbers of people might physically fit within a given structure. Many land use regulations impose costs or put pressure on profitability; this alone is not a fact that determines what a community should do. Understanding costs relative to alternative strategies for achieving various goals makes for better decision making, but in a world of limited resources, decisions still need to be made. To a large extent, as long as everyone has to confront similar requirements, there is no competitive disadvantage to inclusive design, but total resources allocated by society to the built environment may be greater than otherwise.

In conclusion, the built environment, including private residential housing, does not necessarily need to feature exclusionary design elements, such as multiple steps rather than ramps leading to the entranceway or doorways and

---

[36] *See* ROBERT COOTER & THOMAS ULEN, LAW & ECONOMICS 25–26 (3d ed. 2000); MALLOY, LAW AND MARKET ECONOMY, *supra* note 4; MALLOY, LAW IN A MARKET CONTEXT, *supra* note 4; RICHARD A. POSNER, ECONOMIC ANALYSIS OF LAW 279–283 (7th ed. 2007); OZ SHY, THE ECONOMICS OF NETWORK INDUSTRIES (2001).

hallways too narrow for wheelchair accessibility. The shape and the contours of the built environment largely reflect intentional design choices, and we can readily change many of these choices with careful and deliberate planning.

4.2 THE NETWORK NATURE OF INCLUSIVE DESIGN

There is another way to think about inclusive design as it affects the built environment. It may well be that we can learn a lot from thinking in terms of recent work done with respect to network goods[37] and applying some of what is being learned about networks to our understanding of communities and inclusive design.

The market for inclusive design is different from the market for ordinary production goods, and the difference implies further difficulty in expecting private market mechanisms to produce an appropriate level of accessibility across the built environment. First, the built environment, though built of many individual pieces, is itself an integrated network that, with regard to accessibility and sustainability, produces quality-of-life outcomes that are not fully expressed in the design of individual structures. The built environment is a kind of ecosystem that reflects interconnectivity among all of its component parts, even though the parts are produced by a mix of numerous private and public actors. This interconnectivity of the built environment more closely resembles the production of a network good than a typical market good, and this implicates a concern as to the ability of innumerable self-interested individuals to make choices that simultaneously advance the public interest. Second, because of the mixed market activity of private and public development efforts, there is a public goods aspect to the market for inclusive design, and public goods are typically underproduced under normal economic assumptions.[38] Third, certain externalities create a disconnection between the term of use and the useful life of many parts of the built environment such that the people making design choices have difficulty appreciating the long-term costs of their preferences. Fourth, land use decisions are not simply matters of economic calculus; they are informed by a number of factors, including social, political, cultural, and

---

[37] *See* SHY, *supra* note 36; Brett M. Frischmann, *An Economic Theory of Infrastructure and Commons Management*, 89 MINN. L. REV. 917 (2005). BRETT M. FRISCHMAN, INFRASTRUCTURE: THE SOCIAL VALUE OF SHARED RESOURCES (2012); YOCHAI BENKLER, THE WEALTH OF NETWORKS: HOW SOCIAL PRODUCTION TRANSFORMS MARKETS AND FREEDOM (2006); MANUEL CASTELLS, THE RISE OF NETWORK SOCIETY: THE INFORMATION AGE: ECONOMY, SOCIETY, AND CULTURE VOL. I (2020); KECHENG LIU, SEMIOTICS IN INFORMATION SYSTEMS ENGINEERING (2000).

[38] *See* sources cited *supra* note 4; Abraham Bell & Gideon Parchomovsky, *Of Property and Antiproperty*, 102 MICH. L. REV. 1 (2003).

aesthetic values. Fifth, with respect to people with mobility impairment, the law has already concluded that access and inclusion are important civil rights; thus, expressions of consumer-based preferences are largely limited to matters of how best to develop inclusive design communities and not the merits of any right to accessibility.

In considering the built environment as rendered more readily understandable in terms of the various towns, villages, and urban areas in which we live, it can be useful to think of them as a kind of "network enterprise." In this part of the chapter, therefore, discussion centers on the built environment in terms of a network that functions supportively for people of all ages and various capabilities.

At the outset, a network enterprise has certain characteristics that should inform our thinking. Such enterprises involve interrelated goods and services, and consumption is typified by the need to have a system rather than just an isolated good.[39] For example, to get value from a cell phone, you need a network phone service in addition to your communication device, and to get value from a computer, you need to have software to operate it.[40] Likewise, to get value from a DVD player, you need DVDs, and vice versa.[41] This is different than buying a glass of beer, which you might consume and enjoy with or without a hot dog or hamburger, as you can enjoy the beer all on its own. The same goes for something such as a banana or some fresh strawberries; these may be good when mixed with other foods or blended into drinks, but they can be fully enjoyed on their own – such is not the case with a cell phone, a computer, and a DVD player. With the cell phone, computer, and DVD player, the consumer has to look for the best system fit to get use and value out of the component products – and because the component parts of the system can vary by manufacturer and by other factors, the market interactions for network products are different than they are for goods that can be enjoyed on their own.

Before further explaining and applying network ideas to our understanding of the built environment, we must first think of the city as an enterprise, and then think of cities as in competition with each other. A city is a "collective good" – a network system of goods, services, cultural activities, businesses, neighborhoods, schools, housing choices, and integrated infrastructure. In the context of modern property development and land use regulation, consumers of the built environment shop the market for communities in terms of quality-of-life indicators; they do not simply buy a house, for example, by looking at its physical structure removed from its neighborhood and community context. The individual housing structure is given value by its identification with and

[39] Sources, *supra* note 37.   [40] *Id.*   [41] *Id.*

proximity to other valued qualities. Communities, thus, compete across a set of interconnected qualities for residents, businesses, and visitors. The focus on quality of life has enhanced the marketing of lifestyle communities – communities that employ legal covenants, restrictions, and other tools to structure a set of uses and lifestyle themes for particular demographics.[42] This has led to the increased production of planned unit developments, condominiums, subdivisions, and other assorted common interest communities.[43] Within an urban area and as between urban areas, consumers are making complex decisions about lifestyle choices. These decisions are being made not only by residential consumers but also by businesses and others as they think about the quality of life that a particular city can deliver relative to the costs and benefits of its given location, tax structure, climate, and other factors. A city is essentially an integrated system-based product. It is a networked product in the sense that even though component pieces may function without being in a city, the city has no significant meaning absent the bundling of a variety of component pieces. For example, a road or a sewer line can exist in the absence of a city, but a city, as an idealized lifestyle product or enterprise, really does not function in the absence of roads, sewers, and other basic infrastructure; a city is a system, and in buying into a city, one must try to evaluate the interrelated system and not just one component part. A city, as an enterprise, is also a system-based product that many consumers can use at the same time without necessarily diminishing the value and enjoyment of its use to others. I can go to the park at the same time as many others, I can go to the symphony while you go to the ball game, and I can go out to eat while you also go out to eat. Vibrant cities, no matter what their size, offer many choices, and although particular venues have their own constraints and limitations on use, the city as a lifestyle enterprise is very much open-ended and capable of being enjoyed by many people at the same time. In broader market terms, a city functions as a public good even if some of the component parts operate to limit use by private market mechanisms.

As among cities, there is frequently competition: competition to attract new businesses, to have better schools, to boost residential housing opportunities, and to raise revenue while controlling costs. Cities compete for such honors as being ranked in the top 10 for quality of life, for being an "All America" city, for

---

[42] Common interest communities provide a significant number of housing units. These communities are attractive to home buyers in part because they give homeowners a great deal of control over land uses within the community. MALLOY & SMITH, *supra* note 7, at 315–358.

[43] *See generally* Susan F. French, *Making Common Interest Communities Work: The Next Step,* 37 URB. L. 359 (2005); Wayne S. Hyatt, *Common Interest Communities: Evolution and Reinvention,* 31 J. MARSHALL L. REV. 303 (1997); Evan McKenzie, *Common Interest Housing in the Communities of Tomorrow,* 14 HOUS. POL'Y DEBATE 203 (2003).

being a safe city, a green city, a business-friendly city, and just about anything else that creates a positive lifestyle image for the collective and integrated system that makes up the given community.[44] Furthermore, consumers of the built environment value these kinds of distinctions as a way of identifying good lifestyle communities to move into or simply to confirm the quality of the place where they currently live.

With this general idea of a city as a network enterprise, let us develop the concept further by examining the key characteristics of network enterprises as outlined by Oz Shy in his work on networks.[45] These characteristics will help us establish criteria for thinking about a concept of network planning. Shy identified the following characteristics as central to network enterprises:

- Complementarity, compatibility, and standards
- Consumption externalities
- Switching costs and lock-in
- Significant economies of scale in production

In examining these characteristics, we can develop useful insights for understanding network planning with respect to the built environment, even if the idea of the city is not quite the kind of network enterprise on which Shy was focused in his work. The purpose is not to demonstrate a perfect fit between the ideas of network planning and Shy's work on network industries; the point is that the concept of a city as a network enterprise can facilitate useful thinking with respect to developing inclusive design communities that facilitate aging in place.

4.2.1 *Complementarity, compatibility, and standards*

When we think of a given community as a network enterprise, we have to start by mapping out the actual interconnections across the community, without regard to artificially determined legal and political boundaries among

---

[44] *See* Zack O'Malley Greenburg, *America's Most Livable Cities*, FORBES (Apr. 1, 2009, 5:15 PM), www.forbes.com/2009/04/01/cities-city-ten-lifestyle-real-estate-livable-cities. html (last visited Oct 22, 2013); *2014 All-America City Awards*, National Civic League, www.allamericacityaward.com/participate (last visited Oct. 22, 2013); Francesca Levy, *America's Safest Cities*, FORBES (Oct. 11, 2010, 7:10 PM), www.forbes.com/2010/10/11/ safest-cities-america-crime-accidents-lifestyle-real-estate-danger.html (last visited Oct. 22, 2013); Sophie Bushwick, *Top 10 Cities for Green Living*, SCIENTIFIC AMERICAN (Aug. 16, 2011), www.scientificamerican. com/article.cfm?id=top-10-cities-green-living (last visited Oct. 22, 2013); Carol Tice, *You're (Un)Welcome: Best and Worst Cities for Business 2013*, FORBES (April 4, 2013, 12:09 PM), www.forbes.com/sites/caroltice/2013/04/04/ youre-unwelcome-best-and-worst-cities-for-business-2013 (last visited Oct. 22, 2013).

[45] *See* SHY, *supra* note 36.

jurisdictions. Typically, an urban community, for example, includes the city center, outer-city neighborhoods, inner suburbs, and outer suburbs, with some rural connecting points. Within this geographic space, people live, work, shop, and play in various locations. From the point of view of a typical consumer-resident, the community is a seamless web of goods, services, and activities. The city functions as a bundle of complementary goods that collectively operate to give meaning and context to a certain lifestyle. Complementarity exists in the relationships between good residential housing and high-quality public schools; abundant employment opportunities and the ability to purchase good housing; good public infrastructure (such as roads) and the citing of businesses in the community; and high-quality police, fire, and health services and the value of local properties. These are only a few examples of complementarity within a city network. In addition, goods, services, and infrastructure have to function with complementarity across and among different jurisdictional boundaries. Highways, sewers, waterlines, and telephone lines are common examples of infrastructure that need to properly connect across a community for it to function effectively and maximize value for consumers of the overall built environment. The idea of complementarity means that consumers of the city are looking for a system of goods and services and not just one individualized product; housing is valued in relationship to schools, safety, distance from work, and a variety of other factors and not just in terms of a physical structure removed from a given environmental context. This means that cities have a variety of strategies available in figuring how best to compete with each other in offering lifestyle choices that serve a dynamic and ever-changing population.

To effectively manage complementarity, a system needs to have compatibility and standards. Just as a computer application needs to be compatible with the operating system, so too with respect to other complementary goods.[46] The same is true as to electrical current and standardized outlets and plugs. We have a standard protocol in the United States, but we learn from travel abroad that other countries have other operating standards. This means that when Americans travel to Europe or Europeans travel to the United States, they must invest in special outlet attachments to convert between the different electrical standards. It also means that electrical products manufactured in China have to have different specifications depending on the product destination. Such differences are also true in the specifications for automobiles in different countries. Thus, we know that compatibility implies agreed-on and uniform standards but that standards can sometimes vary with market context.[47]

[46] Id.   [47] Id.

In setting compatible and uniform standards, certain protocols have to be agreed on so that such things as high definition (HD) television signals can be picked up properly by all HD sets. Using different protocols for HD as between different television manufacturers and program providers would mean that not all sets could pick up differing HD signals. A compatible and uniform standard makes the overall market more efficient, even if there remains debate as to the best standards as between competing approaches to a given technology.

Compatibility and uniform standards are also important in dealing with property development and regulation. In the urban community context, consider the need to have roads and highways built to compatible standards so that they line up and safely carry traffic without disruption as one travels on a route that transcends several local jurisdictional authorities. Likewise, consider the interconnection of water and sewer lines among individual homes, among residential and commercial developments, and across jurisdictional lines. We do not want a 20-inch water or sewer line flowing into a 6-inch line, nor do we want lines built that do not match up for a proper connection between lines. The same is true with electrical service standards and many other input items that allow our built environment to function seamlessly in generating a certain quality of life for consumers.

In considering the specific problem of mobility impairment and inclusive design, we have very similar concerns. If people with mobility impairment are to effectively navigate a community, we need to make sure that inclusive design standards make various elements of the built environment compatible. If, for instance, doorways only need to be 28 inches wide (too narrow for a typical wheelchair), what good does it do to require interior hallways to be at least 32 inches wide to accommodate a person in a wheelchair? If a person cannot easily and safely enter a structure, it doesn't seem to matter that the hallways are wide enough for wheelchair use. Likewise, if stores and office buildings have to meet certain accessibility standards but houses and transportation systems do not, we end up with truncated networks and a lower quality of life because of the incompatibility. The tricky questions, of course, relate to the setting of appropriate standards and the determination of who should have the authority to set and enforce them. As I noted earlier in the book, there are multiple standards of inclusive design, visitability and universal design, and, within these two broad categories, various approaches promoted by different groups.

One way of approaching the matter of setting design standards begins with recognition that building design is distinguishable from coordination of land use. Accessible design involves setting standards and protocols governing shape, form, and function of the built environment, but standards of design do not necessarily dictate what gets built, where it is located, or how the land is used. In a sense, accessible design standards might be usefully compared to the kind of standards set for such things as HD television, mobile communications, and the Internet. The design and performance standards for these systems permit multiple suppliers to offer products and services in a way that enhances compatibility across the system. At the same time, consumers may enjoy choice in the selection of devices to access the system and may spend more or less on these devices based on the service desired. In the land use context, accessible design establishes the protocols and standards for compliance with minimal standards of functionality that can be used to guide numerous suppliers of buildings, roads, and other assorted property development products. These standards are most effectively provided by an organization or government-related entity with the ability to develop and implement national or global standards, as the case may be. Such standards make it possible for multiple suppliers to use standardized products and property development techniques in a cost-effective way. The actual approval and coordination of local land uses, however, seems more akin to the role of the personalized access devices used with respect to HD television or mobile communications. Control over local property development and coordination of local land uses are best understood and implemented by the people living in these communities. Traditionally, real property and the control of land use are matters of state and local law, and in a federal system such as that of the United States, there is no inherent advantage on the part of a distant federal government to better reflect the needs and preferences of local communities. Consequently, one way to address the setting of accessible design standards is exactly the way that it has been preceding in the United States: with design standards essentially developed and established at a national level, while states and local governments, exercising authority under the police power, control property development and the coordination of land uses.

4.2.2 *Consumption externalities*

The built environment implicates two major categories of consumption externalities.[48] The first of these involves a classic spillover externality, and the second involves a form of network externality. Both types raise concerns for the process of property development and land use regulation.

---

[48] *See* SHY, *supra* note 36, at 3; MALLOY, LAW IN A MARKET CONTEXT, *supra* note 36, at 117; MALLOY, LAW AND MARKET ECONOMY, *supra* note 36, at 97; COOTER & ULEN, *supra* note 36, at 40–42; POSNER, *supra* note 36, at 158–160.

Looking first at spillover externalities, these are the classic kinds of externalities that provide the traditional rationale for public land use regulation. Basically, a spillover externality occurs when a property owner does not have to fully internalize the cost of using her property and her use imposes costs on other, nearby property owners.[49] Sometimes such spillover effects can be significant enough to seriously diminish the use and enjoyment of another property, resulting in a private or public nuisance under the background legal rules of the common law. This may be the case when I use my property to operate a factory and the factory produces unreasonably loud noise or discharges dust and chemical particles into the ambient air, with the particles landing on an adjoining property, making the home dirty and causing respiratory problems for occupants. If I do not have to internalize the costs of the spillover, I do not take such costs into account when I make decisions about opening and operating my factory. If my actions are determined to be a nuisance, my factory may be legally shut down. If my actions are determined to be a threat to the health, safety, welfare, and morals of the public, I may have my use regulated under the state police power. In any event, the key point here is that in dealing with the built environment, we often encounter problems with spillover externalities.

An example to consider with respect to inclusive design involves the problem of dealing with residential housing that is designed with exclusionary features such as narrow doorways and multistep entranceways. Consumers will sometimes assert that they have a preference for such designs and, because it is their money paying for the home, they ought to be able to express their preferences without public interference. The problems with this argument are multiple. First, almost all residential housing is in some way supported or "subsidized" through government-supported mortgages, financial markets, tax incentives, and insurance.[50] All residential owners are to some degree facilitated in their ability to acquire homeownership by the public. Second, in the United States, the typical homeowner stays in a home for about 7 years, whereas the house may remain in the housing stock for upward of 75 or 100 years. The consequences of exclusionary design, thus, ripple across time as a negative eternality affecting the quality of life of potential future owners long after the original owner has moved out. The immediate parties to a residential home construction contract do not internalize the full cost of their design choices because

---

[49] *See* sources cited *supra* note 48. *See also* Brett M. Frischmann & Mark A. Lemley, *Spillovers*, 107 COLUM. L. REV. 257 (2007).

[50] Malloy, *Mortgage Market Reform, supra* note 4; DAVIDSON & MALLOY, *supra* note 26. Malloy & Smith, *supra* note 7, at Chapter 15.

they look at it over a very short time horizon without having to account for potential costs imposed on other third parties over the full life of the structure. As a result of this relationship, private parties are unable to effectively negotiate to an appropriate market outcome, in the absence of public regulation.

The second type of consumption externality is one that Shy identified as a network externality.[51] In Shy's work, he provides examples of network externalities in discussing phone service and the use of a fax machine.[52] He asks us to consider if we would pay for a phone if no one else had a phone, or if we would want a fax machine if no one else had a fax machine. Naturally, the answer to such rhetorical questions is that we would not want to pay for such a device because there would be little to no utility in having a phone or a fax machine if there was no one to whom we might beneficially be able to send and receive messages. As Shy explains, such goods have adoption–network externalities because the utility derived from such goods is affected by the number of other people using similar or compatible products.[53] In the case of cell phones, for example, their utility also depends on the coverage of the network service, with more cell towers providing more utility to customers. Network goods derive substantial value from network connectivity, and this is not the case with drinking a beer or eating some fresh strawberries, as they can simply be enjoyed on their own.

Cities, as examples of the built environment, have their own sort of adoption–network externalities. Although not exactly the same as the adoption externalities in the private market examples of phones and fax machines, cities confront similar problems. One type of network problem involves the fact that the quality of life for a city is composed of a system of mixed, private, and public goods – and as we know, public goods will always be underproduced because private parties cannot capture the full market value of the product and because some goods and services may serve valuable social functions but be difficult to value in dollar terms. This makes traditional economic calculus difficult. A second network problem involves the need for cities to create places that attract user-adopters.[54] These places are the real-world counterparts to virtual world social networks. Cities need to facilitate interaction at various venues of community life, such as at sporting venues, concerts, street festivals, and public squares. A lot of the value from such places is derived from the fact that there are many user-adopters. For example, when people go to a football game, attend a concert, or visit public meeting places such as Times Square in New York City, Jackson Square in New Orleans, and Fisherman's Wharf in San Francisco, they go there to be with other people; they go there for the

---

[51] SHY, *supra* note 36, at 3.   [52] *Id.* at 17.   [53] *Id.* at 17–36.   [54] *Id.* at 1–6.

interactive experience, and the success and value of these places depend on the ability to generate an ample number of user-adopters. If a city is unable to generate enough user-adopters at these locations, they just become empty and unused spaces. A third type of network problem involves connectivity.[55] Much as the value of a mobile phone depends on the connectivity and extent of the available wireless network, cities also have similar networking problems. For example, consider a community effort to provide bike trails. The trails serve as alternative transportation routes, can assist in reducing the local carbon footprint, can add recreational opportunities, and may promote exercise and better health. There are, in other words, multiple reasons for promoting a system of bike trails. One of the key issues in developing a bike trail system is identifying and piecing together the right kind of system that will attract enough adopters. Consider a city that undertakes a bike trail system but offers very few routes, many of which are broken up every couple of blocks because of difficulty in finding space along roadways and sidewalks for including a bike lane. If a bike trail system is short (say, less than a mile) and intermittently disappears such as not to connect any significant venues to anything else, it is not likely to generate many adopters. Simultaneously, the sense that few people will use the bike trail system may hinder the allocation of resources to the project. This is not dissimilar to the mobile phone and cell tower coordination problem.

In the specific context of inclusive design, we also see adoption externalities.[56] Typically, discussions concerning inclusive design may begin with questioning the need for accessible design inasmuch as only a small part of the population uses wheelchairs. When people look at school playgrounds, shopping centers, and parks, they tend to observe that these places are hardly used by people in wheelchairs, thus they ask themselves why they should pay for all kinds of design features that are not really needed. This, of course, ignores two things. First, the fact that people do not generally observe very many wheelchair users in these venues may simply be a testament to the fact that they are not readily accessible. Second, mobility impairment affects people beyond the population needing to make use of a wheelchair. People tend to greatly underestimate the number of consumer adopters in the marketplace because they do not understand the nature of the disability. Instead of affecting less than 1 percent of the population as most people think, the number of families affected by having a family member with mobility impairment approaches 17 percent of the population. Likewise, demographic trends indicate that the population of the United States is aging, and thus, mobility impairment will be a concern of increasing rather than declining importance in the future. Short

---

[55] *Id.* at 117–119.   [56] *See* SHY, *supra* note 36, at 3.

of regulation, many businesses and communities would simply not incorporate widespread inclusive design into the built environment because they do not understand or appreciate the nature of the need (the potential number of adoptive users).

Another undercounted aspect of inclusive design is that people without mobility impairment also enjoy benefits, even though they are not necessarily the direct target of such design efforts. For example, automatic doors that open with the push of a button are frequently used by many people when they are carrying books or a box, and they assist people with sore or weak arms as well as those in wheelchairs. Curb cuts and gradually graded incline ramps installed to assist people in wheelchairs likewise benefit parents pushing a baby in a stroller or pushcart, bicycle riders, and skateboarders. Good design can have many benefits, even if we first think of it as being directed at eliminating barriers for people with mobility impairment, and once we establish a better inclusive design, we find that a number of people no longer have an impairment in the sense that they are now able to access places and spaces that were not available to them under prior exclusionary designs.

4.2.3 *Switching costs and lock-in*

Switching costs and lock-in are related to more traditional economic concepts such as sunk costs and path dependency.[57] The basic idea is that once consumers make a decision to buy into a certain technology or when producers agree on a set of production standards for a product or service, it is difficult to switch to something new. For example, many people get frustrated when they have been using a given computer system and then the place where they work informs them that they all have to switch to a new system. There is a major cost to this switch that goes beyond paying for new equipment and software; switching costs include such things as retraining of personnel and conversion of data. Likewise, once the new system is learned, there will be a tendency to remain with it and avoid the cost of switching out to an alternative technology. Basically, this just means that changing the way we do things is not cost-free. The market for alternative production and consumption patterns is not perfectly efficient because there is friction caused by the emotional, physical, and production cost of moving to an alternative.

In the inclusive design field, this is an important consideration. When we look at the built environment, we see that many construction practices tend to get standardized. For instance, in an effort to lower the cost of production

[57] *Id.* at 4.

and meet building codes, we have standard-sized doors, windows, wiring, and plumbing. Once these standards are adopted, any variation from the standard is a special order and adds considerably to the cost of construction. Builders have priced work on the basis of standard inputs, have coordinated other elements of construction to "fit" with the standards, and have committed to contracts based on the standard. Furthermore, after construction, it is oftentimes extremely difficult to switch standards or products without having to do major structural rebuilding, so lock-in is significant. Once a building is constructed with barriers to safe and easy use by people with mobility impairment, it is often difficult, expensive, and near-impossible to change.

Some aspects of switching costs can be emotional. For example, in residential housing markets, features designed to make a home easier to access and safer to navigate are identified with being designed for the elderly and thus not desired by young buyers. When younger people look at a home with a wheelchair-accessible bathroom and with grab bars by the sink and bathtub, they often think of the house as being one designed for old people and in need of an update. In other words, design creates its own meanings in a society, and these can sometimes function as additional barriers to switching.

4.2.4 *Significant economies of scale*

The idea of economies of scale is that starting up a company and producing the first product may be very costly, but as we produce more units and scale up production, the cost per unit may drop and allow us to make more profit.[58] This means that if start-up and fixed costs are high and variable costs are low, average costs will fall as production increases, up to a point. Taking advantage of economies of scale is something that is important to all businesses, and standard economics deals with calculating the point at which profit is maximized. Shy considered economies of scale in relationship to network goods and argued that the normal economic models are not applicable to economies of scale for network goods. I believe this can be applied to network enterprises, such as the enhancement of accessibility to the built environment.

Shy was looking at information systems.[59] He noted that it takes a lot of time and labor to produce a major encyclopedia, but once it is completed and the information is downloaded to a disk or made available online, it is almost costless to make it available to the people who want it.[60] The same is true with music: once an artist creates and records a song, the reproduction of the song is extremely cheap. Someone can take the song and post it on

---

[58] Id. [59] See generally id. [60] Frischmann, *supra* note 37.

the Internet for millions of people to enjoy for free, and they can all listen at once or at different times. The economies of scale for these types of goods are significant. This is important and unlike many goods and services. For example, production of automobiles goes down on a per unit basis of production as plant and equipment are used more efficiently, but there are still large per unit costs. Similarly, with the making and selling of pizza, the more a person can sell given the fixed cost of a proper oven, the greater the economies of scale, but these economies are nothing like those observed in the information economy. Shy's point is that the market for network goods and services cannot be understood as a competitive price-taking market in the traditional economic sense.

Inclusive design shares some similarities with Shy's example of network goods. Inclusive design is a quality-of-life good that has potential for significant economies of scale. The initial commitment to inclusive design can be costly in terms of learning about and developing appropriate standards for a given community. There can be significant switching costs and a need to persuade constituents of the importance of the need to change; at the same time, the implementation of some aspects of inclusive design in new construction seems to be relatively low cost. For example, building a structure with a standardized 32-inch-wide doorway as opposed to a 28-inch or 30-inch one imposes no additional cost on the project, and likewise with building sidewalks with curb cuts already built in rather than having to make cuts to already existing sidewalks. Once the upfront costs of committing to inclusive design and setting the standards are taken care of, the act of actually building an accessible community may be only a little more expensive than building one that includes barriers to access for people with mobility impairment. Moreover, in terms of economies of scale, the more that inclusive design is integrated across the network, the more useful and valuable the network becomes. As with our earlier example of bike trails, having inclusive design in all housing units, sidewalks, transit systems, office buildings, shopping centers, schools, parks, and public places increases the quality of life for all residents and visitors by making the various venues of community life easily and safely accessible to the greatest possible population of people. Although construction of inclusive design communities is unlikely to have the significant level of economies of scale as experienced in information markets, it should nonetheless demonstrate some important economies of scale.

Recognizing the network nature and interconnectivity of the built environment is useful as it provides us with some important focal points for criteria evaluation: consumption and production externalities; complementarity, compatibility, and standards; switching costs; and significant economies of scale.

The point is not that communities are network goods but that thinking of them in terms of networks can be helpful.

4.3 CONCLUSION

An increasingly important aspect of planning and land use regulation involves facilitating a greater inclusion of people with declining functional mobility and with mobility impairment. Thus, planning must account for accessibility over time so that people can safely and easily age in place. This can be a difficult task because of the complexity of coordinating the development of the built environment and because of the complex market dynamics involved. In part, the market dynamics relate to feelings about the ability of private property owners to express their own preferences in the design choices for the structures that they build and own. This thick sense of privilege with respect to private property is most evident in private residential housing, and it is furthered by the way in which ADA-related legislation treats such property. Consistent with approaches in the civil rights field, the ADA requires less inclusive design regulation in private single-family homes than in places that are categorized as public or as places of public accommodation. As noted in Chapter 1, however, this civil rights focus seems to be misplaced when thinking about the built environment and the regulation of property development and land use because we should want every place to be safe and easily navigable without regard to the way in which it is owned and without regard to the functional mobility level of the potential users.

The privileging of private design preferences are made "thin" when one considers the quasi-public nature of private property, and when one understands the market imperfections that shape self-interested choice. Ultimately, it must be understood that the argument for enhanced inclusive design of the built environment, including private residential housing, is not that a property owner must let uninvited quests on her property but that all property should be safely and easily navigable by any person legally entitled to or invited to possess or make use of it. Moreover, in the context of the broader community, inclusive design is one element of a complex network and system. Networks have their own economic dynamics, and awareness of network implications can facilitate better planning.

5

Additional zoning concepts for inclusive design

A first step in enhancing the planning process for inclusive design is to require all local communities to engage in comprehensive planning with one element of the planning process devoted to developing guidelines and regulations specifically addressed to the issue of mobility impairment and to the ability of people to safely and easily age in place. This element should consider the demographics of the population, expected changes in demographics, and the anticipated changes in economic, social, and other dimensions of the community. The effort should logically include a need to inventory the accessibility of the various properties within the community and the community's capacity to handle the needs of current and future users of the built environment. Attention should be paid to ensuring good and safe access across the entire built environment and should include plans for financing inclusive design infrastructure with continuous upgrading, including plans for dealing with existing parts of the built environment that fall below established standards of accessibility. Planning should also include the coordination of land uses with access to available health care services, fresh and healthy food stores, community activity centers, parks, walking trails, and public transit. In other words, without regard to where the standards on accessibility are set, be they at the local, state, or national level, local officials should still be engaged in a planning process with respect to implementing such standards in accordance with an appropriate plan that is responsive to the future needs of a dynamic community.

The clearest way to proceed with this kind of planning would be to require local accessibility planning or planning for what I have referred to as inclusive design communities; it can also be done as part of a community's effort at developing a sustainability plan.[1] Sustainability plans tend to focus on a

---

[1] *See, e.g.,* DeWitt Town Board, Town of DeWitt Sustainability Policy, *available at* www.townofdewitt.com/documents/308.pdf (last visited Feb. 14, 2013).

variety of environmental objectives, but in reality, one part of a community's sustainability involves planning for its continued accessibility and for the ability of residents to safely and easily age in place. Simply adding accessibility as an element to an already existing effort of a local community to plan for sustainability may be an effective and easy way to advance planning on inclusive design.

As discussed in this chapter, several techniques may be employed to encourage developers and property owners to try new things and go beyond mere compliance with federal disability law. These techniques include variances, amortization of nonconforming uses, density bonuses, TDRs, performance zoning and concurrency, conditional zoning, development agreements, and the use of accessibility impact assessments. A nonzoning tool that is frequently employed involves tax credits, but these are really financial incentives outside of the standard scope of basic land use law.[2]

When planning for inclusive design, it should be kept in mind that zoning and planning techniques may also be used to ensure that accessible construction is aesthetically pleasing. It is within the police power of local government to regulate not only for public health and safety but for the public welfare and morals. This includes regulation of aesthetics.[3] We have all seen the makeshift "handyman" ramps constructed in front of some homes, and we know how aesthetically displeasing some of these can be at times or in particular neighborhoods. Requiring accessible entranceways does not mean that we should have "handyman" 2 × 4 ramps stretching out across the front yard of every residential home in America. Ramps, entranceways, and landscaping design can be regulated by local planning and zoning codes to ensure approved aesthetic outcomes. Inclusive design requirements should fit with the character of the neighborhood and blend in with the style and materials of the surrounding property.

In this regard, it is important to note that many houses in subdivisions and planned unit communities have their own design criteria that are enforced by deed restrictions, covenants, and rules.[4] These are the subject of private

---

[2] *See* Nestor M. Davidson & Robin Paul Malloy, Affordable Housing and Public-Private Partnerships (2009); U.S. Dep't of Hous. & Urban Dev., LIHTC Basics, http://portal.hud.gov/hudportal/HUD?src=/program_offices/comm_planning/affordablehousing/training/web/lihtc/basics (last visited Feb. 14, 2013).

[3] Julian Conrad Juergensmeyer & Thomas E. Roberts, Land Use Planning and Development Regulation Law 43 (3d ed. 2007); Daniel R. Mandelker, Land Use Law § 12:1 (5th ed. 2003). *See also* Anthony Brandt, *Views*, Atlantic Monthly (July 1977), at 46.

[4] *See* Bodine v. Harris Vill. Prop. Owners Ass'n, 699 S.E.2d (N.C. Ct. App. 2012); Turudic v. Stephens, 31 P.3d 465 (Or. Ct. App. 2001); Robin Paul Malloy & James Charles Smith,

property law and are not the same as public land use regulations. Land use planning and zoning involve public law and are enforced by public officials.[5] Private restrictions and covenants are private law and are enforced privately.[6] Oftentimes there is confusion on this point as property owners will make a request for local zoning officials to enforce the private land restrictions that govern their property. Public land use and zoning officials do not enforce these restrictions, and property owners need to read the governing documents to determine how they are made enforceable.[7] With this in mind, it is important to appreciate the fact that public inclusive design requirements would not necessarily eliminate covenants or restrictions otherwise applicable to a property in accordance with private architectural review standards.[8] The public land use regulations should simply constrain some of the potential design regulations that private parties might impose on properties in a common ownership development, such as a subdivision. Private architectural review boards would still be able to review and regulate the design and aesthetic quality of accessible entranceways, for instance, but they would not be able to prevent a property owner from making an entrance fully accessible.[9] A property owner could not simply put up an unattractive handmade wooden ramp in the front yard; she might need to have the design reviewed and approved by the review board. Review boards could still address matters of design, quality of materials, color of finished product or nature of landscaping, and a variety of aspects related to the way in which the inclusive entranceway is constructed and situated on the lot. It would be possible, for instance, to use landscaping or design

---

REAL ESTATE TRANSACTIONS: PROBLEMS, CASES, AND MATERIALS 315–358 (4th ed. 2013).

[5] PATRICIA E. SALKIN, AMERICAN LAW OF ZONING § 6:3 (5th ed. 2013). *See, e.g.,* DEP'T OF STATE, NEW YORK STATE, ZONING ENFORCEMENT (2011).

[6] MALLOY & SMITH, *supra* note 4, at 326. Juergensmeyer & Roberts, *Land Use Planning and Development Regulation Law* §15.1–15.15.

[7] MALLOY & SMITH, *supra* note 4, at 326; Juergensmeyer & Roberts, *Land Use Planning and Development Regulation Law*; Mandelker, *Land Use Law* §15.1–15.15.Id.

[8] Covenants and restrictions running with the land bind future owners and assignees. Eliminating or preventing the enforcement of private covenants and restrictions by state action may raise a variety of legal issues. These issues may vary depending on if a state treats the covenants and restrictions as a property right or as a contract right. The current trend is to treat them contractually. *See generally* Ben W. F. Depoorter and Francesco Parisi, *Fragmentation of Property Rights: A Functional Interpretation of the Law of Servitudes* (2003). JOHN M. OLIN CENTER FOR STUDIES IN LAW, ECONOMICS, AND PUBLIC POLICY, WORKING PAPER 284, http://digitalcommons.law.yale.edu/lepp_papers/284.

[9] In other words, accessibility and architectural control are different. Even when accessibility is required, there can be controls with respect to placement of structures and improvements on the property. These controls might include regulations aimed at controlling color of finish, types of permitted materials, design, and orientation on the property.

features to create a street view of the home as having a wraparound front porch while having a ramping system built behind the porch facade and concealed from view. There are many creative possibilities, from the simple to the elaborate, to accomplish the goal of inclusive housing design, and doing so should not necessarily require the elimination of private covenants, restrictions, and architectural review requirements.

Furthermore, public land use regulations can address accessibility without eliminating a private property owner's right to exclude. Although it is true that one of the fundamental characteristics of property ownership is the right to exclude, this right is not unlimited. For example, one cannot exclude firefighters coming into a home to put out a fire and taking action to reduce potential danger and damage to other nearby properties. Moreover, the right to exclude is not the same as asserting a right to a particular design preference. Public land use regulations for inclusive design do not eliminate the legally enforceable rights of private property owners to exclude others from their property. With inclusive housing design standards, for example, homeowners retain the right to invite or exclude people from their private homes.[10] People do not have to allow uninvited guests into their homes; the homes simply need to be designed so that a person can be invited in without regard to mobility impairment. The real issue is one of regulating the desire to privately contract for design features that exclude approximately 17 percent or more of families from being able to easily and safely visit each other in their respective homes, and to do so under circumstances in which individual property owners fail to account for the full costs of their design preferences.

Planning and zoning for inclusive design addresses concerns beyond aesthetics and questions of a right of exclusion versus a preference for design; planning and zoning addresses basic issues of the public health, safety, welfare, and morals. Inclusive design not only makes for more livable communities, it makes for safer communities. For example, consider some of the basic statistics on safety within the home. Injury from falls in bathrooms and on stairways results in a significant number of deaths and injuries each year in the United States. Some of these injuries and deaths might be prevented with greater use of inclusive design. In 2002, for example, 12,800 people over the age of 65 died, and 1.6 million were treated in emergency departments because of falls.[11] In 2010, one out of three people age 65 or older experienced fall

---

[10] This includes gated communities and other "lifestyle" housing arrangements. People would be required to have inclusive design, not be prohibited from establishing legal criteria for establishing lifestyle.

[11] Robin Paul Malloy, *Inclusion by Design: Accessible Housing and Mobility Impairment*, 60 HASTINGS L. J. 711 (2009) (citing SENIOR FALLS, A HOME FALL PREVENTION

injuries, resulting in 2.3 million visits to an emergency room, with more than 662,000 of these patients being hospitalized.[12] In 2010, the direct cost of falls was $30 billion.[13] In addition, falls are the leading cause of accidental death for the elderly, accounting for about half of all accidental deaths in the home.[14] And approximately 150 children each year die from accidental falls in the home.[15] In 1990, some 1 million people required hospital room treatment from falls occurring on stairs located within the home.[16] For these reasons, the Centers for Disease Control and the Home Safety Council are among those who suggest that all Americans are safer if we install grab bars in all bathrooms, at the toilet, shower, and tub.[17] It is also clear that reducing the number of steps and improving stairways in housing design will enhance safety for all users, without regard to mobility impairment. Thus, from the point of view of local zoning and land use planning authorities, inclusive design is rightly a concern under the police power as well as a matter of concern for disability rights advocates under civil rights law.

A difficulty in planning and zoning for inclusive design at the local level is that communities are networks that oftentimes extend beyond any one local government jurisdiction. Thus, coordinating some aspects of inclusive design across a community will require regional cooperation and will benefit from

CHECKLIST FOR OLDER ADULTS—NCIPC, www.cdc.gov/ncipc/pub-res/toolkit/checklistforsafety.htm (last reviewed Sept. 7, 2006) (noting that although bathrooms and stairways are a primary source of falls, they are not the only ones included in these numbers).

[12] CTRS. FOR DISEASE CONTROL AND PREVENTION, FALLS AMONG OLDER ADULTS: AN OVERVIEW, *available at* www.cdc.gov/HomeandRecreationalSafety/Falls/adultfalls.html (last updated Sept. 20, 2013) (citing M.C. Hornbrook et al., *Preventing Falls Among Community-Dwelling Older Persons: Results from a Randomized Trial,* 34 THE GERONTOLOGIST 16, 16–23 (1994); J. A. Stevens et al., *Gender Differences in Seeking Care for Falls in the Aged Medicare Population,* 43 AM. J. PREVENTATIVE MED. 59, 59–62 (2012)).

[13] CTRS. FOR DISEASE CONTROL AND PREVENTION, *supra* note 12 (citing J. A. STEVENS, FATALITIES AND INJURIES FROM FALLS AMONG OLDER ADULTS—UNITED STATES, 1993–2003 AND 2001–2005, 55 MMWR 1221, 1221–1224 (2006)).

[14] CTRS. FOR DISEASE CONTROL AND PREVENTION, *supra* note 12 (citing Hornbrook, *supra* note 12); *see also* Steve Slon, *Preventing Falls: Nine Guidelines for Caregivers to Keep in Mind,* THE POST STANDARD, Mar. 22, 2011, at C1.

[15] Malloy, *supra* note 11, at 742 (citing OHIO STATE UNIV. EXTENSION, PUBL'N NO. AEX-691.1, FALLS IN THE HOME 1, 2 (1992), *available at* www.cdc.gov/nasd/docs/d000101-d000200/d000131/d000131.pdf).

[16] Malloy, *supra* note 11, at 742 (citing OHIO STATE UNIV. EXTENSION, PUBL'N NO. AEX-691.1, *supra* note 15).

[17] *See* Malloy, *supra* note 11, at 742 (citing SENIOR FALLS, A HOME FALL PREVENTION CHECKLIST FOR OLDER ADULTS—NCIPC, *supra* note 11; HOME SAFETY COUNCIL, BATHROOM SAFETY CHECKLIST, www.homesafetycouncil.org/newpdfs/sg_bathroomNEW_p001.pdf (last visited Oct. 20, 2013).

some national standards. There are, for instance, 3,141 counties in the United States, and within counties, there are often additional entities, such as cities and towns, that may exercise zoning and planning authority.[18] Therefore, local action is one way to advance inclusive design, and it is important to good planning, but it will likely tend to produce varying standards across the country unless guidelines and standards are set at a state or national level. The ADA and related legislation serve this function in establishing standards that address the civil rights of people with disabilities. Local governments can implement planning and zoning regulations that incorporate these civil rights standards in ways that are similar to the way that they regulate land uses that intersect with national standards under the First Amendment and in other areas where there is tension between land use and other fundamental rights.

In this chapter, we explore some additional techniques and concepts in land use regulation that may be useful to advancing our understanding of the relationship between land use law and disability.

5.1 VARIANCES AND RELATED CONCEPTS

The zoning variance is an important concept in land use regulation. A variance involves a request for relief from a requirement of a planning and zoning code on the grounds that the regulation imposes difficulties and hardships for a given property owner.[19] An application for a variance is made by the property owner, and the proceeding is quasi-adjudicative in nature, meaning that the decision of the zoning board is to be based on substantial competent evidence on the record, and appropriate due process protections must be applied. There are two categories of variance: one is typically identified as an *area* variance[20] and the other as a *use* variance.[21] A variance from the code means that the property will have the status of being a legal nonconforming use (its nonconformity with the code is legal because a proper variance has been granted). Generally when a variance is granted, the variance (exemption from compliance with the code) will run with the land and, thus, it will survive transfer of the property.[22] In the situation of a variance granted as a reasonable accommodation for a person with a disability, however, the argument can be

---

[18] Malloy, *supra* note 11, at 743; *see also* U.S. CENSUS BUREAU, USA COUNTIES, http://censtats. census.gov/usa/usainfo.shtml (last visited Oct. 20, 2013).

[19] JUERGENSMEYER & ROBERTS, *supra* note 3, § 5:14; MANDELKER, *supra* note 3, § 6.39. *See* SALKIN, *supra* note 5; Topanga Ass'n for a Scenic Cmty. V. Cnty. of Los Angeles, 522 P.2d 12 (Cal. 1974).

[20] JUERGENSMEYER & ROBERTS, *supra* note 3, § 5:15; MANDELKER, *surpa* note 3, § 6.42.

[21] Sources cited *supra* note 20.   [22] *Id.*

made that this type of variance should be considered "personal" and terminate when the person is no longer using the property (because the variance does not run with the land). This might be appropriate in situations where the particular accommodation requires a design feature not generally applicable to the needs of the community, such as an accommodation that requires the finished side of a wooden yard fence to face the residence of a property owner, even though the zoning code provides for the finished side to face the property of neighbors. Sometimes accommodations of this type are requested to assist in preventing an autistic child from wandering off a property and into the neighborhood. The reasoning is that a fence can be an appropriate barrier to wandering, and the finished side is more difficult to evade than the unfinished side, which has exposed beam supports that facilitate climbing. If a community grants relief in the form of an accommodation variance in this type of situation, it may be appropriate to condition it on the continued presence in the home of the person receiving the accommodation. The granting of such a variance should clearly express the personal nature of the accommodation and make its term conditional, if possible, and appropriate under the circumstances. The expense of bringing the property back into conformity at the termination of the accommodation variance would fall on the property owner. In a situation involving termination of a personal accommodation variance because of a sale of the property, the owner could, of course, bargain to shift to the buyer the cost of bringing the property back into conformity.

The idea of an accommodation variance is at odds with traditional notions of a variance running with the land and would therefore have to be provided for by statute or regulation, or developed in the case law.

5.1.1 *Area variance*

The fence example just discussed involves a type of area variance, and area variances are the more common of the two types of variances. An area variance relates to such things as height, bulk, and setback restrictions as well as to orientation of the improvements on a lot and to the location of driveways, decks, pools, and fences.[23] It can also include such things as the provision for required parking spaces, landscaping, ancillary structures, lot coverage, and density.[24] Traditionally, the application for an area variance involves a permitted use and the assertion that specific requirements of the code pose "practical difficulties" for the owner.[25] In some states, such as New York, the requirements are spelled out in terms of specific criteria. New York applies a

[23] *Id.* [24] *Id.* [25] *Id.*

balancing test that directs a zoning board to consider five factors in balancing
the benefit to the applicant versus the detriment to the health, safety, and
welfare of the neighborhood or community.[26] No one factor is determinate,
and each case is specific to the facts presented. The board is to consider each
of the five criteria but need not make a decision based on deciding any one or
even a majority of the criteria one way rather than another. After considering
each criterion, the board must make a decision based on balancing all of the
factors in the given context. An area variance should be granted if the board
determines that the benefits to the applicant outweigh the detriments to the
neighborhood or community.[27]

In New York, the five factors are as follows:

1. Whether an undesirable change will be produced in the character of
   the neighborhood or a detriment to nearby properties will be created by
   granting the area variance;
2. Whether the benefits sought by the applicant can be achieved by some
   method feasible for the applicant to pursue, other than the area variance;
3. Whether the requested variance is substantial;
4. Whether the proposed variance will have an adverse effect or impact
   on the physical or environmental conditions in the neighborhood or
   district;
5. Whether the alleged difficulty was self-created, which consideration
   shall be relevant to the decision of the board of appeals, but shall not
   necessarily preclude the granting of the area variance.[28]

In a hearing for an area variance, the property owner has the obligation to
present evidence on each of the preceding criteria and to demonstrate that the
benefits of granting the variance outweigh the detriments. The zoning board
will then make its findings as to each criterion and explain its decision as to the
granting or denial of the area variance. The decision of the zoning board must
have a rational basis and be supported by substantial competent evidence on
the record.

The following case, from the state of Maryland, involves an area variance
granted to a property owner as a reasonable accommodation because his
daughter was dealing with mobility impairment. It serves as a good example of

---

[26] N.Y. Town Law § 267-b(3) (McKinney 2006); Wachsberger v. Michalis, 191 N.Y.S.2d 621,
624 (N.Y. Sup. Ct. 1959); Juergensmeyer & Roberts, *supra* note 3, § 5:15; Mandelker,
supra note 3, § 6.42.
[27] Juergensmeyer & Roberts, *supra* note 3, § 5:15; Mandelker, *supra* note 3, § 6.41.
[28] N.Y. Town Law § 267-b(3) (McKinney 2006); Patricia E. Salkin, New York Zoning
Law and Practice § 29:12 (4th ed. 2009).

the process for dealing with an application for an area variance in the context of promoting inclusive design communities, and it includes discussion of the specific criteria required to be evaluated under the relevant zoning ordinance. The discussion of the specific criteria is useful as an example of the kind of work required to comply with local land use law with respect to the granting of a variance.

Mastandrea v. North

760 A. 2d 677 (Court of Appeals of Maryland, 2000)
    Opinion by: Harrell, J....
    Dr. and Mrs. John P. Mastandrea (Appellants) purchased in December 1992 an approximately 12 acre undeveloped, but subdivided, lot with frontage on Glebe Creek in Talbot County. Over the next 4 years or so, the Mastandreas, for themselves and their family, constructed on the lot a home, swimming pool, tennis court, pier, garden, and an extensive set of pathways connecting these improvements. Included in the pathway system, installed personally in 1996 by Dr. Mastandrea and his three eldest sons, were a brick-in-cement path connecting the house and pier and a brick-in-sand path roughly parallel to and within 20–25 feet of the bulkheaded edge of Glebe Creek. A primary reason given for installing the extensive, connecting path system was that the Mastandreas' daughter, Leah, suffered from muscular dystrophy (a progressively degenerative neurological and muscular disease) and was confined to a motorized wheelchair for mobility purposes. In order that she might access all of the property's amenities, and partake of them to some extent with her siblings, the pathways were designed to facilitate her movement by wheelchair. Much of the design and construction of the improvements on the lot also considered wheelchair access as an integral goal.
    The Mastandreas installed the pathways without the benefit of a required building permit from Talbot County (or any form of prior governmental blessing or review) and heedless of the fact that a portion of the pathways were placed within the 100 foot buffer of the Chesapeake Bay Critical Area 2 adjacent to Glebe Creek. The brick-in-cement portion of that path within the Critical Area buffer comprised 711 square feet of surface area. The brick-in-sand portion covered 4486 square feet of the surface of the Critical Area buffer. Together, the surface areas of these two components of the overall path system represented 4% of the total Critical Area buffer identified on the lot. Discovery by the authorities of the unauthorized installation led, among other things, to the Mastandreas filing on 29 January 1998 a variance application with the Board in an effort to validate the pathways constructed within the Critical Area buffer.

Zoning Ordinance § 19.12(b)(5)(iii)(b) defines the Critical Area buffer as being "at least 100 feet wide, measured landward from the Mean Highwater Line of tidal waters and tidal wetlands, and from tributary streams. The need for a variance for those portions of the pathways located within 100 feet of the shore of Glebe Creek is necessitated by Z.O. § 19.12(b)(5)(iii)(c), which prohibits "new development activities, including structures, roads, parking areas and other impervious surfaces" in the buffer.

At the time the Mastandreas filed their variance application, Z.O. § 19.14(b)(3)(iv) required the following favorable findings to be made by the Board before it could grant a variance from the Critical Area regulations:

> (iv) In order to vary or modify the Talbot County Critical Area provisions of this Ordinance, the Board of Appeals must determine that the application meets all of the criteria set forth below.

[a] Special conditions or circumstances exist that are peculiar to the land or structure such that a literal enforcement of the provisions of this Ordinance would result in unwarranted hardship to the property owner;

[b] A literal interpretation of this Ordinance will deprive the property owner of rights commonly enjoyed by other property owners in the same zone;

[c] The granting of a variance will not confer upon the property owner any special privilege that would be denied by this Ordinance to other owners of lands or structures within the same zone;

[d] The variance request is not based on conditions or circumstances which are the result of actions by the property owner nor does the request arise from any condition relating to land or building use, either permitted or nonconforming, on any neighboring property;

[e] The granting of a variance within the Critical Area will not adversely affect water quality or adversely impact fish, wildlife, or plant habitat and the granting of the variance will be in harmony with the general spirit and intent of the Critical Area Law, the Talbot County Critical Area Plan and the regulations adopted in this Ordinance;

[f] The variance shall not exceed the minimum adjustment necessary to relieve the unwarranted hardship; and

[g] The granting of the variance will not adversely affect water quality or adversely impact fish, wildlife or plant habitat, and the granting of the variance will be in harmony with the general spirit and intent of the Critical Area Law, the Talbot County Critical Area Program and the Critical Area provisions of this Ordinance.

At the Board's 11 May 1998 hearing on the Mastandreas' application, the applicants, in support of their principal theme that the variance should be granted as a reasonable accommodation of Leah's disability so that she could access the pier and enjoy the shoreline of Glebe Creek, mustered both testimony and exhibits. They explained that the pathways were located to allow a wheelchair to get close enough that Leah could enjoy the waterfront, but not so close as to be dangerous. According to the Mastandreas, the natural slope and the soil composition of the lot near the shoreline (except for the direct pier access) did not permit wheelchair access directly to the waterfront. Placing the pathways outside the 100 foot buffer, however, would deny a wheelchair occupant access to and enjoyment of the waterfront, they contended. The pathways permitted Leah to enjoy the natural and recreational aspects of her family's waterfront lot and were the only means by which Leah could accompany her brothers and sisters on walks and other activities on the lot. Mrs. Mastandrea testified that her daughter's ability to have access to the waterfront is one of the few pleasures that she still is able to enjoy due to the physical effects of her disorder.

The (brick-in-concrete) pier access pathway was designed to prevent a wheelchair from gaining momentum on the natural downslope from the house to the water. A pathway constructed in a straight line from the house to the pier, without the slope break provided by the Mastandreas' construction, would create a dangerous situation for a person confined to a wheelchair.

Dr. Mastandrea testified that in constructing the brick-in-sand pathway parallel to Glebe Creek his sons removed about six inches of turf, surface soil, and clay, and replaced it with three to five inches of sand. An environmental consultant, Ronald Gatton, testified that he was familiar with the Mastandreas' property and the intent of the Critical Area laws to reduce the amount of runoff into the Chesapeake Bay and its tributaries. Mr. Gatton testified that the soil of the lot was one of the heaviest clay soils that he had ever tested. He conducted an infiltration test on the brick-in-sand path and determined that water permeated the brick-in-sand pathway faster than the surrounding undisturbed soil, making the path three times as permeable as the surrounding lawn. Mr. Gatton stated that because the natural soil conditions in the area tended to be very stiff, with a "plastic" quality, it was his opinion that the pathway parallel to the creek actually intercepts much of the runoff from the lawn between the house and the path before entering Glebe Creek . . .

The Critical Area Commission (the Commission) presented one witness in opposition to the variance request. Mr. Gregory L. Schaner, a Natural Resources Planner for the Commission, opined that the requirements for granting a variance were not met by the Mastandreas. Mr. Schaner restated the position of the Commission, previously set forth in a 9 April 1998 letter to the Talbot County Planning Commission, that the Commission recommended denial of the variance request and that the Mastandreas be required to remove all portions of the pertinent pathways, except for an immediate perpendicular access from the house to the pier. As to the house-to-pier connection, Mr. Schaner recommended that the Board require that the Mastandreas remove all portions of the pathway, including the circular, wheelchair "break" areas designed to reduce a wheelchair's momentum on the way toward the pier, and suggested that the Board allow only a single, straight-line path from the house to the pier. He acknowledged that the Commission had not conducted any environmental impact studies or tests to ascertain the actual impact, if any, of the relevant pathways in the Critical Area buffer on the lot or the water quality of Glebe Creek. Mr. Schaner also acknowledged that there were, at that time, no provisions in the Critical Area regulations (State or county) or the Z.O. variance provisions expressly taking into account handicapped access considerations.

The Board, in split decisions rendered on 27 July 1998, voted to grant legitimizing variances for the existing pathway from the house to the pier (by a 4–1 vote) and for the existing pathway parallel to Glebe Creek (by a 3–2 vote). Essentially, the Board majority in each instance concluded that the paths provided reasonable access to the waterfront for handicapped persons and were reasonable accommodations for Leah's disability. The Board majority was impressed also with the mitigation effects of the Mastandreas' plantings and the permeability enhancement of the brick-in-sand pathway. Accordingly, the Board made written findings on 21 October 1998 favorable to the Mastandreas' application, as required by Z.O. § 19.14(b)(3)(iv) . . .

Even though there was scant reference to the ADA in the record before the Board and no express reliance on the ADA in the Board's written findings of fact and conclusions of law granting the variance, it is clear that the Board considered and relied on Leah's disability in its application of the Critical Area variance standards in Z.O. § 19.14(b)(3)(iv). The Board's pertinent conclusions of law stated:

- There are special conditions or circumstances which exist that are peculiar to the subject property such a literal enforcement of the provisions of the ordinance would result in unwarranted hardship to the property owner. The property is a large parcel with a substantial amount of waterfront. A walkway only to the pier on this property does not provide reasonable access to the entire waterfront area of the property if a walkway is the only means by which a resident can gain access to the waterfront. Part of the reasonable use of such a property is access to the entire waterfront, not just the pier. The lateral walkways within the buffer providing such access to a handicapped resident of the property amount to only about four percent of the entire surface area of the buffer, an amount which can easily be offset by mitigating plantings on the property and the Applicant appears to have already mitigated much of the potential increase in runoff from the lateral walkway by existing and planned landscaping . . .

- A literal interpretation of the ordinance will deprive the property owner of rights commonly enjoyed by other property owners in the same zone. Access to the waterfront of the property for the Applicant's daughter is limited by her disability. Most people fortunate enough to live on waterfront property have access to the entire waterfront without having special walkways disturbing the buffer zone vegetation. The special circumstances of this resident will deprive her of that access commonly enjoyed by others.

- The granting of the variance will not confer upon the property owner any special privilege that would be denied by the ordinance to other owners of lands or structures within the same zone. The walkways constructed by the Applicants are a reasonable accommodation for the special circumstances of the Applicants and should be granted to all owners of land in similar circumstances.

- The variance request is not based on conditions or circumstances which are the result of actions by the property owner. By their actions, the Applicants purchased the property and placed the walkways where they are. However, they simply desire equal access to as much of the enjoyment of the property for their handicapped daughter as reasonably possible. The walkways are the least objectionable means to that end to accommodate her special circumstance which, of course, is not a result of their choice. The request does not arise from any condition relating to land or building use, either permitted or nonconforming, on any neighboring property.

- The proposed variance will not adversely affect water quality or adversely impact fish, wildlife, or plant habitat and the granting of the variance will be in harmony with the general spirit and intent of the Critical Area Law, the Talbot County Critical Area Plan and the regulations adopted in the Ordinance. While the walkways exceed that which is normally required to provide direct access to a pier on the property the excess is minimal and can easily be mitigated . . .

Our role in reviewing whether the Board, as an administrative agency, correctly reached the conclusions required by the Zoning Ordinance for the grant of a variance in the Critical Area buffer "is precisely the same as that of the circuit court." This means we must review the administrative decision itself.

We have stated that "the correct test to be applied [to the judicial review of zoning matters] is whether the issue before the administrative body is 'fairly debatable,' that is, whether its determination is based upon evidence from which reasonable persons could come to different conclusions." For its

conclusions to be "fairly debatable," the Board's decision to grant the variance must have been based on substantial evidence . . . Under the substantial
evidence test, "the heart of the fact-finding process often is the drawing of
inferences made from the evidence . . . The court may not substitute its judgment on the question whether the inference drawn is the right one or whether
a different inference would be better supported. The test is reasonableness,
not rightness" . . .

The Board in this case, therefore, did not have to consider whether denying
the variance would have denied the Mastandreas a reasonable and significant
use of the "entire" lot. Rather, the Board was required to (and did) consider
whether the property owners, in light of their daughter's disability, would be
denied a reasonable and significant use of the waterfront of their property
without the access that the path provided. There is substantial evidence in the
record establishing that, without the path, a person in a wheelchair could not
enjoy the waterfront portion of the property . . .

The Board recognized that a literal application of the Z.O. would deprive
Leah of an ability to enjoy the property on which she resides as others in the
area similarly situated may enjoy theirs without the need for a similar path.
By providing a reasonable accommodation for Leah's special circumstances,
the Board prevented discrimination by virtue of her disability and thereby
provided her with a reasonable use and enjoyment of the property . . .

Conclusion

In conclusion, we find that the Board considered all of the factors required
under Talbot County Zoning Ordinance § 19.14(b)(3)(iv) and, after weighing
the evidence before it, permissibly decided to make a reasonable accommodation of Leah Mastandreas' disability in granting the variance for the pathway
in the Critical Area buffer parallel to Glebe Creek . . . Judgment of the Circuit
Court for Talbot County reversed; case remanded to the Circuit Court with
directions to affirm the decision of the Board of Appeals of Talbot County.

5.1.2 *Use variance*

A use variance involves the authorization of a use that is otherwise not permitted on a particular property.[29] The use variance is traditionally granted to

---

[29] JUERGENSMEYER & ROBERTS, *supra* note 3, §5:15; MANDELKER, *supra* note 3, § 6.43;
SALKIN, *supra* note 28, § 29:4.

a property owner when the applicable use restrictions are found to impose an "unnecessary hardship."[30] The variance, when granted, permits a different use for the property than that otherwise required by the zoning code.[31] For example, a property owner might seek a use variance to permit a multifamily residential use in a single-family residential zone or to have a small coffee shop in an area that otherwise prohibits food and beverage retail uses. The property owner must demonstrate that the permitted uses under the code impose an unnecessary hardship on him, and this is typically based on the assertion of unique circumstances with respect to the property.[32] Obtaining a use variance is traditionally more difficult than obtaining an area variance.

In the state of New York, the traditional test of unnecessary hardship has been clarified by statute and requires that the applicant demonstrate the following:

1. The applicant cannot realize a reasonable return [for every permitted use of the property], provided that lack of return is substantial as demonstrated by competent financial evidence;
2. The alleged hardship relating to the property in question is unique and does not apply to a substantial portion of the district or neighborhood;
3. The requested use variance, if granted, will not alter the essential character of the neighborhood; and
4. The alleged hardship has not been self-created.[33]

Unlike the requirements for an area variance, the use variance does not involve a balancing test.[34] The applicant must demonstrate the presence of all four elements for a use variance to be granted.[35]

Let us consider two types of requests that might arise in an inclusive design context. First, consider a neighborhood of single-family residential properties all with homes built on lots of a minimum lot size of one acre. Property owner Paul has an aging mother who lives in a nearby city in a large home of her own, and she is having difficulty maintaining it and navigating it because of its size and because of the various stairways in the house. Paul makes an application to the zoning board asking for a variance to permit him to construct a small,

[30] N.Y. Town Law § 267-b(2) (McKinney 2006); Juergensmeyer & Roberts, *supra* note 3, § 5:15; Mandelker, *surpa* note 3, § 6.44; Salkin, *supra* note 28, § 29:6.
[31] Juergensmeyer & Roberts, *supra* note 3, §5:15; Mandelker, *supra* note 3, § 6.42; Salkin, *supra* note 28, § 29:4.
[32] Juergensmeyer & Roberts, *supra* note 3, § 5:20; Mandelker, *Land Use Law* § 6.46; Salkin, *supra* note 28, § 29:8.
[33] N.Y. Town Law § 267-b(2) (McKinney 2006); Otto v. Steinhilber, 24 N.E.2d 851 (N.Y. 1939); Juergensmeyer & Roberts, *supra* note 3, § 5:15; Mandelker, *supra* note 3, § 6.43. Salkin, *supra* note 28, § 29:6.
[34] Salkin, *supra* note 28, § 29:7.   [35] *Id.*

single-story, ranch-style home on his lot as an ancillary structure for his mother. Paul has an architect and an engineer who have demonstrated that the lot is large enough to easily contain the small cottage that Paul proposes to build, and they demonstrate that high-quality building materials will be used so that the home will be attractive and blend in with the look of Paul's house and others of the neighborhood. The zoning code limits use of residential lots to a single-family home and ancillary structures, with ancillary structures defined as a shed or pool house. Additional residential structures are not a permitted use. At the outset, Paul is seeking a use variance and not an area variance. Paul wants permission for a use that is otherwise prohibited (placing more than one residential structure on a lot). It is highly unlikely that Paul can demonstrate that all four of the preceding criteria apply to his situation; in fact, he will likely have difficulty demonstrating that any of them are applicable to his request.

As another example, consider the situation of Margaret. She owns a one acre lot in an area zoned for single-family residential. The area was zoned for this use about 20 years ago. Since that date, things have changed in the community. A new highway was constructed nearby, a large subdivision went in behind her house, and a gas station and firehouse were built on the corner adjoining her lot. The area is no longer a quiet or peaceful suburban setting. Margaret has tried to sell her home for the past year and a half but cannot find any buyers for it at a price anywhere close to her asking price. Her real estate broker tells her that no one wants a single-family home in this location anymore because of traffic and noise. Margaret has received a number of inquiries from potential buyers interested in acquiring the property if it can be used for a higher-intensity use such as for professional office space, retail, or for a restaurant or bank. Margaret has found one potential buyer who has put an offer on her property at a reasonable price providing that the property can be granted a variance for use as a professional office. The buyer plans to keep the structure looking like a single-family home on the exterior but will remodel and use it as a professional office. At the location, he plans to provide physical therapy to people with various types of low functional mobility. Office hours will be between 9:00 AM and 6:00 PM, and parking will be limited. No more than two staff members and three clients are expected to be on location at any given hour. Margaret applies for a use variance, seeking to permit the property to be used for a professional office building for physical therapy. In this situation, unlike that of Paul, Margaret may have an opportunity for success in seeking a use variance because she has several factors going for her. She will need to substantiate in real dollar-and-cents terms evidence to support a claim that the property has no economic viability for any of the uses currently permitted under the zoning code (single-family residential),[36] and if she can do this, she will then have an opportunity to make out the other elements in support of her application. She may not be successful, but at least it appears that her application has much more potential for success than the one Paul might submit.

In considering an application for a variance, it is important to remember that zoning is covered by federal disability law. This includes the variance process and the decision-making activities of planning and zoning boards; it is not limited to the legislative act of developing and enacting a zoning code. Consequently, the guidelines offered in Chapter 3 are applicable to the zoning actions addressed here in Chapter 5. In particular, in dealing with a variance request that includes facts indicating a need for consideration of a reasonable accommodation, attention must be paid to the following factors (similar to those identified in Chapter 3):

1. In granting or denying the variance, explain the outcome with reference to the specific criteria for a variance applicable in the jurisdiction.

2. When dealing with matters that raise potential disability law issues, be certain to account for federal disability law requirements under the ADA, FHA, RA, and related legislation. In evaluating the application for a variance pursuant to an accommodation of a disability, for example, engage in fact finding as to (1) the reasonableness of a requested accommodation; (2) the necessity for an accommodation; (3) the extent that an asserted difficulty with the code is different in kind from that experienced by the general public; and (4) with respect to housing, the ability of the property owner to obtain an equal opportunity to obtain housing in the absence of an accommodation ("but for" the accommodation, the person with a disability would not have an equal opportunity to obtain housing in violation of the FHA).

3. In rendering a decision, make specific fact-based findings as to listed criteria, including the requirements of federal disability law. Quasi-adjudicative decisions, as in those made by a zoning board of appeal, must be supported by substantial competent evidence on the record; thus, be certain to document the fact finding and the rationale for supporting a decision. (Legislative acts, as in developing a comprehensive plan and the zoning code, are subject to review on a rational basis standard.)

---

[36] *See* Passucci v. Town of West Seneca, 542 N.Y.S.2d 74 (N.Y. App. Div. 1989); Benway Stadium Inc. v. Town of Volney, 510 N.Y.S.2d 342 (N.Y. App. Div. 1986); Vill. Bd. of Vill. of Fayetteville v. Jarrold, 423 N.E.2d 385 (N.Y. 1981); SALKIN, *supra* note 28, § 29:8.

4. If a variance is granted as a personal accommodation for a person with a particular disability and the variance is for a specific purpose not of general applicability, the law should permit local governments to condition the accommodation and to revisit the matter when the person accommodated is no longer at the property. In some jurisdictions, this may be problematic if local law holds that a variance must, by definition, run with the land. In such jurisdictions, either the law must recognize that federal disability law has changed the nature of particular types of variances or a new class of variance must be authorized to address the needs of people entitled to accommodation (perhaps called "accommodation variances"). Accommodation variances are granted because of the personal characteristics of a user of the property (a disability) and are therefore unlike traditional variances from inception. Conditioning the term of the variance based on the continued presence of the person being accommodated should be considered an inherent characteristic of such a variance. Another way to look at the situation is by concluding that making a reasonable accommodation in accordance with federal disability law does not involve the granting of a variance. One might conclude that when a reasonable accommodation is asserted in connection with seeking exemption from a code requirement, it is simply a request for a zoning board to exercise its authority to interpret the code provisions. In essence, the zoning board is asked to determine if the code fully applies to the given situation, and if it concludes that an accommodation is required, it determines that the code has been displaced by federal disability law. Consequently, it then functions not to grant a variance but to develop a reasonable accommodation consistent with the needs of the individual and the requirements otherwise announced in the code. Inasmuch as the zoning board is developing an accommodation and not granting a variance per se, the accommodation is rationally linked to the continued presence of the accommodated party at the location of the property.

5. The record must reveal a fair and unbiased process; consequently, to the extent that public hearings produce potentially discriminatory testimony, such as in the recording of discriminatory comments made by a member of the public at a public meeting, decision makers should clarify, on the record, that a decision is in no way influenced by such impermissible comments or considerations. Decision makers in such situations should counter any biased comments and confirm that a decision is based on a fair and complete evaluation of the full and *relevant* information on the record.

6. Decisions should be reviewed periodically to ensure that the application of facially neutral criteria does not, in fact, result in disparate treatment of people with disability. The considerations relative to disparate treatment and disparate impact analysis applicable in the variance context are the same as in the context of the six criteria as set out in Chapter 3.

5.1.3 *Nonconforming uses, grandfather clauses, and amortization*

A nonconforming use can be thought of in a couple of ways. The typical situation of a nonconforming use involves a change in the zoning code. For example, consider a zoning code that in time period 1 designates a given street as a location for two-family homes, and these homes are required to be set back from the street line by at least 30 feet. Then, in time period 2, the code is updated, and it changes the use designation for the street such that only single-family homes are permitted. This change makes any of the two-family homes on the street nonconforming uses; they do not conform to the requirements of the current code.[37] These preexisting homes are nonconforming uses, but in most cases, they are permitted to continue on the property because the use is said to be "grandfathered."[38] A grandfathered use is one that is allowed to continue as a nonconforming use because it was a conforming use in an earlier time period.[39] Generally, a grandfathered use is permitted to continue so long as it is not expanded, substantially replaced, or abandoned.[40]

A nonconforming use may also include zoning criteria related to an area variance and not to use. In our preceding example, assume that the zoning code change did not eliminate the two-family residential use but merely changed the street setback requirements, which now require homes to be set back by at least 45 feet from the street line. This means that all new homes have to be built with a setback from the street line of at least 45 feet, but it also means that homes built under the prior code requirements that are only set back by 30 feet are now nonconforming. As is the case with a use, the nonconforming setback will be grandfathered.

Another common way that a nonconforming use arises is through the variance process. In a situation where an area or a use variance is granted, the resulting use is a permitted nonconforming use: a use made legal and permitted

---

[37] *See* City of Los Angeles v. Gage, 274 P.2d 34 (Cal. Dist. Ct. App. 1954); JUERGENSMEYER & ROBERTS, *supra* note 3, § 4:31; MANDELKER, *Land Use Law* § 5.78; SALKIN, *supra* note 28, § 10:2.

[38] *See* JUERGENSMEYER & ROBERTS, *supra* note 3, § 4:32; MANDELKER, *supra* note 3, § 5.78; SALKIN, *supra* note 28, § 10:2.

[39] Sources cited *supra* note 38.   [40] *Id.*

by the fact that the variance was granted. The variance once granted runs with the land, but as with a grandfathered use, there will be general limitations on the running of the variance, as it generally cannot be freely expanded or rebuilt, and it may be lost if it is abandoned for a given period of time.

In some states, a grandfathered nonconforming use may be subject to termination after a certain number of years; this process of termination is known as amortization.[41] The idea is one of estimating the remaining and useful economic life of a use that was conforming at the time it was established and calculating the number of years it will take to provide the property owner with a reasonable investment-backed return on the use that became nonconforming with a zoning change. An amortization provision should have clear criteria, and a board asked to set a termination date will need to consider real economic information on the cost of the property and the remaining useful life of the use. In an amortization situation, a board may evaluate the useful remaining value of a small business, such as a barber shop, at $100,000 and may determine that the property owner can get a reasonable investment-backed return out of his investment in the barber shop by being permitted to operate it as a grandfathered nonconforming use for another five years. In a state permitting amortization, the barber shop owner could have the continued operation of his nonconforming use terminated at the end of a five-year period rather than having it run indefinitely. Amortization is designed to facilitate the need for change in land use planning and zoning for a dynamic community while protecting the reasonable investment-backed expectations of property owners. Amortization is a potentially useful tool in dealing with the need to upgrade properties (including residential properties) to enhance accessibility. For example, property owners might be given a set number of years in which to add accessible features to a currently inaccessible structure; barriers to access would be amortized and required to be eliminated.

5.2 ZONING AMENDMENT AND SPOT ZONING

An alternative to seeking a zoning variance is to seek an amendment to the zoning code. In such an instance, the property owner requests a change in the code itself rather than a variance from a code provision. A key difference is that a zoning amendment is not a quasi-adjudicative act; it is a legislative

---

[41] *See* Modjeska Sign Studios, Inc. v. Berle, 373 N.E.2d 255 (N.Y. 1977); JUERGENSMEYER & ROBERTS, *supra* note 3, § 4:39; MANDELKER, *supra* note 3, § 5.82; SALKIN, *supra* note 28, § 10:2. *See generally* Margaret Collins, *Methods of Determining Amortization Periods for Non-Conforming Uses*, 3 WASH. U. J. L. & POL'Y 215 (2000).

act.[42] This means that a request needs to go to the legislative authority for the community rather than to an adjudicative board or panel. It also means that an amendment must be consistent with a comprehensive plan and cannot be directed at one or a very small number of properties.

Whenever consideration is given to a potential zoning amendment, some attention ought to be given to the matter of "spot zoning."[43] Spot zoning is impermissible and involves treating a given property or a very small number of properties differently than surrounding properties, oftentimes by permitting a more intense use on a given parcel of land than that permitted on surrounding properties.[44] Consider as an illustration of spot zoning, the preceding example of Paul requesting a use variance to place a small ranch home on his property for his mother to live in. If Paul is unsuccessful with the variance application, or if Paul feels that he will be more successful with the city commission (the legislature for his community) than he will be with the zoning board, he may seek a zoning code amendment to permit the use on his property. If Paul obtains an amendment to the zoning code to permit his requested use, he will have a new zoning code classification. The amendment would permit his intended use as consistent with and conforming to the new code provision. Paul would be permitted to have two homes on one lot while everyone around him retains the use restriction of one single-family residential unit per lot. This kind of change may be illegal spot zoning. Enacting a zoning code is a legislative act, and it must be pursuant to a comprehensive plan. Focusing on a specific use on a particular property outside of consideration of a comprehensive plan for the entire community is generally a quasi-adjudicative act, and when it results in a more intensive use or a beneficial use for one property owner singled out with respect to surrounding properties, it may be considered illegal spot zoning.

A kind of corollary to spot zoning is something that some people refer to as "reverse spot zoning." This can result from amending a zoning code and may also be raised in connection with the granting of variances. In many ways, reverse spot zoning raises issues of due process and equal protection, but it is generally a reference to a situation involving the grant of a change in zoning or of a variance from zoning to a large number of property owners surrounding a particular property owner who is denied a request for a similar change.

---

[42] JUERGENSMEYER & ROBERTS, *supra* note 3, § 5:6, 5:9; MANDELKER, *Land Use Law* § 6.26; SALKIN, *supra* note 28, § 10:2.
[43] JUERGENSMEYER & ROBERTS, *supra* note 3, § 5:10; MANDELKER, *supra* note 3, § 6.28; SALKIN, *supra* note 28, § 10:2.
[44] Sources cited *supra* note 43.

In the area of working to advance inclusive design through the enactment of zoning changes and the flexible granting of area and use variances, it is important to be careful to avoid illegal spot zoning.

5.3 PERFORMANCE ZONING AND CONCURRENCY

An alternative to use-based zoning is performance zoning. Instead of regulating uses, performance zoning focuses on regulating externalities and spillover effects.[45] It is based on the idea that in many situations, the regulation of categories of use is really a proxy for attempting to regulate the perceived externality consequences of the use. For example, certain industrial uses may be placed in a traditional zoning category permitting only heavy industrial uses, and this zone may be established on the basis of heavy industrial uses being noisy, dirty, and generating a lot of large truck traffic. Such uses could rationally be placed outside of zones for schools, residential housing, or community recreational facilities. The zone is defined around the uses permitted. In contrast, performance zoning attempts to focus on the externalities and spillovers that we actually want to control. In performance zoning, we might have a zone that simply says that any uses within the zone must meet certain standards for noise levels, traffic, and particle discharge into the ambient air. As long as a use fits the criteria for the zone performance standard, there would be little concern for how one defined the use. In most cases, performance zoning has been used in dealing with commercial and industrial uses or in regulating with respect to environmental concerns.[46] In the environmental context, one might regulate performance standards for rain water runoff, for example. In any event, performance zoning might be a useful tool for addressing inclusive design. As long as properties met certain inclusive design standards, they would be permitted. These design-based performance standards might relate to making all housing accessible to people in a wheelchair without having to specifically address building codes or particular use categories. Performance standards might, thus, be used to require that all residential housing meet certain local performance standards, even if federal disability law does not require it.

Concurrency is another concept that might be useful for a growing community with new development under way or anticipated. Concurrency in the

---

[45] JUERGENSMEYER & ROBERTS, *supra* note 3, § 4:19; MANDELKER, *supra* note 3, § 5.41; SALKIN, *supra* note 28, § 10:2. *See also* LANE KENDIG, PERFORMANCE ZONING (1980); Chris Duersken, *Modern Industrial Performance Standards: Key Implementation and Legal Issues*, 18 ZON. PLAN. L. REP. 33 (May 1995).

[46] Sources cited *supra* note 45.

land use and zoning context refers to regulating growth to match the development of infrastructure.[47] In the area of inclusive design, concurrency might be used to regulate development of new residential housing and other uses to be concurrent with expansion of accessible sidewalks and public transit. To be enforceable, concurrency requirements must be related to reasonable efforts to approve and construct the needed infrastructure. In other words, a community cannot use a concurrency requirement simply to stop property development; there must be an effort to address the provision of future infrastructure that will be needed for the changing development needs of the community.

As long as the criteria for performance zoning and concurrency are rational and advance a legitimate state interest in protecting the public, health, safety, welfare, and morals, they are generally enforceable.

5.4 INCENTIVE ZONING

Various zoning and land use tools might be used to create incentives for advancing inclusive design. A couple of the techniques that might be used include density bonuses, fast-track zoning approval, and TDRs. Incentives such as these might be offered to encourage developers to build beyond a level of simple compliance with federal disability law. This may include adding more inclusive design features to a given property or making accessibility a key consideration in properties not otherwise covered by extensive inclusive design requirements (such as private single-family residential housing). Incentives might also be used to encourage private developers to include accessible sidewalks, easily configured roadways, and safer and more abundant crosswalks within private developments such as large-scale residential subdivisions or major mixed-use developments.

These three examples of incentive zoning can be described briefly. Density bonuses permit developers to build out a property with higher-level density in exchange for providing something valued by the community but not otherwise required.[48] So, for example, a zoning code might provide for a building density of two housing units per acre but also have criteria providing that if a developer is willing to include certain inclusive design features that go beyond mere compliance with federal disability law, the developer will be granted a density bonus permitting three housing units per acre rather than two. Fast-track

[47] *Id.*
[48] JUERGENSMEYER & ROBERTS, *supra* note 3, § 4:18; MANDELKER, *supra* note 3, § 7.27; SALKIN, *supra* note 28, § 10:2. *See also* John J. Costonis, *The Chicago Plan: Incentive Zoning and the Preservation of Urban Landmarks*, 85 HARV. L. REV. 574, 576 (1972).

zoning approval recognizes that the zoning and planning approval process for property development can be a long and slow process – sometimes taking years for major projects.[49] In recognition of this fact, some communities will offer a fast track in the process as an incentive to developers willing to provide certain desired benefits to the community, such as greater accessibility. This might reduce the time to approval by 25 to 30 percent and result in real cost savings to the developer. TDRs are another tool for providing incentives and were discussed in the *Penn Central* case covered in Chapter 2.[50] In the context of inclusive design, a developer willing to go beyond simple compliance with federal disability law on accessibility might earn specified development rights useable on other properties in the community. This could include earning something, such as a density bonus, but the key difference would be that the density bonus could be applied to a different property located somewhere else and not simply to the property in question. The ability to apply the incentive to a property other than the one that is the immediate subject of a planning and zoning matter is what gives the TDR a special kind of value. The TDR, once created, may also be able to be banked and traded or sold to other property owners, and this gives it even more flexibility and potential value.

5.5 OTHER ZONING CONCEPTS

5.5.1 *Conditional zoning*

Another possible technique for advancing inclusive design involves conditional zoning. In the zoning process, conditions can be placed on development approvals and on the granting of variances, and some uses may require a special use permit in a given zone. Generally, reasonable conditions will be upheld. Conditions can be used as a way to require the meeting of certain accessibility standards for a property. Conditions can be used to advance certain goals but should be evaluated in terms of the essential nexus between the condition and the stated public interest in health, safety, welfare, and morals.[51] The cost imposition of meeting a condition should also fall within constitutional guidelines for rough proportionality so as not to amount to an unlawful taking.[52]

---

[49] Sources cited *supra* note 48.
[50] Penn Cent. Transp. Co. v. New York City, 438 U.S. 104 (1978). *See also infra* Chapter 2.
[51] Koontz v. St. John's River Water Mgmt. Dist., 570 U.S. ___, 133 S. Ct. 2586 (2013); Nollan v. Cal. Coastal Comm'n, 438 U.S. 815 (1987).
[52] *Koontz*, 570 U.S. ___, 133 S. Ct. 2586 (2013); Dolan v. City of Tigard, 512 U.S. 374 (1994).

5.5.2 *Vested rights and development agreements*

Given the dynamic nature of planning and zoning, and the amount of time it takes to complete property development, there is a legitimate concern for avoiding changes in development requirements during the time it takes to complete a given project. Property owners invest time and resources into development projects, and designing projects to comply with all regulatory guidelines is an important task. Changing designs to meet changing guidelines is expensive and can undermine the reasonable investment-backed expectations of the property owner. Therefore, property owners strive to achieve a high level of certainty as to the rules and regulations that will apply to a given project, with a hope that these rules and regulations will not change once significant commitments are made. The property owners seek to fix the law that will be applicable to a project and, in legal terms, may assert vested rights in the law as it existed at the time they commenced an undertaking.[53] Vested rights are important not only because they establish the rules and regulations applicable to the project but also because, once vested, the property development rights will be subject to a potential takings claim if changed.[54] Vested rights bring a level of certainty to the development process and facilitate development.

Different jurisdictions have different approaches to vested rights. Some jurisdictions may have a concept of early vesting, whereas others may be referred to as having a late vesting process.[55] A typical early vesting approach fixes the applicable land use regulations as of the date of filing for project approval with the local land use and planning officials. A late vesting approach may fix the applicable land use regulations as those in effect as of the date that a final permit is issued for the project to go forward. Various dates or criteria may be used to fix the applicable land use laws to govern a project. Vesting is critical in large-scale and complex property development where completion of a project may be several years or even decades down the road. Complex and multiphase developments, such as large-scale residential developments covering thousands of units to be built out over many years, may have multiple vesting dates that correspond to the dates when specific development phases are undertaken.

---

[53] JUERGENSMEYER & ROBERTS, *supra* note 3, § 5:27; MANDELKER, *supra* note 3, § 6.12; SALKIN, *supra* note 28, § 10:2. *See* Avco Cmty. Developers, Inc. v. South Coast Reg'l Comm'n, 553 P.2d 546 (Cal. 1976).

[54] Sources cited *supra* note 53.

[55] JUERGENSMEYER & ROBERTS, *supra* note 3, § 5:28; MANDELKER, *supra* note 3, § 6.12; SALKIN, *supra* note 28, § 10:2.

Traditional law in this area has held that government cannot simply contract away its authority and its obligation to change the law as needed to protect the public health, safety, welfare, and morals.[56] Consequently, traditional land use law prohibited what is referred to as *contract zoning*.[57] Older cases provided that local government could not contract away the right to change planning and zoning rules and to require developers to adjust to the changes. These older cases pose technical problems for modern-day land use and planning professionals, but for the most part, they do not prevent local government from effectively working with developers to facilitate stability and predictability in the development process.[58] In general, the problem has been finessed by referring to agreements on fixing the law applicable to a given project as *development agreements* rather than as contracting for specific zoning.[59] As a practical matter, a development agreement is a modern-day approach to the goal of contract zoning, but the change in name and coverage has allowed courts to treat it differently than contract zoning. Typically, a development agreement covers more than the fixing of the land use law applicable to the project and includes a number of additional understandings between the public and private parties to the agreement. In this way, the development agreement is positioned as different from contract zoning, and the old cases that disfavored contract zoning are conveniently sidestepped. In reality, this simply reflects a move away from the rigidity of traditional Euclidian zoning to modern planning and zoning based on flexibility and negotiated arrangements among public and private entities pursuant to stated criteria and procedural requirements.

The idea of the development agreement can be useful to the goal of advancing inclusive design in our communities. A typical development agreement can provide for a number of elements and may function as a kind of "mini-comprehensive plan" for a major development project. For example, a development agreement for a major regional shopping mall may include requirements for hiring and training local residents for employment positions at the mall and may include hiring targets designed to encourage a diverse workforce at the property. The agreements might also include provisions for paying

---

[56] JUERGENSMEYER & ROBERTS, *supra* note 3, § 5:11; MANDELKER, *surpa* note 3, § 6.62; SALKIN, *supra* note 28, § 10:2.

[57] Sources cited *supra* note 56. *See* Durand v. IDC Bellingham, LLC, 793 N.E.2d 359 (Mass. 2003).

[58] Though the law still technically prohibits contract zoning, we obtain a similar result with development agreements. JUERGENSMEYER & ROBERTS, *supra* note 3, at 180–183; MANDELKER, *supra* note 3, § 6.23; SALKIN, *supra* note 28, § 10:2.

[59] Sources cited *supra* note 56.

workers a stated "living wage" and other things. The point is that development agreements are negotiated arrangements that typically go beyond simply fixing the vesting date of the applicable land use law. As such, development agreements may be a vehicle for negotiating for inclusive design requirements that go beyond minimal compliance with federal disability law.

5.5.3 *Accessibility impact assessments*

A modern trend in planning and zoning includes the development of *Health Impact Assessments*.[60] These assessments are similar to Environmental Impact Statements but focus more on policy and on creating a framework for the deliberative process.[61] The idea in the land use area is that land use regulations and goals should be evaluated in terms of potential health impacts and in terms of corresponding goals for improving health quality.[62] In a similar way, Accessibility Impact Assessments might focus attention on the way that land use regulations and particular proposed property developments impact the accessibility of a community. Focus would be on the integration of inclusive design across the community and on the ability of people to safely and easily age in place. Communities could develop their own accessibility policies, consistent with federal disability law, much as some now develop sustainability policies to guide deliberation on future growth and planning. This could be done as part of the comprehensive planning process or independently as a focused inquiry, again, as is frequently done with respect to sustainability. Moreover, property owners seeking to do developments of a certain size or density might be required to prepare and submit an Accessibility Impact Assessment that identifies the specific steps to be taken on the property to make it inclusive and the potential impact of the proposed project on overall accessibility in the community. These assessments might also include details with respect to connecting this particular project with a network of other properties and uses in the community. In particular, attention could be given to landscape and building design for accessibility as well as to connective infrastructure such as sidewalks, crosswalks, and transit. Considerations as to street layout and traffic patterns might also be included to assess the relative ease and safety of a project's relationship to accessibility across the community network.

---

[60] Pamela Ko & Patricia Salkin, *What Every Land Use Lawyer Should Know About the Emerging Use of Health Impact Assessment and Land Use Decision Making*, 13 N.Y. ZONING LAW & PRAC. REP. 1 (2013).
[61] *Id.*   [62] *Id.*

Accessibility Impact Assessments might also serve as one way of facilitating local community based *Olmstead planning* pursuant to federal disability law.[63] Olmstead planning refers to a requirement articulated in *Olmstead v. L.C.*, 527 U.S. 581 (1999), and subsequently mandated in federal disability legislation.[64] Olmstead planning requires communities to plan for the best ways to deliver services to people with disabilities in settings that enable them to interact with nondisabled people to the fullest extent possible.[65] Olmstead planning expresses a desire to move away from using institutional settings for delivery of services to people with disabilities and promotes greater integration of people and services across the community.[66] An Olmstead plan must have specifics and not simply be a list of vague or aspirational goals.[67] In addition, the plan must include strategies for funding and implementation. Olmstead planning requires local communities to adjust their services to accommodate people with disabilities so long as a requested modification does not fundamentally alter the service, and thus, to avoid making an adjustment, the local government has the burden of showing that any proposed modification will fundamentally alter the service.[68] Budget constraints and potential shortfalls in financing are not necessarily defenses to implementing community-based plans.[69]

While many planning and zoning officials might not see Olmstead planning as directly related to their activities, it seems that some sort of specific planning as to accessibility across an integrated community network could be required because zoning and planning are considered services covered by the ADA. Such services are not limited to specific zoning decisions such as those related to an application for a variance. Planning and zoning services involve planning for the future and the taking of legislative action to advance particular planning goals. In setting goals and working to achieve them, consideration needs to be given to the ways that property development

---

[63] See U.S. Dep't of Justice, Statement of the Department of Justice on Enforcement of the Integration Mandate of Title II of the Americans with Disabilities Act and Olmstead v. L.C. (June 22, 2011), *available at* www.ada.gov/olmstead/q&a_olmstead.htm#_ftnref9.

[64] Olmstead v. L.C., 527 U.S. 581 (1999); 28 C.F.R. § 35.130(d) (2010, amended 2011); Exec. Order No. 13,217, 3 C.F.R. 774 (2002), *reprinted in* 42 U.S.C. § 12131 (2006).

[65] See U.S. Dep't of Justice, Statement of the Department of Justice on Enforcement of the Integration Mandate of Title II of the Americans with Disabilities Act and Olmstead v. L.C. (June 22, 2011), *available at* www.ada.gov/olmstead/q&a_olmstead.htm#_ftnref9; Samuel R. Bagenstos, *The Past and Future of Deinstitutionalization Litigation*, 34 Cardozo L. Rev. 1 (2012); J. William Cain, *The "Most Integrated Setting" Regulation of the Americans with Disabilities Act*, 34 Ark. Law. 8 (1999).

[66] See U.S. Dep't of Justice, *supra* note 65.   [67] *Id.*; 28 C.F.R. § 35.130(b)(ii)(7).

[68] U.S. Dep't of Justice, *supra* note 65.   [69] *Id.*

and land use regulation ensure access to people with mobility impairment. The planning process should include taking reasonable steps to enhance the ability of people with mobility impairment to continue to meaningfully participate in community life. In particular, planning should include an element directed at making residential housing easier and safer to navigate as people age in place. Reducing barriers to navigation can facilitate the ability of elderly Americans to remain in their homes longer and to thereby remain connected to the community for a greater period of time. Making housing more accessible, and making goods and services more accessible at the community level, will reduce the need for premature relocation to the institutional settings of a typical assisted-living or nursing home facility. This is exactly the kind of planning that Olmstead requirements are designed to facilitate. Thus, engaging in Accessibility Impact Assessments, or including accessibility assessments as part of more traditional comprehensive planning, is one way of providing for greater inclusive design and for making certain that planning and zoning activities appropriately account for the needs of people with disabilities.

5.6 CONCLUSION

A number of strategies ought to be employed to advance inclusive design in our communities. These strategies involve cooperation at local, state, and national levels. Some strategies can be driven by specific regulatory requirements, and others can include incentives for encouraging the voluntary addition of inclusive design features to a given property development project. This chapter covered a number of land use devices and techniques that should be understood in working to advance inclusive design. Undoubtedly, other strategies and techniques might be included in a full inventory of land use law and regulation, but the preceding reflect the most significant considerations for modern property development.

6

Conclusion

In seeking to understand the implications of mobility impairment, it is important to appreciate the relationship between it and the design of the built environment. Unless we are in the middle of a national park or in a nature preserve, we can generally think of the built environment as everything we see when we look around: the buildings, streets, sidewalks, parks, warehouses, factories, schools, harbors, airports, rail lines, sewer lines, cable and fiber-optic lines, and just about everything else that makes up the environment in which we work, live, and play. To a large extent, the built environment is about the places and spaces that we call home, and much of this environment is the product of two interrelated areas of property law: real estate development and land use planning and regulation.

The way in which we design and construct the built environment is important because it gives shape and meaning to our understanding of mobility impairment. In the literature concerning disability law and policy, attention is often focused on understanding disability in the context of constitutional and civil rights law rather than in terms of land use law and planning. Consequently, analysis of the design of the built environment frequently centers on questions of access and on issues of exclusion. Lack of access and the process of exclusion are linked to unequal treatment and discrimination, thus raising concerns under constitutional and civil rights law. We can readily appreciate the importance of this focus when we read the opening narratives to this book involving Pauli, Ann, Celia, and Tiffany. In each case, there is a sense of unfairness and inequality. In each case, we know that technology exists to design the built environment differently and that, if we were to eliminate barriers to free and easy movement, the people involved would be able to participate much more fully in their community. In short, we can understand that design can function to exclude and discriminate against people in ways similar to legal exclusions based on race, gender, religion, and ethnicity. The exclusionary design of buildings and infrastructure that raises barriers to social participation by people with mobility impairment diminishes the opportunity for meaningful participation in community life and discriminates against them.

What is often missed in looking at these scenarios is that they are also problems of land use law and planning. When we talk about someone having a constitutional right to be included, and about the need for inclusive design in the way we approach the built environment, it seems that we often forget that the actual process of making the built environment more accessible involves a need to regulate and control property development and land use. Planning for the future needs of a community, therefore, requires thoughtful attention to changing demographics, economic development trends, traffic patterns, and a variety of other factors. Good planning is not the product of a disability rights lawsuit; the result of such litigation is simply corrective action, after the fact.

To effectively plan for inclusive and sustainable communities, we must understand that mobility impairment is not just a matter of civil rights; it is also a matter of concern to local land use and planning law. Consequently, local planning and land use professionals need to be made active and valued participants in the process of building inclusive design communities. Local land use professionals need to work closely with disability rights advocates, and disability rights advocates need to appreciate the underlying land use and planning law issues involved in making the built environment more inclusive. Working across professional disciplines and among alternative frameworks will prove beneficial to making progress on inclusive design. It is also important to reinvigorate local government in the planning process for inclusive design. This means requiring local comprehensive planning with respect to mobility impairment and with respect to the needs of people aging in place. Such planning must be consistent with national requirements on accessibility under the ADA and its related legislation and should be responsive to local input and implementation.

In a federal system of governance, it is not always easy to work on the legal relationship among national and local governments, but the process of doing so is nonetheless important. The interconnected environments in which individuals tend to operate seldom obey the strict political and legal definitions of jurisdiction that we transcribe onto the local geography. People live and operate in a networked set of relationships that can cross from city to suburb, to countryside, and back again. For many people, daily and weekly activities take them between various villages, towns, counties, and other jurisdictional subdivisions, but they seldom have need to pay any attention to these legal demarcations. Most people tend to understand their activity as going from home to work or from work to the office or shopping. They know how to get there but generally have no reason to pay attention to the crossing of political boundaries that fix the local land use and development authority within a given political subdivision. They just want the local landscape to work well as an integrated system, with roads, lighting, sewer, and other services functioning as a seamless web of infrastructure and design. Consequently, land use planning and regulation must be done in an integrated way that responds to a networked web of human activity and not just to the artificial jurisdictional boundaries drawn on a map. This requires careful consideration of the appropriate relationship that should exist among local, state, and federal regulatory authorities. Moreover, it requires thoughtful and intentional comprehensive planning to achieve acceptable goals for inclusion and sustainability so that people might safely and easily age in place.

Cases cited

Table of primary cases discussed in the text. Cases identified in italics appear in the text as an edited version of the case opinion. Cases in regular font are discussed in the text but are not included in edited form. The table does not include cases cited only in the notes or cases cited only in the body of an included edited case opinion.

Index

Made in the USA
Middletown, DE
23 December 2018